Transforming Leaders Into
PROGRESS**MAKERS**

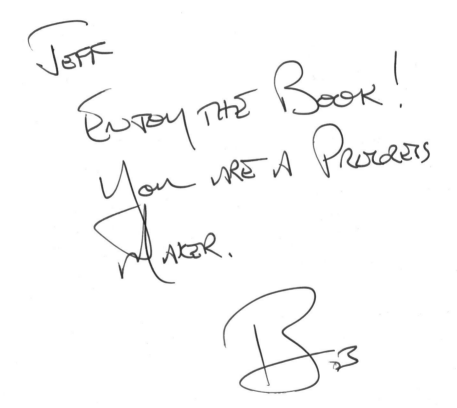

Jeff

Enjoy the Book!

You are a Progress

Maker.

B ob

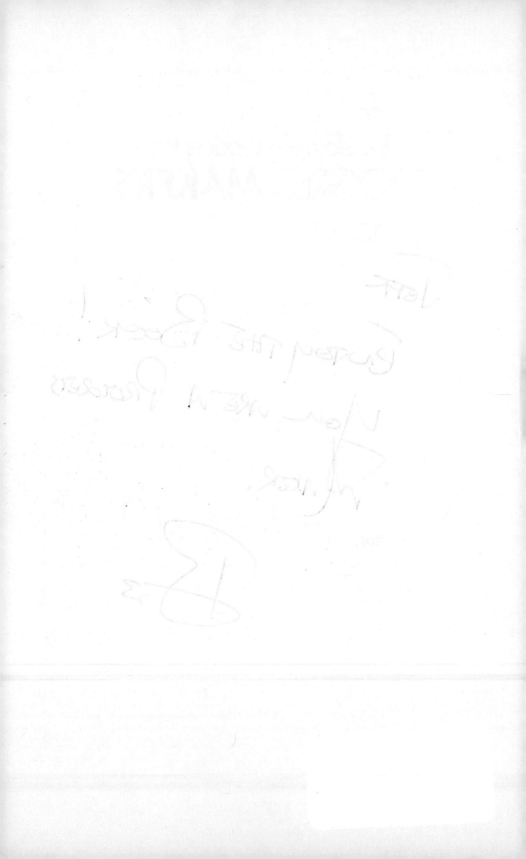

Transforming Leaders Into
PROGRESS**MAKERS**
Leadership for the
21st Century

Phillip G. Clampitt | Robert J. DeKoch

University of Wisconsin, Green Bay   *The Boldt Company*

Los Angeles | London | New Delhi
Singapore | Washington DC

For information:

SAGE Publications, Inc.
2455 Teller Road
Thousand Oaks,
  California 91320
E-mail: order@sagepub.com

SAGE Publications India Pvt. Ltd.
B 1/I 1 Mohan Cooperative
  Industrial Area
Mathura Road, New Delhi 110 044
India

SAGE Publications Ltd.
1 Oliver's Yard
55 City Road
London EC1Y 1SP
United Kingdom

SAGE Publications Asia-Pacific Pte. Ltd.
33 Pekin Street #02-01
Far East Square
Singapore 048763

Printed in the United States of America

Library of Congress Cataloging-in-Publication Data

Clampitt, Phillip G.
Transforming leaders into progress makers : leadership for the 21st century / Phillip G. Clampitt, Robert J. DeKoch.
    p. cm.
Includes bibliographical references and index.
ISBN 978-1-4129-7468-4 (cloth)
ISBN 978-1-4129-7469-1 (pbk.)
    1. Leadership. 2. Communication in management. I. DeKoch, Robert J., 1952- II. Title.

HD57.7.C53 2011
658.4'092—dc22   2010013968

This book is printed on acid-free paper.

10   11   12   13   14   10   9   8   7   6   5   4   3   2   1

Acquisitions Editor:	Todd R. Armstrong
Editorial Assistant:	Nathan Davidson
Production Editor:	Libby Larson
Copy Editor:	Gillian Dickens
Typesetter:	C&M Digitals (P) Ltd.
Proofreader:	Theresa Kay
Indexer:	Terri Corry
Cover Designer:	Candice Harman
Marketing Manager:	Helen Salmon

CONTENTS

FOREWORD

———•◆•———

M any of the contemporary contributions that attempt to address the subject of leadership have the intellectual heft of a bumper sticker. They are often based on pithy suggestions such as "lead, follow, or get out of the way," or "when in charge take charge." Then there is the "leadership secrets of . . ." genre that suggests that we too would be great leaders if we would emulate the actions of some notable historical figure. At a higher level of sophistication, but equally problematic, are overly engineered competency-based models that list a series of traits or skills that promise the consistent production of excellent leaders if we could just master the list. It's not that there is anything inherently wrong with such observations. There is something to be said for proverbs, truisms, and rules of thumb. The problem arises when well-intentioned academics teach them without thinking critically about them and when practitioners try to apply them in their practice. I'm reminded of a conversation with Dickinson College President William Durden, who responded to a student's question, "What leadership books do you recommend?" with the statement, "For goodness sake, don't read anything with the word *leadership* in the title."

When it comes to leadership, the results achieved from applying formulaic approaches are often disappointing if not downright harmful.

Leadership is a complex and dynamic social phenomenon. What works for one person doesn't work for the next. What works in one situation is inappropriate for another. That's not to say that we should remain silent about leadership. There are patterns that can surely be discerned, studied, and applied. We should seek out these patterns, but we should also maintain a healthy skepticism when faced with definitive statements about how to influence other people.

Most leadership scholars would agree that influence is at the heart of leadership. The most we may be able to hope for are probability statements that generally hold true while maintaining the possibility of exceptions. As Clampitt and DeKoch note, probability statements use terms such as *usually, sometimes, often, frequently, rarely,* and *occasionally.* The study of leadership may well attract those who are comfortable with uncertainty. The lack of clear and unambiguous answers will undoubtedly frustrate some and send them running in search of the universal laws of the natural sciences. Those who remain, who can handle paradox and uncertainty, will find their studies most gratifying.

Phillip Clampitt and Robert DeKoch understand something about the promises and the pitfalls of trying to decipher the truths of leadership. In *Transforming Leaders Into Progress Makers: Leadership for the 21st Century,* they engage in some high-order patterning, yet they also avoid the trap of declaring universal truths. They provide real-life examples to illustrate their points without falling prey to hero worship. In this book, we can see the reflection of their book *Embracing Uncertainty: The Essence of Leadership.* I have often assigned that 2001 contribution as an example of a refreshing alternative approach to traditional depictions of leadership. *Progress Makers* is far more than a rehash. There is indeed new wine in this bottle. Beyond its useful treatment of uncertainty and platforms, it touches upon one of the great questions of leadership studies by including the notion of progress as a central theme.

Almost 20 years ago, the late Joseph C. Rost, a founder of the field of leadership studies, struggled to capture the definition of leadership. The result was the seminal book *Leadership for the Twenty-First Century.* After reading hundreds of books on the subject of leadership and criticizing most of them for a lack of definition, Rost proposed that leadership is "an influence relationship among leaders and followers who intend real changes that reflect their mutual purposes."[1]

In Rost's definition, we see the importance of change and the characterization that leadership is more than simply raw influence. Change, however, can just as easily be for the bad as the good. Rost's definition makes no distinction between the leader of the criminal enterprise that works to the detriment of society and the public servant that works for the public interest. Here's where Clampitt and DeKoch come in. They sagely avoid the highly doubtful proposition that an influence relationship that results in a bad outcome is something other than leadership. Instead, they focus on progress—a hopeful term that connotes something inherently positive and worthy, and they describe the kind of leadership that is most likely to result in progress. Once again, with a level of candor that is rare in published works, they assert that progress is not an inexorable linear advancement but a messy process full of fits and starts.

I suggest that this work contains concepts and insights that advance the study and practice of leadership. It is to be celebrated equally for its humility as well as its assertions. An example of intellectual humility appears in the conclusion where they caution the reader that none of the strategies and tactics in the book should be considered sacrosanct. Here there are no false claims of certainty, demonstrating that the authors practice what they preach. Instead of punctuating their work with a declarative statement of truth, they enjoin the reader to refine and explore. Yet just as we accept the caveat and invitation, we should not overlook the helpful exploration that lies within the cover of this book. The authors are in search of a more sustainable form of leadership, a project that could be the next great platform of leadership theory.

George E. Reed, PhD
Department of Leadership Studies
University of San Diego

NOTE

1. J. Rost, *Leadership for the Twenty First Century.* Westport, CT: Praeger, 1993, 102.

ACKNOWLEDGMENTS

In Chapter 11, we discuss how to engender progress by thoughtfully "enlarging the circle" or building the right team in the proper way. We were fortunate that the right people chose to be part of our circle. We begin the acknowledgments with the first member to join the Progress Maker circle. The authors are deeply grateful for the support of Laurey Clampitt, who is one of the world's best "refiners" and masterfully guides "explorers" in their progress-making quests. She devoted enormous amounts of her time to challenging the ideas, critiquing the manuscript, and improving the writing, time she took away from her new business, *Totally Twisted* (Dining Designs). Moreover, she developed all the content for the book's Web site (www.imetacomm.com/pm). In short, this project would not have been completed without her guidance and assistance. Lee Williams (Texas State University) also provided thoughtful commentary on numerous chapters during the embryonic stages and developed several research projects highlighted in several chapters and Appendix B. He also serves as a valued mentor, colleague, and friend to one of the authors (Phil). Cal Downs also deserves recognition for his ongoing influence on Phil's career and life.

The *Progress Maker* research team was headed by Tiffany Jensen with the assistance of Kim VandenAvond, Ryan Hartwig, and Kylene Pankratz (all proud graduates of the Communication program at the University of Wisconsin–Green Bay). They unearthed obscure research on a 24/7 basis that enriched the final product. Todd Armstrong at Sage Publications along with his assistant Nathan Davidson guided this project with professionalism and enthusiasm. They selected a number of insightful and thoughtful reviewers who greatly enhanced the final manuscript. Those reviewers were Angela Laird Brenton (University of Arkansas at Little Rock, College of Professional Studies), Charles D. Allen (United States Army War College, Department of Command, Leadership, and

Management), Angela D. Boston (The University of Texas at Arlington, Department of Management), Sue Currey (St. Edward's University, New College), Larry M. Edmonds (Arizona State University, Interdisciplinary Humanities and Communication), Gary F. Kohut (The University of North Carolina at Charlotte, Department of Management), Lance Kurke (Kurke & Associates, Inc., and Carnegie Mellon University), H. John Heinz III (Graduate College of Public Policy and Management), George E. Reed (University of San Diego, Department of Leadership Studies), Meir Russ (University of Wisconsin–Green Bay, Department of Business Administration), and W. Robert Sampson (St. Petersburg College, College of Technology and Management). An additional word about one of the reviewers: George Reed agreed to write an insightful foreword to the book that reflects both his thoughtfulness about leadership and commitment to the project. We are grateful for his support, friendship, and service to the nation. In Chapter 14, we discuss the importance of error detection and correction. This team of distinguished scholars did their best to make sure we avoided errors and seized relevant opportunities. Finally, we want to thank our wonderful black belt copy editor, Gillian Dickens (aka "Little Dickens"). She, along with Libby Larson and Aja Baker, were instrumental in refining the final version of this book and the ancillary material. The book is dedicated to two special and extraordinary people who continue to be a source of inspiration as we progress through life together—Laurey and Debbie.

ABOUT THE AUTHORS

Phillip G. Clampitt (Ph.D., University of Kansas) is the Hendrickson Professor of Business at the University of Wisconsin–Green Bay, where he teaches in the Information Sciences program. The *Wall Street Journal* and *MIT Sloan Management Review* recently highlighted his work on "Decision Downloading," which details how companies can effectively communicate decisions to those not involved in the decision-making process. He is the author of a Sage Publications best-seller, *Communicating for Managerial Effectiveness* (fourth edition; see www.imetacomm.com/cme4) and coauthor of *Embracing Uncertainty: The Essence of Leadership.* Along with being on the editorial board of numerous professional journals, his work has been published in a variety of journals, including the *MIT Sloan Management Review, Academy of Management Executive, Management Communication Quarterly, Journal of Business Communication, Communication World, Journal of Broadcasting, Journal of Communication Management, Ivey Business Journal,* and *Journal of Change Management.* In addition to many guest speaking opportunities in the United States, he has also been invited to speak internationally at the University of Pisa, University of Aberdeen, and University of Ulster, as well as to numerous multinational businesses and professional organizations. As a principal in his firm, Metacomm, he has consulted on communication issues with a variety of organizations, such as PepsiCo, Manpower, Schneider National, American Medical Security, Dean Foods, The Boldt Company, Stora Enso, The U.S. Army War College, Appleton Papers, Foremost Farms, Thilmany Paper, Dental City, and Nokia (see www.imetacomm.com).

Robert J. DeKoch received his bachelor of arts degree from Lawrence University and his master's degree in Business Administration from the University of Wisconsin–Oshkosh. His career has spanned numerous manufacturing industries where he has held various management positions in operations, engineering, and research. He is currently the president and chief operating officer for a major U.S. construction services firm, The Boldt Company (see www.theboldtcompany.com). He is also co-chairman of the board of New North, Inc., a regional economic development initiative in northeastern Wisconsin. The initiative's mission is to harness and promote the 18-county region's resources, talents, and creativity for the purposes of sustaining and growing the regional economy (see www.thenewnorth.com). Throughout his career, Mr. DeKoch has focused on developing work environments for high involvement and continuous learning. He has instituted progressive communication processes in the workplace to promote understanding, focus, and alignment. He strives to build organizational relationships that foster innovative thinking, recognition of achievement, and genuine teamwork. He coauthored the book *Embracing Uncertainty: The Essence of Leadership* and leadership articles in various journals.

To Laurey, who infuses my life with joy, wisdom, and richness
—Phil

and

To Debbie, my wife, my best friend, and my lifelong partner
—Bob

ELEMENTS OF
PROGRESS MAKING

✹ 1 ✸

INTRODUCTION

————✦•✦————

*What is the use of living, if it be not to strive for noble cause and
to make this muddled world a better place for those who will live
in it after we are gone? How else can we put ourselves in harmo-
nious relation with the great verities and consolations of the infi-
nite and the eternal? And I avow my faith that we are marching
towards better days. Humanity will not be cast down. We are going
on—swinging bravely forward along the grand high road—and
already behind the distant mountains is the promise of the sun.*

—Sir Winston Churchill

C lick on your favorite search engine and enter the word *leadership*. You'll
find thousands of books on the subject. Upon closer examination, you
would find that they fall into three categories.

First, there are authors who focus on the skills and attributes of leaders.[1] Great
leaders are intelligent, visionary, inspiring, persistent, knowledgeable, driven,
ethical, and confident. They are also emotionally intelligent, effective time
managers, skilled communicators, strategic thinkers, exceptional problem solvers,
and socially skilled, to name a few.[2] Who wouldn't want their leaders to possess all
these characteristics? Yet, short of Superman or Wonder Woman, is it even possible for a single person to possess all these skills and attributes? In fact, some business finance scholars believe that the long-term growth of new companies
hinges more on the horse (the business idea) than the jockey (the leader).[3]

Second, there are authors with a more academic orientation.[4] They tend to either review the relevant leadership research or propose a particular leadership theory. Many readers find the academic debates exhilarating and enlightening. Yet, the theoretical debates often leave little room for discourse on strategies and the related tactics. What should the aspiring leader *do* based on these ideas?

In more recent years, a third category has emerged that focuses on the leadership "secrets" of successful leaders.[5] An almost dizzying array of titles has emerged. There are the leadership secrets of Jack Welch, Elizabeth I, Winston Churchill, Abraham Lincoln, Hillary Clinton, Mahatma Gandhi, General Patton, Alexander the Great, and even Harry Potter. Apparently, many readers find this "admire and emulate" strategy quite attractive. Yet, how does a leader know when a situation requires a Gandhian or Churchillian approach? After all, they deeply disliked and distrusted one another.[6] We wonder how many of the "secrets" are mere platitudes wrapped around the lives of these extraordinary leaders. We suspect that their secrets may still be safely locked away in one of Harry Potter's magic chambers.

Troubling questions aside, aspiring leaders could clearly benefit from any one of these three approaches. Many leaders have been enriched by thoughts gleaned from one or more of these approaches. Yet, often the advice from one approach appears at odds with that from another. For example, the merits of lean thinking (i.e., taking out waste or "muda") seem to be in conflict with those of innovative thinking that celebrates some seemingly "wasteful" practices. What should leaders do when faced with advice that appears to be illusory or contradictory? As we pondered that question, the inklings of an idea emerged around a major gap we discovered in the literature.

What is the gap? Here's the way to discover it. Go back to the search engine and enter the word *progress*. You'll find considerably fewer books on this subject. Enter the words *leadership* and *progress* together and discover fewer still (see Figure 1.1). For the moment, put aside this admittedly crude research technique.[7] Aren't these results a bit odd? Aren't leaders supposed to make progress? And that's the gap. *Progress* should be at the center of any discussion of leadership. Yet relatively few leadership experts devote much attention to the issue.

Why is there virtual silence on the subject of progress? First, many authors are far more interested in tilling up the old ground than in suggesting something novel. They may well reason that it worked in the past; all we need is a new package. Second, defining progress proves to be a difficult and thorny task. Does it mean growing the company? Innovating? Continuously improving?

Figure 1.1   **Book Title Search**

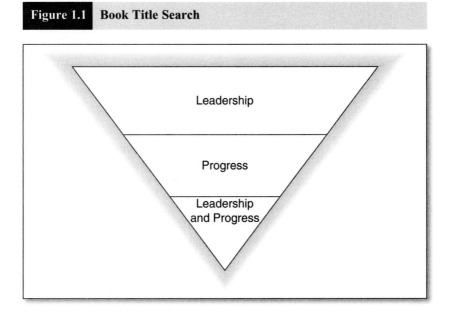

Being a market leader? All of the above? Third, explaining how to achieve progress cannot be summed up in catchy one-line admonitions. We even lack a solid lexicon for discussing progress.

OUR PURPOSE

We wrote this book to answer these questions and bridge the gap. We wanted to reconcile the seemingly contradictory advice and overly simplistic lessons provided to aspiring leaders. Yet, we sought in this book to abide by Einstein's dictum, "Make everything as simple as possible, but not simpler." In short, we wrote *Transforming Leaders Into Progress Makers: Leadership for the 21st Century* and created the related Web site (www.imetacomm.com/pm) to advocate a more enlightening and actionable perspective on leadership. And most important, we want to help those in leadership positions become progress makers.

Progress Makers advances five basic arguments:

- Leaders must possess certain skills and a desire to lead, but more important, they must move their organizations to new and more vibrant platforms.

- Progress is a function of meeting the ever-changing challenges of an evolving environment and moving an organization to seize those challenges.

- The most fundamental leadership judgment is determining when the organization needs to explore new opportunities and when it needs to improve (or refine) current practices.

- Leaders who are willing to embrace certain strategies and tactics can become progress makers.

- There are many people in leadership positions who are not progress makers.

We weave our support for these contentions throughout the chapters. In some cases, we offer case study examples; in others, we reveal the findings of the special research projects developed for this book.

OUR APPROACH

Exploring. Refining. Platforms. In Section I, we explain these concepts, the foundational ideas for the Progress Model. These three cornerstone concepts provide the basis for understanding how to make progress. But you need a deep, intense, visceral kind of understanding of these three ideas to act with confidence. Merely checking the right box on a classroom quiz will not do. Almost anyone can learn to do that. As we shall see, great leaders—the progress makers—not only know the quiz answers but also know how to make the kind of progress their organizations need at a particular point in time.

Then we thoroughly discuss the notion of progress and the Progress Model. Next we discuss how explorers and refiners make progress. Hint: They take very different approaches. We conclude the section with a chapter on progress makers.

In Section II, we sketch out the strategies and tactics that will enable you to become a progress maker. These are not the normal recommendations found in some leadership books. In fact, some may sound vaguely paradoxical. That's a hint. As we shall see, progress makers embrace seemingly contradictory and paradoxical positions.

The seven strategies (and related tactics) we highlight emerged by synthesizing three different "pools of insight": (1) leadership literature, (2) reflections on our personal leadership experiences, and (3) special research projects developed for this book. Numerous ideas worthy of discussion flowed from the pools of insight. We then filtered out the redundant and inconsequential, channeling the remaining into seven essential insights that form the basis for the second section of *Transforming Leaders Into Progress Makers* (see Figure 1.2).

One of the special research projects involved interviewing leaders who we deemed to be progress makers. We used three criteria to select these people. First, they must have assumed leadership positions over an extensive time period. Second, they must have moved their organizations forward by both exploring and refining. Third, they must have had extensive experience moving from one platform to another. We crafted these extraordinarily compelling interviews into Progress Maker Profiles, which are sprinkled throughout the book.

In Appendix A, we compiled a list of all the progress makers we researched, discussed, or profiled. We invite you to take a deeper dive into the lives of the progress makers you find most intriguing (see the book's Web site at www.imetacomm.com/pm). You can do this by reading or listening to their life stories. We would be thrilled if *Progress Makers* inspires you to go on a biography reading binge. As you study the lives of other progress makers, you can often find deep parallels to the struggles you face as a leader. Oprah Winfrey, for instance, certainly meets our criteria as a progress maker. While she started her career in the

Figure 1.2   Progress Makers Insight Pools

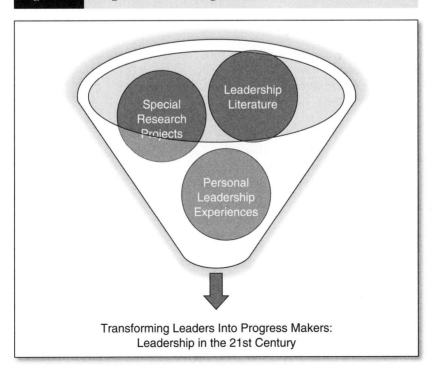

Transforming Leaders Into Progress Makers:
Leadership in the 21st Century

news business, she established her first major platform with *The Oprah Winfrey Show.* As the host and supervising producer, she "entertained, enlightened, and uplifted millions of [TV] viewers."[8] That was only the beginning. In the spirit of a progress maker, she went on to establish other successful platforms, including Harpo Studios, *O, The Oprah Magazine,* and OWN: The Oprah Winfrey Network. When Oprah announced that she was ending her TV show, many devoted fans were saddened, some dismayed, and others completely bewildered.[9] But that decision, too, represents the spirit of a progress maker. Why? Progress makers know when a particular platform (e.g., *The Oprah Winfrey Show*) has run its course and when it's time to devote energy to other endeavors (e.g., The Oprah Winfrey Network).[10] We will have more to say about this mind-set in the following chapters.

Transforming Leaders Into Progress Makers revolves around time-tested insights, everyday entrepreneurs, and a few high-profile leaders, such as Oprah. The right people armed with the right insights can change our world. It all starts with a click. The instant you see a link between leadership and progress, something clicks in your mind, snapping on a light that illuminates the way forward. We hope that *Progress Makers* shines a bright beam on your path to the future.

NOTES

1. See, for example, J. Maxwell, *The 21 Indispensable Qualities of a Leader: Becoming the Person Others Will Want to Follow.* Nashville, TN: Thomas Nelson, 1999.

2. D. Tourish, personal communication, June 6, 2009.

3. S. Kaplan, B. Sensoy, and P. Strömberg, "Should Investors Bet on the Jockey or the Horse? Evidence From the Evolution of Firms From Early Business Plans to Public Companies." *Journal of Finance* 64, no. 1 (2009): 75–115.

4. See, for example, P. G. Northouse, *Leadership: Theory and Practice.* 4th ed. Thousand Oaks, CA: Sage, 2006.

5. See, for example, W. Roberts, *Leadership Secrets of Attila the Hun.* New York: Business Plus, 1990.

6. A. Herman, *Gandhi & Churchill: The Epic Rivalry That Destroyed an Empire and Forged Our Age.* New York: Bantam, 2008.

7. We are making the defensible but tenuous assumption that book titles tell us something important about the content and perspective of the authors.

8. See http://www.oprah.com/article/pressroom/oprahsbio/20080602_orig_oprahsbio (accessed November 19, 2009).

9. See http://www.chicagotribune.com/news/chi-oprah-winfrey-show-end-link, 0,6527512.story (accessed December 1, 2009).

10. "Brand Royalty." *The Economist.* November 28, 2009, 78.

⚜ 2 ⚜

EXPLORING

———•◆•———

*The world needs risk takers. They inspire, challenge, and encour-
age. They set off sparks, igniting fires that burn long after their
passing. They dare the impossible. But not without cost.*

—Maria Coffey

Explorers dominate the topography in almost every field of human endeavor. They shape the landscape for all: Their accomplishments tower over others, and their spirit prods us to further feats. Their achievements are chronicled in textbooks in every language. The mere mention of names such as Magellan, Queen Elizabeth, Einstein, or Beethoven elevates our spirit while raising our gaze to the possibilities of human accomplishment. It was Magellan who led the expedition that was the first to circumnavigate the world, literally shattering the worldview of those who believed the earth was flat. It was Queen Elizabeth who ushered in England's Golden Age of artistic and military supremacy.[1] It was Einstein who challenged conventional wisdom about the nature of space and time, spurring inquiries into bewildering phenomena such as black holes that are still being investigated to this day. It was Beethoven whose music built the musical bridge connecting musicians of the classical period to those from the romantic period. Explorers like these in countless fields of human activity stand like mountaintops influencing all, inspiring many, and challenging others to scale new heights. They set the standards of accomplishment while laying the groundwork for future ventures into the unknown.

Yet, to say that explorers are a rare breed is unfair. We need not be overly awed by some figurative "Mount Magellan" or "Elizabeth's Precipice" because anyone can discover a new vista or seize an opportunity. We all have the spirit of an explorer. Any parent knows that a 2-year-old has an almost unquenchable spirit of discovery.[2] Sometimes it's endearing. Sometimes it's not, like the discovery that an antique glass vase can explode into a million pieces with a mere nudge.

Over time children learn about the risks of curiosity, discovery, and exploration. The shattering vase brings glee but also cuts. The candle flame entices but also burns. This is reward and punishment at its most primal and influential. Discovery can thrill, but it can also kill. So, we learn from experience, the admonitions of parents, and the lessons of our teachers about the boundaries of exploration. The message becomes clearer and stronger over time—"exploring is dangerous, avoid it." Silently, unconsciously, children moderate their naturally inquisitive and curious natures.

Taming children's natural curiosity protects them from harm but also can stifle something in their spirit that may be vital. Youngsters who fail to explore the possibilities of different professions than their parents may well be heading down a path to the unemployment line. Adults who suppress their natural inquisitiveness risk falling into personal and professional ruts that diminish their capacity for personal fulfillment and professional relevancy. The business that fails to explore innovative practices risks stagnation and potential extinction.[3]

The lesson is basic: Most things in life are like gravity. As any bicyclist can tell you, sometimes gravity is your friend, and sometimes it's your worst enemy. Likewise, exploring may be the most exhilarating activity in the world, but it may also turn into a deadly obsession. That is, in fact, Maria Coffey's warning that begins this chapter. She knows from deep personal experience about the tragedies of exploring. She lost the love of her life, mountain climber Joe Tasker, on the Northeast Ridge of Mount Everest.[4] Exploring can wound, maim, and destroy. Dr. Beck Weathers lost fingers, toes, and his nose on his "intrinsically irrational" quest to climb Mount Everest.[5] A survey of British expeditions over 7,000 meters notes that there was "at least one death every fifth expedition."[6] Death rates on K2, the second tallest mountain in the world, are equally frightening. The chances of dying on K2 are almost 12%; those odds come "perilously close to the odds of dying in Russian roulette."[7] Those odds might cause pause in any potential mountaineer. But the notion stretches beyond the mountaintops to any number of different exploratory enterprises. For example, only 10% to 20% of new products or services endure for longer than 2 years.[8] Therefore, as we discuss the explorer's characteristics below, be mindful of the dangers as well as the promise.

ATTRIBUTES OF EXPLORERS

Explorers come in all shapes, sizes, and temperaments. Edmund Hillary and Tenzing Norgay were the first to go beyond the death zone, ascend Mount Everest, and return home. The New Zealander Hillary towered over his climbing partner, Sherpa Norgay. Einstein, the jovial genius, played practical jokes, while Beethoven, the introspective loner, brooded. So putting together a list of characteristics and aptitudes is a dicey matter and partially dependent on the arena of expertise. Explorers of the Arctic regions clearly need to have a certain physiological constitution to endure bone-chilling temperatures and wind chills registering in the triple digits. Likewise, a ground-breaking physicist must have a special mental acumen.

We put those special, but obligatory, abilities aside and reviewed the exploits of great explorers in a wide variety of fields. We asked a simple question: What common aptitudes, if any, do these people have? We found four that we believe capture the essence of explorers regardless of their area of specialty. Think of it as the "explorer's job description."

Embrace Uncertainty

Explorers gravitate toward the unknown, chaotic, vague, random, and complex (see Figure 2.1). When confronted with uncertainty, they don't try to minimize it or chop it down to size; instead, they investigate and seek to understand it. They are invigorated, not daunted, by it. Their doubt and lack of understanding stimulates inquiry and action rather than fear and complacency. During the 1930s, for example, the highly honored British explorer Freya Madeline Stark was "attracted to the blank spots on maps of the Middle East."[9] The Royal Geographical Society bestowed the prestigious title of "Dame" on Ms. Stark in part because she ventured into and wrote

Figure 2.1	Uncertainty Continuum

Certainty	Uncertainty
◎ Known	◎ Unknown
◎ Law-like	◎ Chaotic
◎ Sure	◎ Unsure
◎ Clear	◎ Vague
◎ Predictable	◎ Random
◎ Absolute	◎ Provisional
◎ Simple	◎ Complex
◎ Stable	◎ Turbulent

about territories few Europeans dared to travel. She once explained her passion for exploring some of the most remote and dangerous areas of Persia by noting, "The lure of exploration still continues to be one of strongest lodestars of the human spirit, and will be so while there is the rim of an unknown horizon in this world or the next."[10]

Sometimes explorers possess a whimsical streak. Consider, for example, Richard Feynman, the Nobel Prize–winning physicist. He conceived of the unconventional but exceedingly influential Feynman diagrams that visually lay out the paths of subatomic particles. One day, he opened an atlas and blindly put his finger on a random spot on the map and promptly planned a journey there. His exploits are wonderfully chronicled in a delightful book, *Tuva or Bust!*[11] Professor Feynman may represent the extreme end on the "uncertainty embracer" scale, but it does give us a sense of the helter-skelter-like mind-set of some explorers.

An explorer would never believe the old adage "curiosity killed the cat," and even if she did, she would certainly think she has more than nine lives to expend on the quest. Professor Feynman perhaps captured his sentiments best in this revealing statement: "I feel a responsibility to proclaim . . . that doubt is not to be feared, but that it is to be welcomed as the possibility of a new potential for human beings. If you know that you are not sure, you have a chance to improve the situation."[12] For explorers, uncertainty almost mysteriously energizes them, beckoning them forward. If you see someone energized by a mystery or tough problem, then you are probably looking at a person with the soul of an explorer. They nod their heads in agreement with historian

Daniel Boorstin's quip, "The most promising words ever written on the maps of human knowledge are *terra incognita*—unknown territory."[13]

Question the Conventional

Questions are not as innocent as they appear. Some are merely veiled objections—"Why do we have to scrap a perfectly good product and invent a new one?" Others lead down blind alleys of inquiry—"What are the physical properties of aether?" Centuries ago, physicists were obsessed with determining the character of aether—a substance that presumably invisibly occupied all of space. Scientists believed it would explain the nature of magnetism, electricity, and light. Today, few scientists believe that it exists.[14] Other questions are grounded in dubious assumptions—"How can we make a better floppy disk drive for personal computers?" A few turn out to be meaningless—"What does an odorless perfume smell like?"

Explorers, on the other hand, have acquired the ability to ask the right questions. They take to heart CEO Wilbur Ross's maxim that "the biggest risk is the question you forgot to ask, because the danger is always something you don't know."[15] The explorer's journey often emerges from asking penetrating questions that go to the crux of the matter. Explorers endeavor to perceive the essential character of the uncertainty and then take action. The goal-oriented climber wants to get to the mountaintop; the explorer wants to find a new path up.

Scientists are particularly effective at formulating the penetrating questions that expand our knowledge into new realms. As David Gross, Nobel Physics Laureate, said, "One of the most creative qualities a research scientist can have is the ability to ask the right questions. . . . Science is shaped by ignorance."[16] No wonder that the 125th anniversary issue cover of *Science* is boldly emblazoned "125 Questions: What Don't We Know?" Inside are 125 significant scientific questions that are testable or answerable, such as

- What is the universe made of?
- What is the biological basis for consciousness?
- Are we alone in the universe?
- Is an effective HIV vaccine feasible?
- What can replace cheap oil—and when?

Explorers love tough, big, and unconventional questions like these. They are not afraid to ask them, and they tenaciously pursue the answers.

Trust Their Intuitions

By necessity, an explorer relies on a well-honed intuition. The necessity emerges from the fact that any exploration into the unknown entails contingencies that simply cannot be anticipated. Explorers recognize that waiting to get *all* the facts straight or a plan for *every* possibility is impossible. Working under the illusion that you can gather *all* the facts or plan for *every* possibility only delays action. Indeed, researchers have shown that gathering too much information can actually undermine organizational effectiveness.[17] That said, successful explorers do not recklessly dash into the unknown completely unprepared. Intuition works best when sharpened by extensive experience.[18]

Intuition is the name we give to sensibilities that are beyond our awareness or cannot be easily articulated. These sensibilities emerge from gleaning essential patterns behind a wide variety of related experiences. After scaling many peaks and avoiding many accidents, expert mountaineers develop an innate sixth sense of what slopes to avoid for fear of avalanche.[19] Likewise, An Wang of Wang computers had been through so many business cycles that he intuitively recognized that the days of high-priced calculators were numbered. In the face of strong internal opposition, Wang moved the company away from a business that was, at the time, a major profit center.[20] Today, companies give away calculators as promotional items that cost hundreds of dollars years ago.

These sensibilities are not easily communicated to others. A bullet-point list of insightful instructions on a PowerPoint slide will never hone intuition like a sustained string of good and bad experiences. That's why pilots spend hundreds of hours in simulators. Without the requisite experiences, even the most intuitively gifted make really foolish mistakes. What else could explain British explorer Captain Robert Scott's decision to use Shetland ponies (not sled dogs) and boots (not skis) to make his assault on the South Pole?[21] He was simply not as familiar with sled dogs and skis as his competitors farther north in Norway. Indeed, that may be why the Norwegians won the race to the South Pole and back. And, sadly, why Scott perished.

Delight in the Adventure

What happens to explorers when they are not exploring? They are not happy for long. They get agitated, impatient, and gnarly. The mundane bores and tires the true explorer. The first climber to ascend all 14 mountain peaks over 8,000 meters,

Reinhold Messner, put it this way: "Endurance, fear, suffering cold, and the state between survival and death are such strong experiences that we want them again and again. We become addicted. Strangely, we strive to come back safely; and being back, we seek to return, once more, to danger."[22] He reveals a deep insight: It's not the conquered mountain, the initiative completed, or the contest won that fulfills the explorer. Rather, the satisfaction emerges from acting in the here-and-now and thinking about, managing, and conquering uncertainties. Explorers labor on the precipice of their abilities, infusing their being with strength, vitality, and joy.

Conquering an intellectual mountain brings a similar joy. Physicist Victor Weisskopf played a pivotal role in the creation of first atomic bomb and made noteworthy scientific contributions in a variety of fields. In his autobiography, *The Joy of Insight: Passions of a Physicist,* he explains his pervasive inspiration:

> The joy of insight is a sense of involvement and awe, the elated state of the mind that you achieve when you have grasped some essential point; it is akin to what you feel on top of a mountain after a hard climb or when you hear a great work of music.[23]

The stereotypical physicist doesn't use words like *joy* and *passion*. But these are indeed the expressions of one with a restless mind, intent on exploring in the rarified air of intellectual activity that few dare to challenge.

EXPLORING AND PROGRESS MAKING

The passions and attributes of well-known explorers provide the backdrop for our discussion about the relationship between exploring and progress making. There are a variety of skills associated with exploring: scanning, integrating, imagining, hypothesizing, and brainstorming. As people and organizations master those skills, they learn to embrace uncertainty, trust intuitions, question the conventional, and delight in the adventure. In this sense, exploring, like planning, represents both an individual skill as well as a strategic activity of an organization.

Exploring represents one of the essential features of progress making, though not the only one. The other features—refining and platforms—are synthesized in the Progress Model and discussed in subsequent chapters. Exploring may or may not result in progress making. Einstein, for instance, clearly fits the profile of an explorer. Was he a progress maker? Early in his career, absolutely. His exploring led to a world-shattering new way of thinking about the universe. He established several new explanatory platforms, including the special and general theories of relativity. Others helped refine those ideas. After these singular achievements (e.g., platforms), he spent many years seeking to develop a unified field theory.[24] Unfortunately, he explored this idea but never made much progress. The lesson: Brilliant explorers often make progress, but there are no guarantees.

Our world produces relatively few Einsteins. Most leaders we will discuss in this book work more intimately with other people than Einstein did. Today, nearly all scientific progress happens when teams of committed people explore new revolutionary ideas. For example, Kazumi Shiosaki, the CEO of Epizyme, leads a team of scientists seeking to develop treatments for cancer, Alzheimer's, and other pernicious diseases through the science of epigenetics.[25] Press reports tout the promise of genetic engineering for preventing these diseases by directly altering the DNA of genes. Her company took a different path than directly altering genes.[26] Instead, Epizyme researches ways of suppressing the biochemical triggers of our genes.[27] If her team can develop drugs that impact the triggers, then the gene cannot express latent disease characteristics. Such fascinating explorations may well lead to a new revolutionary platform. Never heard of epigenetics? You are not alone. Explorers often work in obscurity for long periods of time; sometimes, though, life-changing progress emerges from the shadows of anonymity.

CONCLUDING THOUGHTS

Everybody has innate exploring tendencies. As philosopher René Descartes put it, "Wonder is the first of all passions."[28] How intensely does the exploring fire smolder in humans? In some people, it burns red hot. In others, it simmers below the surface, waiting to be fueled. Just as we all possess some degree of athleticism, we all possess some degree of curiosity. Are there people who are simply naturally gifted explorers? Sure. These are the people who explore because it is so deeply ingrained in their being that they are compelled into the unknown. Mountaineer George Mallory was mysteriously driven to Everest time and time again, only to die in the quest. Before his death, though, a reporter asked him why he kept returning. He famously replied, "Because it's there."[29] And to those with the soul of the explorer, that is all there is to it. End of story. When something this deep defines your essence, it becomes almost inexplicable.

That said, just as everyone can get in better physical shape, everyone can improve their skills as an explorer. In fact, most people are explorers in one part of their life and not in others. For example, some people love to explore new vacation spots but may be reluctant to explore a new way to conduct business at work. Everyone has a capacity to explore, but these abilities are often underused in certain settings. Understanding that dynamic and how to develop employees' abilities may well be one of the greatest leadership challenges. Leaders have an obligation to stoke the exploring embers of their supporters. Yet they must know when to explore and when not to. Extreme explorers need some kind of counterbalance if they hope to survive. Refiners perfectly moderate the explorer's potential excesses. That's the issue we consider in the next chapter.

NOTES

1. D. Starkey, *Elizabeth: The Struggle for the Throne.* New York: HarperCollins, 2001; M. Hart, *The 100: A Ranking of the Most Influential Persons in History.* New York: Hart Publishing, 1978.

2. F. P. Hughes, *Children, Play, and Development.* Thousand Oaks, CA: Sage, 2010.

3. C. Brogan and J. Smith, *Trust Agents: Using the Web to Build Influence, Improve Reputation, and Earn Trust.* Hoboken, NJ: John Wiley, 2009 (see pp. 64–65).

4. M. Coffey, *Where the Mountain Casts Its Shadow: The Dark Side of Extreme Adventure.* New York: St. Martin's Griffin, 2003.

5. J. Krakauer, *Into Thin Air.* New York: Villard, 1997, xiii.

6. Coffey, *Where the Mountain Casts Its Shadow,* 14.

7. Ibid., 15.

8. C. Carlson and W. Wilmot, *Innovation: The 5 Disciplines for Creating What Customers Want.* New York: Crown Business, 2006.

9. Quoted in R. Sale, *Explorers: A Photographic History of Exploration.* London: HarperCollins, 2005, 118.

10. Quoted in Sale, *Explorers,* 119.

11. R. Leighton, *Tuva or Bust! Richard Feynman's Last Journey.* New York: Norton, 2000.

12. R. Feynman, *The Meaning of It All: Thoughts of a Citizen-Scientist.* New York: Basic Books, 2005, 28.

13. D. Boorstin, *The Discoverers.* New York: Random House, 1983, xvi.

14. A. Einstein, translated by R. W. Lawson, *Relativity: The Special and General Theory.* New York: Crown Publishing, 1952.

15. W. Ross, "Good Execution Beats a Bad Idea." *Fortune,* November 23, 2009, 42.

16. D. Gross, cited by T. Siegried, "In Praise of Hard Questions." *Science,* July 1, 2005, 76–77, p. 76.

17. K. M. Sutcliffe and K. Weber, "The High Cost of Accurate Knowledge." *Harvard Business Review* 81, no. 5 (2003): 74–82, p. 78.

18. E. Dane and M. Pratt, "Exploring Intuition and Its Role in Managerial Decision Making." *Academy of Management Review* 32, no. 1 (2007): 33–54; C. Miller and D. Ireland, "Intuition in Strategic Decision Making: Friend or Foe in the Fast-Paced 21st Century?" *Academy of Management Executive* 19, no. 1 (2005): 19–30; G. Gigerenzer, *Gut Feeling: The Intelligence of the Unconscious.* New York: Viking, 2007.

19. E. Viesturs, *No Shortcuts to the Top: Climbing the World's 14 Highest Peaks.* New York: Broadway Books, 2006.

20. A. Wang, *Lessons: An Autobiography.* Reading, MA: Addison-Wesley, 1986.

21. D. Crane, *Scott of the Antarctic.* New York: Knopf, 2006.

22. R. Messner, quoted in Coffey, *Where the Mountain Casts Its Shadow,* 6.

23. V. Weisskopf, *The Joy of Insight: Passions of a Physicist.* New York: Basic Books, 1991, viii.

24. W. Isaacson, *Einstein: His Life and Universe.* New York: Simon & Schuster, 2007.

25. S. Ante, "Fertile Ground for Startups." *Business Week*, November 23, 2009, 46–54.

26. See www.epizyme.com.

27. The "Epi" refers to the biochemical processes that occur at a level above the gene.

28. R. Descartes, translated by E. S. Haldane and G. Ross, *Passions of the Soul.* Cambridge, UK: Cambridge University Press, 1931, 358.

29. See Coffey, *Where the Mountain Casts Its Shadow,* for a discussion of this famous dictum.

⇘ 3 ⇙

REFINING

————•◆•————

Efficiency is doing better what is already being done.

—Peter Drucker

The well-worn adage "better, faster, cheaper" best characterizes the refiner's mind-set. Refiners are the editors who sharpen a memo to better clarify the meaning of a key phrase. They are the technicians who squeeze steps out of a manufacturing process to get the product to the marketplace faster. They are the financial analysts who figure out ways to deliver quality service more cheaply. They are, in short, the people who try to improve or upgrade what already exists or what we already do.

We all have some degree of refining tendencies. In his thought-provoking essay "Definition of Man," the philosopher Kenneth Burke makes the wry observation that we are all "rotten with perfection."[1] Most refiners would be comfortable with a nod toward perfection. But the word *rotten* raises more than a few eyebrows. What does he mean? He explains, "A given terminology contains various implications, and there is a corresponding 'perfectionist' tendency for men to attempt carrying out those implications."[2] For example, if you choose the term *human resources* to describe your employees, there would be a natural tendency to treat people like one manages financial resources, fuel oil, shipping docks, and the like. He draws our attention to the fact that our innate desire to perfect or refine can have a dark side.

So when we discuss the characteristics of refiners in the following section, we need to recognize both sides of their character. Even the perfect apple rots without special care.

ATTRIBUTES OF REFINERS

Explorers tend to garner more headlines than refiners. After all, refiners are the ones who diligently work behind the scenes. In this section, we identify some of the common characteristics of those who are particularly skilled at refining. As in the previous chapter, we asked a simple question: What common characteristics, if any, do these folks have? We found four characteristics that we believe capture the essence of refiners regardless of their area of specialty. Again, think of it as the "refiner's job description."

Gravitate Toward Certainty

Refiners lean toward the predictable, known, and stable. They enjoy making what already works better. They improve the world from the solid ground of proven laws and established principles. They improve fuel efficiency by decreasing the weight of our vehicles (law of energy conservation). They increase the speed of customers through the checkout lane by changing the layout of the grocery store (principles of time and motion). They enhance our odds of winning at blackjack by teaching us about probabilities (law of probabilities).

Yet, they are unlikely to invent a hybrid engine to run your car, conceive of barcode readers to speed your visit at the grocery store, or even recommend buying a casino to ensure that the odds are in your favor. They, in fact, make progress incrementally, not with revolutionary (and uncertain) notions. Most refiners would agree with Voltaire's aphorism: "Perfection is attained by slow degrees; it requires the hand of time."

Strongly Value Order

Will Shortz is not a household name, but he has superstar status with crossword puzzle fans across the world. In fact, he has been the editor of crossword puzzles for the *New York Times* since 1993. He has a curious background. For instance, he graduated from Indiana University with a one-of-a-kind, personally designed degree in enigmatology. Puzzling major? Exactly; it's the study of puzzles and games in their cultural context. His house is filled with shelves of esoteric puzzle memorabilia such as "crossword drink coasters, crossword postcards, crossword board games, and crossword jewelry."[3] For all this seeming playfulness, he has a rather strict sense of order. For instance, when he became the editor, he set up a classification system for puzzles from easy to difficult. On Mondays the easiest puzzle appears, Tuesday the next easiest, and so on until the killer on Sundays. This had not been done before Shortz came along. And some puzzle aficionados were not particularly happy about the change.

That sense of orderliness and tidiness pervades most crossword puzzle fans. Marc Romano, also an avid puzzler, immersed himself in the arcane world of competitive crossword puzzlers. These are the kind of people who can do the *New York Times* Sunday crosswords in less than 30 minutes; mere mortals tally time in hours, not minutes. Romano opines in his entertaining book, *Crossworld,* "I suspect that, deep down, people who do lots of crosswords are attempting to create order by proxy."[4] We can extend that thought to most refiners. They are agitated by clutter and incompleteness. They love order and everything in its proper place or space (particularly when doing a crossword puzzle). And that may even mean not attempting the Sunday crossword puzzle for fear of not completing it.

Enamored With Precision and Clarity

In recent years, Rosalind Franklin has started to receive much deserved recognition for aiding in the discovery of the structure of DNA. It was Watson and Crick who received the Nobel Prize, but that would not have happened without Dr. Franklin. She took the exquisite X-ray diffraction pictures that led to the unraveling of the DNA mystery.[5] Her method tells us much about the qualities of great refiners. She made numerous pictures while making tiny adjustments to her equipment. Her quest was to make the clearest, most detailed pictures ever. And she succeeded by almost every measure. In fact, one fellow scientist put it this way:

> As a scientist Miss Franklin was distinguished by extreme clarity and perfection in everything she undertook. Her photographs are among the most beautiful X-ray photographs of any substance ever taken. Their excellence

was the fruit of extreme care in preparation and mounting of the specimens as well as in the taking of the photographs.[6]

Dr. Franklin's story reveals qualities that define the essence of great refiners. It shows how refiners take the existing equipment (or process) and push it to the extreme in a quest for greater clarity. It reveals the enormous power and influence that can emerge from more precise information. In this case, it was Watson and Crick's Nobel Prize. It also demonstrates how refiners often have a natural passion for their craft. In Rosalind Franklin's case, she went to the university over her father's strong objections. He believed women did not belong in college. She, of course, proved him wrong. And, like any refiner, she had the precise facts to back her up.[7]

Pursue Correctness

Refiners want to "get it right." Unlike the explorer, an approximation will not do. Refiners exhibit a Sherlock Holmes–like inquisitiveness as they track down the right answer. The mythical Sherlock Holmes pursued his cases with a logical relentlessness that marvels fans to this day. He once mildly rebuked his partner, Dr. Watson, with this revealing admonition: "I have no data yet. It is a capital mistake to theorise before one has data. Insensibly one begins to twist facts to suit theories, instead of theories to suit facts."[8] This kind of careful, logical deduction characterizes most refiners. It is a kind of curiosity that drives the refiner to the *only* rational solution to a mystery.

The refiner believes that if you fit all the pieces of the puzzle together, the correct answer emerges. (Of course, the problem is that you may not have all the pieces.) Unlike the explorer, they are not heavily reliant on intuition or hunches. Indeed, like Holmes, they wait to form their impressions until after all the facts have been gathered, analyzed, and pieced together. They trust the systematic, methodical, and thorough approach.

That's why refiners are constantly tinkering with their procedures and processes to improve accuracy. Highly regarded pollsters, for example, tend to have a refining orientation and an obsession with exactitude. They want to predict with reliable accuracy who will win a given election. Almost anyone could call up a random list of voters and ask, "Who are you going to vote for?" but for the pollsters, their credibility is at stake. Pollsters face many challenges in "getting it right." At the top of the list is the problem of distinguishing between those who *say* they are going to vote and those who *will actually* vote.

One of the key distinctions between different pollsters is how they qualify people to be included in their poll. The best pollsters have a series of qualifying "gates" they use before they actually count respondents' opinions. Fine-tuning this process is time-consuming and costly, but it does tend to increase the reliability of their prognostications.[9]

REFINING AND PROGRESS MAKING

The sensibilities and characteristics of high-profile refiners discussed in the previous section frame our discussion of another essential progress-making activity. As with exploring, refining represents both an individual skill and a strategic direction. Both individuals and organizations can make progress through refining. However, unlike exploring, the refining process tends to produce incremental and evolutionary progress. We will have more to say about this issue in later chapters.

For now, though, we want to highlight the progress-making possibilities of the refining activity. Consider, for example, one of the most successful collegiate coaches in history, Pat Summitt. As the head coach of the Lady Vols at the University of Tennessee, she became the first Division One men's or women's coach to reach 1,000 career wins. Equally impressive, her players win accolades as students: 100% of them who complete their athletic eligibility graduate from the university. Early in life, Pat was driven to perfection. How else do we explain her spotless attendance record from kindergarten through high school?[10] Achievement through dedication, hard work, and a passion for improvement defines her career in equal measure to her basketball IQ. As a young coach, she earnestly studied the coaching lessons of the collegiate greats such as Dean Smith and Bobby Knight. She adapted and refined their approaches to the women's game. She summed up her philosophy best: "I look at how do we get better all the time. Success drives me, but failure drives me more."[11] This is not a mere headline but something the preacher practices every day. And she has the record to prove it.

The crowd roars approval when one of Pat's players lobs the ball into the air and sends the game-winning shot swishing through the net. Yet far from the eyes of the crowds are the countless hours spent sharpening the footwork, honing the upper body, and conditioning the psyche to take the pressure shot. The cycle of practicing, critiquing, and correcting deepens the understanding of the physical and psychological aspects of any task. That's why so many products in the world just keep getting better and better; the cars we drive today are safer and more fuel efficient than their predecessors. Like Pat, refiners reach the summit of their careers with an almost religious-like fervor to these progress-making activities.

CONCLUDING THOUGHTS

Refiners naturally excel at organizing, categorizing, systematizing, scheduling, dissecting, optimizing, and streamlining. Perhaps no other person better captures this orientation than an American mechanical engineer described as having a "greater effect on the private and public lives of the men and women of the twentieth century than any other single individual."[12] His near obsession with optimization led him and his stopwatch-equipped colleagues to determine the best size and weight of shovel for each specific task. And that was just the beginning. If you could do that for shovels, what about other tools and processes? His biographer summed up this man's philosophy of work: "You had to do it the one best way prescribed for you and not in your old, idiosyncratic, if perhaps less efficient way."[13] This was the scientific way to manage a factory, mill, mine, office, and even a tennis match (he won the 1881 U.S. Open Tennis Championship in doubles).

And so it was that Frederick Taylor and his scientific management approach held sway over business in the late 1800s and early 1900s, eliminating wasted motion, escalating efficiency, and dramatically increasing profits.[14] He had some notable detractors, such as union workers and their supporters in the U.S. Congress who complained about the de-humanizing impact of a by-the-numbers management style. The modern descendants of Taylorism such as reengineering and Six Sigma soften the rough edges of scientific management and address many of the concerns raised by critics. Yet, Taylor's ideas still weave a magician-like spell in today's push for efficiency and quality. In sum, refiners, like explorers, can point to some remarkable successes of their approach.

Clearly, some people don't naturally gravitate toward the refiner's viewpoint. Yet, Taylor advocated what others do today. Namely, most people can learn refining skills and apply them to a host of problems. In order to do so, refiners need a launching pad. They can find it in something we call a "platform," the subject of the next chapter.

NOTES

1. K. Burke, *Language as Symbolic Action: Essays on Life, Literature, and Method.* Berkeley: University of California Press, 1968, 16.

2. Ibid., 19.

3. M. Romano, *Crossworld: One Man's Journey Into America's Crossword Obsession.* New York: Broadway Books, 2005, 42.

4. Ibid., 216.

5. H. Judson, *The Eighth Day of Creation: Makers of the Revolution in Biology.* New York: Cold Spring Harbor Laboratory Press, 1996.

6. J. D. Bernal, "Dr. Rosalind E. Franklin." *Nature,* July 19, 1958, 154.

7. B. Maddox, *Rosalind Franklin: The Dark Lady of DNA.* New York: HarperCollins, 2002.

8. A. C. Doyle, *Sherlock Holmes.* Secaucus, NJ: Castle Books, 1978, 13.

9. S. Igo, *The Averaged American: Surveys, Citizens, and the Making of a Mass Public.* Cambridge, MA: Harvard University Press, 2007.

10. See http://www.utladyvols.com/sports/w-baskbl/mtt/summitt_pat00.html (accessed November 28, 2009).

11. L. Gregg, "Trailblazer, Icon, and Living Legend." *Women in Business,* August/September 2009, 28–31, p. 31.

12. J. Rifkin, *Time Wars: The Primary Conflict in Human History.* New York: Henry Holt & Co., 1987, 106.

13. R. Kanigel, *The One Best Way: Frederick Winslow Taylor and the Enigma of Efficiency.* New York: Penguin, 1997, 209–10.

14. In one respect, Taylor could be characterized as an explorer because he advocated a revolutionary way of improving productivity. In this chapter, though, we focused more on his advocacy of efficiency and incremental improvements.

4

PLATFORMS

All that is human must retrograde if it does not advance.

—Gibbon

The word *platform* originated from the Middle French word *plate-forme.* The first syllable, *plate,* signifies a plate or something flat and conveys a sense of stability. The second syllable, *forme,* suggests an underlying form or structure. The two concepts intermingle to form a wonderful visual and conceptual image. No wonder the word has been picked up and used in so many different contexts:

- When the train conductor yells "all aboard," you embark from a *platform* or a structure that is relatively flat and stable.
- When software engineers develop an operating system, such as Microsoft's Windows 7 or Google's Android, they are creating a *platform* for users to launch a wide array of other applications.
- When politicians want to communicate their guiding principles or ideals to the public, they create a *platform* that provides a sense of identity and stability amid the ever-variable political winds.
- When petroleum engineers want to extract oil from under the sea bed, they construct drilling *platforms* designed to withstand even more powerful winds.

At the core, a platform offers stability and structure to both protect us from disarray and project us forward. In short, platforms are a set of closely bundled notions, practices, procedures, activities, or decisions that provide a springboard for action.

HOW PLATFORMS EMERGE

People create platforms by exploring, refining, and consolidating. It all starts with exploring a new way to manage a situation, produce a product, or solve a problem. Consider, for example, the fight against a cruel and insidious malady that afflicted over 50,000 people in the United States in 1952. At the time, people were treated with a hodgepodge of medicines and voodoo-like home-spun remedies that were as varied as they were ineffectual. The truth was, once it struck, nobody knew what to do. Some people—especially children—died; others were crippled for life. Sadly, all the scientific energy focused on a cure for polio resulted in little progress.[1]

Such circumstances often provide fertile ground for someone to develop an entirely new approach or platform. Fortunately, there was someone who had the courage to address the problem from an unusual angle. His experience in creating an influenza vaccine made him uniquely qualified to pursue a radical new method. He reasoned, since we can produce a flu vaccine, why not develop a polio vaccine? Yet, as with any new platform, there were plenty of naysayers. In fact, on the eve of deploying his vaccine to the masses, famed journalist Walter Winchell falsely alarmed parents by "reporting" that the new polio vaccine "may be a killer."[2] Today, of course, the polio vaccine is considered one of the greatest medical success stories of all time.

How the vaccine was developed proves instructive. The new platform emerged from a combination of *instinct, insight,* and old fashioned *hard work.* The *instinct* came from a unique individual with a special medical background that could be used to respond to this malady. The *insight* came after repeated trial-and-error experiments. Even after the key insights were gleaned in the laboratory, *hard work* was needed to overcome the technical production problems. Indeed, the more vaccine the lab produced, the better they got at producing it by clarifying instructions and setting up more rigorous quality standards and other typical refining activities. Consequently, parents throughout the world rejoiced. And they have one platform creator to thank: Jonas Salk. Without him, who knows how many more would have suffered.

We represent a platform with a *series of nodes.* The story of Jonas Salk's polio vaccine illustrates the essential dynamics of how the first node (1.1) of a platform is established. It starts with some special individual's or team's instinct about how to approach a problem in an entirely novel way. They *explore* a number of options to glean the essential insights. They often analyze data and test out options during this phase. After they have settled on an acceptable solution, they start *refining* it through a series of improvements. Cycles of exploring (upward direction) and refining (downward direction) ultimately lead to the development of a fairly stable terminal point that temporarily provides enough certainty to launch the plan, market the product, or administer the vaccine (see Figure 4.1).

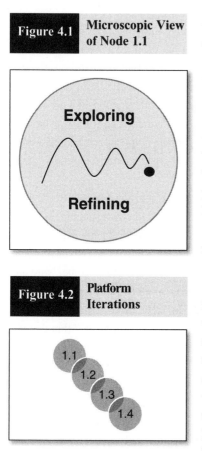

Figure 4.1 **Microscopic View of Node 1.1**

Figure 4.2 **Platform Iterations**

Usually, platforms are subsequently refined or upgraded. It's not a "once and done" type of exercise. The successive iterations of the platform are displayed in nodes 1.2, 1.3, and so on (see Figure 4.2). Computer users know that their operating system (e.g., platform) requires routine updating to protect against new viruses and fix minor glitches. Each upgrade would be considered a refinement of the existing platform. However, when Microsoft encouraged Windows XP and Vista users to move to Windows 7, it advocated a shift to a new platform, not a mere refinement of an existing platform.

FEATURES OF PLATFORMS

Often people resist new platforms by actively opposing them or passively ignoring them. One of Salk's favorite maxims was,

> When you're arguing for an unpopular idea [platform], there are three stages
> of truth. First, your opponents say it can't be true. Next they say if it's true, it
> can't be very important. Finally they say well, we've known it all along.[3]

He vividly reminds us that new platforms spawn both victims and victors. But
how long does one remain a victor? After all, radio dramas yielded to silent
movies, which in turn yielded to talkies, and so on. Each new platform sup-
plants or significantly changes its predecessor. Two insightful scholars discuss
this phenomenon in a wonderfully titled book, *Beware the Winner's Curse:
Victories That Can Sink You and Your Company:*

> All of us are susceptible to the Winner's Curse: we can overpay for something
> we passionately want to acquire or, if we are successful, we rest on our lau-
> rels and let complacency carry us along when we really should be taking
> action. . . . The Winner's Curse is not automatic nor is it guaranteed. Those
> who, for whatever reasons, do not respect the Curse are likely to experience
> it and some potentially costly consequences. By remaining suitably humble
> and taking (the right) steps, you can become an observer of the Winner's
> curse rather than a victim.[4]

General managers of professional sports teams face both prongs of the
winner's curse. They must avoid overpaying for a prized player for several
reasons: (1) Sometimes that player can't deliver on the high expectations, and
(2) the funds used on the star player diminish the money that can be paid to
the supporting cast. Likewise, the managers must avoid retaining star players
who are past their prime playing days.[5] The winner's curse puts in sharp focus
the perils facing the victor as well as the hopes left to the vanquished. Neither
should be ignored.

Progress makers remember the lessons of the winner's curse because they
recognize three essential features of platforms:

1. **Platforms are temporary, but they are often treated as permanent.** Richard Feynman, the Nobel Prize–winning physicist, was
   fond of reminding people, "The first principle is that you must not
   fool yourself—and you are the easiest person to fool."[6] Platforms,
   especially profitable ones, create the ideal conditions for building a
   fool's paradise. A false sense of stability and sustainability imbues all
   who work at maintaining and profiting from the existing platforms,
   particularly those who appear to dominate the competitive landscape.

For example, at one point, General Motors sold half of all the cars in the United States. The subsequent market failures and bankruptcy in 2009 led the editors of *The Economist* to dig up the fossil record and cleverly dub the collapse "Detroitosaurus Wrecks."[7] And that is exactly what happens to outmoded platforms: They slowly die out like the ancient dinosaurs they've become.

2. **Platforms don't necessarily lose their stability, but they often become irrelevant.** Platforms provide focus at the expense of concealing other options. Kodak film is a wonderful product, but who needs it now? Digital cameras make traditional camera film irrelevant. In fact, digital photographic products account for 70% of Kodak's revenues, and the company no longer produces Kodachrome film.[8] And frankly, most people could care less what product they use to take their pictures—all they want is a photograph to share with others.

   Traditional newspapers may face a similar fate. People want news at the right place and at the right time. That's why successful newspapers must grapple with the implications of the Internet and 24-hour cable TV news. Failing to do so may result in oblivion through irrelevancy. One encouraging sign for newspapers is the push to electronically publish content and make it available on devices such as Amazon's Kindle. In fact, later in the book, we profile one progress maker, Laura Hollingsworth, who is successfully grappling with these concerns. She, unlike other leaders, recognizes the inherent threat posed by what an organization doesn't recognize or understand.

3. **Platform improvements can create deceiving illusions.** The problem can be stated simply: How do you judge whether an innovation is merely an *improvement* to an existing platform (moving from version 1.3 to 1.4) or a *jump* to a new platform (leaping from 1.4 to 2.1)? The answer, though, cannot be discerned as easily. For example, does a new encyclopedia edition with numerous new articles on pop culture count as an improvement to an existing product or a jump to a new platform? What about dramatically changing the packaging and design of a cola product? In both cases, developers may feel like they are engineering a radical transformation or platform shift. In hindsight, though, we realize they were not. In effect, these were cosmetic changes to an existing platform. The potential deception creeps in when leaders fail to assess the need for

an evolutionary and revolutionary platform change. That's a more subtle way to inadvertently fall prey to the winner's curse.

On the other hand, consider Wikipedia, the encyclopedia collaboratively written by volunteers and freely available on the World Wide Web. Wikipedia ushered in an entirely new platform and competitor to traditional publishers such as Encyclopedia Britannica.[9] Likewise, sports drinks and assorted fruit drinks revolutionized soft drink markets by moving masses of thirsty consumers away from traditional colas. In both cases, these represent new platforms that compete against older, although improved, platforms.

Leaders may reorganize, shift resources, and establish new priorities in an attempt to make their organizations more relevant to the times. Often such changes are necessary and consequential. For example, when Ruth Kirschstein became the first woman director of the U.S. National Institutes of Health, she used her leadership skills to shift resources to basic research and establish innovative programs such as the Minority Access to Research Careers (MARC) program. Her colleagues describe the impact of her programmatic shifts as "incalculable."[10] Few could argue with her success. Some of her successes emerged from refining existing platforms such as increasing funding to basic research. Other successes surfaced by establishing new platforms such as the MARC program. She built a winning organization without falling prey to the winner's curse.

CONCLUDING THOUGHTS

Platforms shape, improve, and limit our lives in countless ways. The automobile literally shaped the landscape because we built roads and freeways to accommodate the vehicles. Global Positioning System (GPS) devices improved our ability to navigate. Yet even as platforms shape and improve, they limit. For example, Google and other search engines revolutionized our ability to expediently locate lots of information, but they also tend to limit our searching. For many students, if it does not exist on the Internet, it does not exist. In fact, for some people, if it can't be located on the first page of the search engine results page (aka SERP), it doesn't exist. That's why some consulting companies specialize in "search engine optimization"; in other words, these consultants figure out ways to push your company higher up the Google,

Yahoo, or Bing search engine results page. Ironically, the search engine's power and speed seem to limit many individuals' willingness to search for other useful information in other venues such as books, personal networks, or other less accessible information sources.

Platforms dominate the landscape of our work-a-day world like the buildings in a vibrant city. Some are small and charming such as Trek's distinctively stylized carbon-fiber Madone bicycle.[11] Others loom large like the Internet. Still others have "Caution: Work in Progress" signs posted around the platform such as genetic engineering protocols. Like any lively cityscape, some platforms retain their stately prominence while others are torn down to make way for the modern. The dynamic interplay between stability and change, tradition and innovation, characterizes the forces that shape progress in our cities as well as in our lives. And that idea provides the focal point of the next chapter.

NOTES

1. J. Kluger, *Splendid Solution: Jonas Salk and the Conquest of Polio.* New York: Putnam, 2004.

2. Ibid., 264.

3. Ibid., 317–18.

4. G. Anandalingam and H. Lucas, *Beware the Winner's Curse: Victories That Can Sink You and Your Company.* New York: Oxford University Press, 2004, 232–33.

5. S. Leahy, "Parity Goes Only So Far in Today's NFL." *USA Today,* November 27–29, 2009, A1–2.

6. R. Feynman, "Cargo Cult Science: Some Remarks on Science, Pseudoscience, and Learning How to Not Fool Yourself." Caltech's 1974 commencement address. See http://calteches.library.caltech.edu/51/2/CargoCult.htm (accessed June 10, 2009).

7. "Detroitosaurus Wrecks." *The Economist,* June 6, 2009, 9.

8. M. Copeland, "Photo Finish." *Fortune,* July 20, 2009, 12.

9. A. Lih, *The Wikipedia Revolution: How a Bunch of Nobodies Created the World's Greatest Encyclopedia.* New York: Hyperion, 2009.

10. H. Schachman and M. Cassman, "Retrospective: Ruth L. Kirschstein (1926–2009)." *Science,* November 13, 2009, 947.

11. R. Karlgaard, "Three Joy-Giving Products." *Forbes,* June 22, 2009, 21.

⚜ 5 ⚜

PROGRESS

————•◦•————

The art of progress is to preserve order amid change and to preserve change amid order.

—Alfred North Whitehead

The idea of progress appeals to most people. It creates buzz by summoning our attention and enticing us forward with the promise of something better. Yet, many have stumbled over that phrase "something better." Is the car a better mode of transportation than a horse? Those are exactly the kinds of value judgments that some people don't like to make. Indeed, you do not hear historians talk much about progress these days. Why not? Ronald Wright, in his book *A Short History of Progress,* captured the essence of the conundrum:

> The atomic bomb, a logical progression from the arrow and the bullet, became the first technology to threaten our whole species with extinction. It is what I call a "progress trap." But much simpler technologies have also seduced and ruined societies in the past.[1]

His argument beckons us to ponder some difficult issues. What does "better" actually mean? What end are we pursuing? Perhaps the nuclear holocaust scenario seems a bit extreme. Yet, the basic argument might resonate if we tinker with a few words: "Fully automated plants, a logical progression from the assembly line and machine-assisted manufacturing, may become the technology that threatens much of a company's workforce with extinction." Perhaps this characterization helps provide some perspective on the historian's cautions about the concept of "progress."

In this chapter, we jump into the progress debate. We do so because progress makers should (1) know what they are trying to achieve and (2) understand both the risks and rewards of making progress. That said, we are unapologetically pro-progress. No surprise there. What may cause you pause are the five observations we make in this chapter about progress.

DEFINING PROGRESS

Traditionally, the notion of progress has been linked to concepts such as moving forward or advancing. For example, a geometric progression is a sequence of numbers (e.g., 1, 3, 9, 27, 81 . . .) obtained by multiplying the previous number by a constant factor (in this case, a 3). The notion of progress has been used in a variety of ways, usually with positive connotations, but not always. Consider the following: A progressive income tax is one that gradually increases. Of course, politicians—but not necessarily high-income taxpayers—may consider this "progressive." Companies like geometrically increasing revenues, but no one wants geometrically increasing cancer cells (a progressive disease). Progressive jazz was the name given to the jazz of the 1950s that involved experimentation with rhythms and harmony. Some were hits, but most were not.

We celebrate the educational progress of a student who graduates from high school and subsequently from college. At the very least, the student has cleared some major hurdles and set herself up for future success. Hurdling obstacles to grasp the diploma captures one sense of progress. It entices us with images of moving forward toward a particular goal or end state.[2]

But progress making implies something else as well. The other sense of progress focuses on grasping new and unknown possibilities. This type of progress is harder to visualize than hurdling toward a predetermined outcome. Yet, we hear inklings about this perspective in the commencement speaker's challenge that beckons graduates to envision and create a better world. In short, *we believe that the notion of progress embodies two images: the hurdler and the visionary.* The problem: People use the same word to describe two distinctly different types of progress.

Some readers, no doubt, flinch at the suggestion that a horse might be a better mode of transportation than a car. One might ask, "Do you really expect me to bring home the groceries on the back of horse?" Well, of course not, unless you happen to live on a narrow mountain pass without paved roads. This simple thought problem, though, vividly illustrates the conundrum anyone faces when deciding what counts as progress. Everyone defines progress based on a particular set of circumstances and conditions. Horses are a useful way to navigate around the mountains. They certainly represent a progressive mode of transport when compared to hiking to and fro to gather provisions. But most folks would still prefer the family car for the trek down the old Pony Express route from Missouri to California.

This whimsical example has a serious point. Namely, organizational leaders often view progress from very different vantage points as they see various circumstances coming into play. These differences translate into divergent definitions of progress. The lexicon may be the same, but what counts for progress for one executive many not count for another. The horse represents progress for one and the fighter jet for another. After all, a former secretary of defense for the United States began his influential essay on "transforming the military" with a stirring account of the "first U.S. cavalry attack of the twenty-first century" by U.S. Special Forces operators.[3] It was not the world's most sophisticated warfare technology that proved decisive in the battles with the Taliban in the Afghanistan war. It was the horse. Yet Special Forces operators were never trained how to mount, ride, and shoot from a horse. The soldiers had to clasp the reins of an *old* "battle field technology"—the horse—to make progress against a new foe. The horse allowed them to project power into places that cutting-edge tanks or even jets could not reach. Mastering the horse—not the latest and greatest technical gizmo—became the symbol of military progress.[4] Such are the strangely twisting mental gyrations necessary to make a judgment about what counts as progress.

How do you get a handle on the true nature of progress? That question prompted us to go beyond the standard dictionary definition of "moving forward." At the most basic level, we believe progress occurs when four conditions have been met:

1. *Results emerged from conscious decision making and deliberate choices.* This provision rules out inertia and happenstance as sources of progress. What about the organization that seizes a serendipitous

opportunity? Would that count as progress? Yes. It falls within the parameter because the organization made a deliberate choice to pursue the opportunity. Consider what emerged from a conversation with TV host Johnny Carson and Wolfgang Puck while Puck was running Spago's. The celebrated chef discovered that Johnny would take his pizzas home, freeze them, and rewarm them later. The indignant gourmet's first reaction was, "How can you do that to my pizza?"[5] Then he tried it himself and realized "it wasn't bad."[6] In fact, he eventually turned that unforeseen conversation and moment of insight into a multimillion-dollar pizza business.

2. *Something—or some condition—has improved the status quo.* An organization, product, or social movement makes progress when it moves beyond the current state of affairs. Often planned changes represent improvements over the status quo. Putting an eraser on the end of pencil improved its functionality and ease of use.[7] However, all changes do not result in improvements because unintended negative consequences may crop up. Expanding the number of features of a software system may please a few power users but at the same time slows the boot-up process to a slug-like crawl.

3. *The improvements are legitimately sustainable.* The improvements should be sufficiently stable and endure long enough to serve as a platform. In short, they should be resistant to rapid regression. This provision rules out the Riccardo "the Cobra" Ricco-type performance enhancements. His remarkable 2008 Tour de France exploits abruptly ended when officials discovered he was using a banned performance enhancer.[8] He earned his nickname for his quick-hitting venomous attacking style of cycling. He turned out to be a snake of a different sort. Doping to enhance athletic performance—like cooking the books to enhance financial performance—results in artificial progress. In due course, deceit-driven gains prove to be undeserved, unstable, and unsustainable. They often prove as deadly as a cobra's strike to a career or an organization.

4. *The improvements occurred through either exploring or refining.* This provision stipulates the fundamental types of actions that drive improvement. We will have more to say about this issue in later chapters.

These four conditions provide a framework for understanding the underlying nature of progress. To be sure, our definition does not answer all the specific questions related to defining progress in a particular circumstance.
Organizational leaders, for example, define progress in a variety of ways.
Some possibilities, to name a few, include defining it in terms of profitability,
adaptability, innovation, growth, market share, return on investment, prestige,
and social consciousness. Which is correct? That depends on the organization's environment, philosophy, and strategy at a particular point in time. A
university, for example, might define progress in terms of prestige, while a
consumer products business might characterize progress in terms of market
share. Even within a particular organization, one division might describe
progress in terms of innovation while another division might define it by profitability numbers. Effective leaders collaborate with others to define progress
for their organizations or communities. Those deliberations should be informed
by the implications discussed in the next section.

IMPLICATIONS OF THE PROGRESS DEFINITION

Assessing the Degree of Progress Requires a Complex Act of Judgment

Even if a reasonable consensus emerges about the meaning of progress,
another problem surfaces. Could a company, for example, make more
money than the previous year and still not be making progress? Of course.
If general market conditions are favorable, then the business might be riding a basic industry trend. During the early 1990s, a lot of mutual fund managers looked pretty good, boasting double-digit returns. How much of this
was due to the skill and great insight of mutual fund managers and analysts?
How much to generally favorable market conditions? Teasing out answers to
questions like these presents the fundamental challenge in assessing progress.
This requires an act of judgment by people well acquainted with all the relevant conditions. This assessment cannot be made by simply looking at the
bottom-line numbers.

Good financial results do not necessarily equate with progress. Likewise,
poor results do not necessarily equate with stagnation. Could a sports team
have a losing record and still be making progress? Certainly. Perhaps the players and coaches learned some valuable lessons that could serve as the basis for
future success. The win/loss record or statistics can never tell the complete

story. For example, the Los Angeles Lakers basketball team lost to the Boston Celtics in the 2008 NBA finals. Basically, the same team returned the next season, dominated, and won the 2009 NBA championship. The team's coach, Phil Jackson, noted that MVP Kobe Bryant learned from past defeats about how to be a better leader through "giving."[9] Even hard-core sports fans would find it difficult to locate the exact statistic to reflect that leadership quality.[10]

Progress Always Creates New Challenges

Progress agnostics are those people who tolerate progress (they usually drive cars instead of ride horses) but are not quite sure they believe in it. Their lament was best argued by historian Ronald Wright:

> Hope drives us to invent new fixes for old messes, which in turn create more dangerous messes. Hope elects the politician with the biggest empty promise; and as any stockbroker or lottery seller knows, most of us will take a slim hope over prudent and predictable frugality.[11]

Professor Mazlish of MIT echoes the concern: "What seems to be a step forward often leaves us standing still, or even moves us backward. Dr. Guillotine invented his machine to make executions more humane, but we know to what use it was put."[12] Dr. Edward Tenner makes a similar argument in his fascinating book, *Why Things Bite Back: Technology and the Revenge of Unintended Consequences.* He points out that for almost every step forward, some new problem has emerged. Yes, antibiotics have saved countless people from suffering, but new kinds of bugs have emerged that are even more deadly and resistant to antibiotics. Likewise, "rigid molded ski boots have helped prevent ankle and tibia fractures at the cost of anterior cruciate ligament injuries."[13] The Internet has expedited communication around the world but ushered in computer viruses, spam, and concerns about privacy invasions.

Our response: So what? There are problems (challenges) and costs associated with the status quo, as well. The only difference is that we often know more about the costs associated with the status quo than we do about something entirely new. It really boils down to what kinds of problems you want to deal with. Any championship sports team faces a strong possibility that other teams will try to poach their players, enticing them with bigger salaries and special perks. Does that mean you stop trying to win the championship because you might face this new challenge? No one in their right mind would take such a position. Yet, that seems to be precisely the argument of many progress agnostics.

You can be optimistic or pessimistic about progress. As professor of history, Robert Friedel perceptively noted, "At every step along the way in (our) history there have been debates, sometimes quiet, often violent, about improvement. Who should define it? Who should benefit from it? Who must pay the inevitable costs?"[14] The pessimists usually get most of the press coverage. Fair enough. We need to know about the possible downsides of purported progressive new technology, government programs, or business ventures. Humans, after all, are peculiarly sensitive to the downside.[15] Behavioral psychologists call it the "loss aversion" tendency, whereby fear of loss often trumps potential pleasure of gain.[16] It's part of our survival mechanism. Nevertheless, our natural instincts and a pessimistic press (bad news always leads) should not obscure a sober analysis of the possibilities presented by progress. And we may even choose not to adopt certain so-called progressive ideas. That's fair, as well. After all, the scientific community stepped away from human cloning. However, the likelihood, and indeed inevitability, of new challenges (or problems) emerging from something progressive should not impede our quest to make things better.

Progress Is Not Inevitable

For many people, progress seems to be almost inescapable and preordained. This is particularly true in the technological realm. The march from the phonograph, to the eight-track tape, to the CD, to the iPod may appear to follow a perfectly linear and totally predictable path. But that obscures the reality. A complex series of interrelated events produced this seemingly straight evolutionary track. Indeed, there was nothing inevitable about the iPod. Sure, many of the technologies were available, but someone had to package them together with expert marketing to make it a commercial success. And many other companies tried but failed. As CEO Steve Jobs acknowledged, even Apple almost missed the boat because his attention was focused on refining the video editing programs on the Mac.[17]

Believing in the inevitability of progress obscures the central role people have in generating progress. There was nothing inevitable about the civil rights movement. It never would have taken hold in the United States without Rosa Parks, Martin Luther King Jr., and others leading the way. There was nothing inevitable about the World Wide Web; the basic protocols and structures had been around for over 20 years. Rather English computer scientist, Sir Timothy John Berners-Lee, brainstormed the idea and developed it. And there was nothing inevitable about putting a man on the moon. It only happened because of the tireless efforts of engineers and the leadership of President Kennedy. Without his speech committing the nation "to achieving the goal, before this decade is out, of landing a man on the Moon and returning him back safely to the earth," the United States would never have done so.[18] In short, progress does not equate with the passage of time.

Progress Rarely Follows a Straight Line Leading From Point A to Point B

Parents know that there is nothing orderly or tidy about how their children learn their native language. Language acquisition occurs in fits and starts; one day they are saying "goo-goo" and the next, "Google it." The typical child possesses a working vocabulary of 10 words for the first 13 to 15 months of life and then it spikes up in the second and third years. By 4 years, the "young human has a linguistic ability close to that of an adult."[19] Parents intuitively know this, so you don't see too many of them shouting, "Jane, you've only learned 2 new words in the last month—that's not good enough!" One child may have a working vocabulary of 20 words by 10 months; another child may have the same number a year later. No worry; parents just need to set up the right conditions for progress, and the child's brain will do the rest.[20] After all, Albert Einstein was "slow in learning how to talk," and he ended up doing pretty well in life.[21]

This means that progress may not always occur on a predetermined timetable or meet the quarterly business goals. It suggests that progress may occur behind the scenes, out of view of outside observers, and not provide immediate, visible results. Progress often occurs in small, almost inscrutable, steps before it reaches an inflection or "tipping" point.[22] In retrospect, everyone sees the growth curve. But the pre–tipping point period, with all the false starts, miscalculations, and blunders, presents a vexing emotional challenge to any progress maker.

Consider, for example, an irritant that Sir Isaac Newton, Johannes Kepler, and millions of school kids around the world grumbled about for years. Nobody cherished adding, subtracting, multiplying, and dividing by longhand. Everyone coveted a simple-to-use pocket calculator. Many people tried, but

Thomas de Colmar had the first "success." He "built an adding machine the size of a piano for the 1855 Paris Exhibition."[23] Attempts to shrink the size met with limited success (a refining activity). The "lightweight model" weighed 34 pounds and was lugged around in large suitcases.

What was needed was an entirely new platform, and fortunately there was someone with the insight to craft it. Unfortunately, it was conceived of in one of the most despicable places in the world—the Buchenwald Nazi concentration camp. It was there that Curt Herzstark drew up plans for the "most ingenuous calculating machine ever to grace an engineer's hand: The Curta calculator."[24] This entirely mechanical gizmo resembles a small pepper grinder and, for some basic tasks, offers greater precision than the slide rule. The Curta enjoyed a large and loyal following for over 20 years before it was eventually replaced by electronic calculators. The tale of the Curta demonstrates the circuitous route progress often takes. The upward slanting straight arrow of progress is a myth.

Progress in One Arena Can Influence Progress in Other, Seemingly Unrelated, Arenas

Could any puzzle rival the popularity of the daily crosswords that appear in newspapers across the world? Years ago, that would have been hard to imagine. But a new rival has appeared on the scene: the Sudoku puzzle. The uniquely addictive logic puzzle "consists of a 9 × 9 grid that has been subdivided into 9 smaller grids of 3 × 3 squares. Each puzzle has a logical and unique solution. To solve the puzzle, each row, column and box must contain each of the numbers 1 to 9."[25] This puzzle may well be the perfect cultural icon for the deeply and surprisingly interconnected world that we live in. Sudoku puzzle solvers soon learn that a number in one part of the grid will have a surprising and often nonobvious link to another part. The connections are far more subtle and stronger than you would find in a crossword.[26]

Likewise, teasing out the often subtle interrelationships between different fields of human endeavor can be maddeningly difficult but immensely satisfying. Often progress in one seemingly unrelated field will have a tremendous impact on another. For example, one way to reduce drunk driving and other dangerous driving behaviors would be to assign more police to patrol the roads. That often works, but it is costly. But a surprising development in another arena has resulted in a significant increase in reports of misbehaving drivers. What is it? The cell phone. We often hear about how the cell phone has led to more distracted drivers. True, but it is also responsible for an increase in reporting driver misconduct. In other words, the cell phone has spawned some unintended positive consequences, as well. Whether you are a puzzle fanatic or a leader wishing to make progress, progress can often be achieved by working to see the connections between seemingly unconnected domains.

CONCLUDING THOUGHTS

We started this chapter by noting the difficulty of nailing down a definition of progress. The struggle involves making complex judgments, fighting the complacency of those who believe in the inevitability of progress, looking for deep interconnections between different arenas, and coming to grips with the unintended positive and negative consequences of moving forward. The mental and psychological enormity of these tasks may seem overwhelming. But it all starts with a seemingly simple question: What does it mean to move forward? As you will see in the following chapters, explorers, refiners, and progress makers answer this question in very different ways.

PROGRESS MAKER PROFILE

OSCAR BOLDT AND THE BOLDT COMPANY

The whirring B-24's propeller blades cutting through the air failed to suppress his anxiety, apprehension, and tinge of excitement. Bumping along the cloud tops high over Austria, 20-year-old O. C. Boldt was on his first combat mission of World War II and scared to death. His job was to navigate to a target and drop bombs. But something happened in the sky over Vienna as dense clouds obscured any view of the target. Consistent with United States policy, you don't drop the bombs unless you can visually identify the target. So the experienced pilot and crew started heading toward another target—in Yugoslavia. Boldt was momentarily disappointed, distressed, and more than a little disoriented. It took him a while to regain his composure, refocus on the tasks at hand, and carry on with the new mission. He heard something in the voices of the experienced pilot and crew that startled him at first. As they spoke in a calm, deliberate, and matter-of-fact tone, they moved on to the alternative target. No drama. No panic. No second guessing. No looking back. No regret. No needless emotions. "Flip the switch," and just move on to the next target. This rapid mind-emotion shift made a deep impression on this young navigator. And it may help us understand his later successes as the CEO of the Boldt Company.

After the war, he returned to Wisconsin to earn a degree in civil engineering from the University of Wisconsin–Madison. Shortly thereafter, he returned to the family construction business. In 1950, he took over the business his grandfather founded. The company grew in depth and scope under his leadership. The depth emerged through making major investments in construction equipment that some naysayers questioned. The scope enlarged as the company moved into new types of construction projects such as industrial factories, hospitals, and sports arenas. In 1980, *Healthcare Magazine* named Boldt one of the United States' top 10 health care builders. Boldt expanded thereafter, opening offices around the country. In 1987, O. C. Boldt passed the leadership helm over to the fourth generation of the Boldt family when his son, Tom, was named CEO of the growing company.

Those are the historical milestones of O. C. Boldt's leadership. What happened behind the headlines? This is what we sought to understand when we interviewed O. C. about those years. For someone who has experienced and achieved so much, he is remarkably humble and equally self-effacing. He refers to himself as an "odd combination of spare parts that needed to be remodeled and fashioned to fit into the right spot." The military experience provided the "remodeling," the CEO position the "right spot."

In our discussions, he often linked his business philosophy and decisions to the lessons learned as a young Air Force navigator. For instance, he believes a "flip the switch" mentality is vital in moving beyond the inevitable disappointments involved in bidding on projects. Despite your best efforts, you end up losing many contract bids. To be sure, the sales staff needs to look back at lessons learned from failing to get the contract. But at some point, too much retrospective examination debilitates the move forward. No need to let past setbacks stand in the way of directing your effort toward the task at hand. Flip the switch, and move on to the next opportunity. We discuss this idea in further depth in the chapter about "focused flexibility."

(Continued)

(Continued)

O. C. Boldt's World War II experience also taught him about the nature of progress. In rare circumstances, as a navigator he had to determine the plane's location and proper flight path using a sexton, a mechanical navigation device that uses celestial objects as reference points. Back then, pilots could not rely on radar or GPS to navigate. The stars were the guide. What happened when the clouds obscured the view of the sky? O. C. explained that he just took readings whenever he could and trusted that he had the plane headed in the right direction. There was always time to refine the measure when conditions permitted.

He used similar sensibilities to guide the company. He couldn't always determine the exact location but always had to know the company was headed in the right direction. So he took measurements when he could. For example, he noted at one point in the 1970s that the company was "too small to be big and too big to be small." So the company selected a strategy and stuck with it.

He fondly recalls a serendipitous meeting with a Saudi Arabian prince in Appleton, Wisconsin. As a board member of Pierce Manufacturing, Inc., he was invited to the reception to review the progress on a fleet of Pierce fire trucks for the Saudi National Guard. By chance he struck up a conversation with the agent who had set up the Saudi sale. The agent asked Oscar about his company, and it so happened that the agent needed someone to build a maintenance facility for the fire trucks in Saudi Arabia. Would Boldt be interested? A smaller company would decline. A small company looking to become big might jump on the opportunity. A wise, small company looking to become big would seriously contemplate and discuss the matter. And that's exactly what Boldt did. He laughs, recalling that "half the Boldt employees thought we were nuts, the other half were thrilled with the opportunity." O. C. notes that just like the navigator of the B-24, he couldn't take a precise measurement at the time of the decision. But "I knew we were headed in the right direction."

Time would prove him right. The company continued to grow. Shortly thereafter, an owner of a Memphis hospital complex was interviewing Boldt about building a new hospital. The owner was nervous about the distance between Boldt's Wisconsin headquarters and Memphis, Tennessee. Oscar grins when he reminisces about his retort: "We are over in Saudi Arabia right now, so it would appear that Memphis will be a little less challenging." It was an accurate, confident, and reassuring rejoinder that was only possible because Oscar and his team heeded the lessons he learned while flying in a B-24.

LESSONS LEARNED

- **Leaders try to instill a "flip-the-switch" mentality in their employees.** Why? It provides the needed focus to maximize your effectiveness for the next challenge. Too much energy devoted to dwelling on an already lost situation takes away energy from the future.

- **Avoid obsessing about taking precise measurements of your current position.** Sometimes you just have to take measurements when you can and momentarily trust you are moving in the right direction.

- **Implement improvements (refinements) as you move forward.** Everything doesn't have to be perfectly in place to launch a new platform. Setting up operations in Saudi Arabia required much improvisation.

NOTES

1. R. Wright, *A Short History of Progress.* New York: Carroll & Graf, 2004, 30.

2. G. Moskowitz and H. Grant, eds., *The Psychology of Goals.* New York: Guilford, 2009.

3. D. Rumsfeld, "Transforming the Military." *Foreign Affairs,* May–June 2002, 20–32, p. 20.

4. D. Stanton, *Horse Soldiers: The Extraordinary Story of a Band of U.S. Soldiers Who Rode to Victory in Afghanistan.* New York: Scribner, 2009.

5. W. Puck (L. Welch interview), "Wolfgang Puck: From Potato Peeler to Gourmet-Pizza Tycoon." *Inc.,* October 2009, 87–88, p. 88.

6. Ibid., p. 88.

7. D. Baron, *A Better Pencil: Readers, Writers, and the Digital Revolution.* Oxford, UK: Oxford University Press, 2009.

8. See   http://www.guardian.co.uk/sport/2008/jul/17/tourdefrance.cycling3 (accessed November 29, 2009).

9. J. Zillgitt, "Man on a Mission: Bryant Revels in Victory, Finals MVP." *USA Today.* http://www.usatoday.com/sports/basketball/nba/2009–06–15-bryant-finals-mvp_ N.htm (accessed June 15, 2009).

10. Some might argue that this quality could be measured by the number of assists. Those statistics, though, show that he averaged almost an identical number of assists in the 2008 and 2009 finals (5.6 vs. 5.5 per game). However, L.A. finished the playoffs 6–1 after starting 10–6 (and struggling with Houston). One reason might be that Kobe averaged 7.9 assists in the last 7 games (6–1) after averaging only 4.4 assists

in the first 16 games (10–6). Bottom line: The assist statistic may or may not be a good indicator of Kobe's newly discovered "giving" quality. Michael Sadoff, of Sadoff Investments, provided this insight and background research (June 15, 2009).

11. Wright, *A Short History of Progress,* 123.

12. B. Mazlish, "Progress: A Historical and Critical Perspective." In *Progress: Fact or Illusion?* edited by L. Marx and B. Mazlish. Ann Arbor: University of Michigan Press, 1996, 27–44, p. 40.

13. Dr. Edward Tenner makes a similar argument in his fascinating book, *Why Things Bite Back: Technology and the Revenge of Unintended Consequences.* New York: Knopf, 1996, 255.

14. R. Friedel, *A Culture of Improvement: Technology and the Western Millennium.* Cambridge, MA: MIT Press, 2007, 543.

15. D. Ariely, *Predictably Irrational: The Hidden Forces That Shape Our Decisions.* New York: HarperCollins, 2008.

16. Loss aversion may seem at odds with our natural optimism. Note, however, that loss aversion focuses more on preserving what we now possess while optimism focuses on more on our hopes for the future.

17. B. Schlender, "How Big Can Apple Get?" *Fortune,* February 21, 2005, 65–76.

18. J. F. Kennedy, "Special Message to the Congress on Urgent National Needs." May 25, 1961. John F. Kennedy Library. http://www.jfklibrary.org/Historical+Resources/Archives/Reference+Desk/Speeches/JFK/Urgent+National+Needs+Page+4.htm (accessed March 18, 2010).

19. S. Greenfeld, *Brain Story.* New York: Dorling Kindersley, 2001, 158.

20. This may seem contrary to our third observation. It's not. There has been abundant research indicating that children deprived of the right stimuli will become linguistically stunted.

21. W. Isaacson, *Einstein: His Life and Universe.* New York: Simon & Schuster, 2007, 8.

22. M. Gladwell, *Tipping Point: How Little Things Can Make a Big Difference.* New York: Little, Brown, 2000.

23. C. Stoll, "The Curious History of the First Pocket Calculator." *Scientific American,* January 2004, 92–99, p. 94.

24. Ibid., 92.

25. M. Mepham, *The Book of Sudoku #2.* New York: Overlook Press, 2005, vii.

26. J. Delahaye, "The Science Behind Sudoku. " *Scientific American,* June 2006, 81–87.

⋇ 6 ⋇

THE PROGRESS MODEL

———————◦•◦———————

To change and to improve are two different things.

—German proverb

Authors are fond of adorning the mastheads of their book chapters with an attention-grabbing quip or maxim from some well-recognized person. The sayings fly above the chapter title, flagging down our attention, beckoning our minds to focus on some critical issue. We use this device, as well, but in this chapter, we take a different slant. For starters, consider the following list of quotations from famous people that are clever as well as illuminating.[1]

"A place for everything and everything in its place. Order is wealth."—Samuel Smiles	"The most beautiful order is a heap of sweepings piled up at random." —Heraclitus
"Knowledge is the only meaningful resource today."—Peter Drucker	"Imagination is more important than knowledge."—Albert Einstein
"Customers are your future, representing new opportunities, ideas, and avenues for growth."—Michael Dell	"The popular slogan, stay close to your customers, appears not always to be robust advice."—Clayton Christensen

(Continued)

(Continued)

"Preparation is everything. Noah did not start building the ark when it was raining."—Warren Buffett	"Strategic planning can neither provide creativity nor deal with it when it emerges by other means." —Henry Mintzberg
"Action to be effective must be directed to clearly conceived ends." —Jawaharlal Nehru (Former Indian Prime Minister)	"Have faith and pursue the unknown end."—Oliver Wendell Holmes

There is a problem, though, with this table of quotes. Read them carefully, side-by-side. The maxims in the right column seemingly contradict their cousins in the left column. What's going on? There are three possible explanations.

First, these successful people don't have any idea what they're talking about. But that's not likely; they have all achieved a degree of success and presumably wouldn't write down something trivial or ill-advised. Second, one of the ideas is actually superior to the other. For example, maybe chaos is actually better than order. While we won't address it now, it is certainly possible to provide convincing arguments for any of these quips. But a third and more intriguing explanation seems more likely. Namely, the ideas in each column are essentially correct but are circumstance dependent. Knowledge, for example, may be useful at some times but not at others. Ignorance and imagination might, in fact, be valuable to an organization in certain situations.

This is, in fact, our position. We believe that if you understand the dynamic tension between the thoughts in the first and second columns, you realize what it means to make progress in any organization. Wise leaders instinctively know this but sometimes find it difficult to make the argument or lack the language to explain this dynamic tension. Consequently, their decisions may appear contradictory, their actions nonsensical, and their motives suspect. And employees may respond with cynicism, passive resistance, or even latent hostility. In short, organizational leaders need a framework and a vocabulary to explain the dynamic tension represented by columns 1 and 2. The Progress Model provides both.

HOW THE PROGRESS MODEL WORKS

Figure 6.1 brings together all the elements we've discussed in the previous chapters. Recall that people *explore* when they try something totally new and innovative. Exploring means taking a step into unknown, unpredictable, and uncertain territory. People *refine* when they are working to improve existing ways of doing business. They generate greater certainty and predictability.

Progress can be made either by *refining* (column 1 quotes) or *exploring* (column 2 quotes). But enduring progress can only occur if you do both. And that's why chaos is sometimes good, and at other times, it's not. And why knowledge is sometimes enlightening and at other times blinding.

As people explore and refine, they establish *platforms.* It could be a particular way of completing a task (e.g., a company procedure or protocol), organizing information (e.g., weather reports), representing knowledge (e.g., a theory), providing a service (e.g., cell phone network), or meeting a consumer need

Figure 6.1   The Progress Model

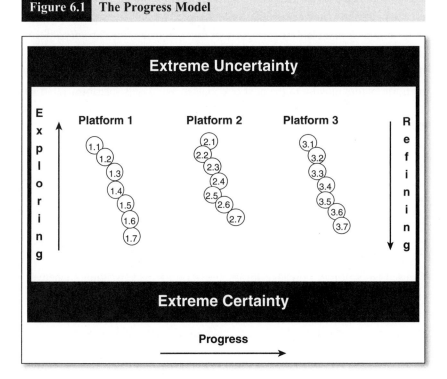

(e.g., packaged food). Most people build better, faster, and cheaper platforms over time by refining existing modes of thought or ways of doing something. We represent this feature of progress with overlapping nodes 1.1, 1.2, and so on.

Sometimes, though, people or organizations chose to push aside an existing platform and jump to a new one. We illustrate that feature with a new node labeled 2.1. The leap from 1.7 to 2.1 would be like jumping from a slide ruler to a calculator. You simply do not know what might happen or what new problems you might encounter with a new platform. Typically, platform jumpers encounter more uncertainty than those in the refining mode; after all, slide rulers won't run out of power at inconvenient moments.

The progress arrow on the bottom of the figure indicates that progress can occur either by refining or exploring. However, the degree and type of progress is limited by each activity.

Perhaps the quintessential example of progress making involves one of the most wonderful success stories of the modern era, namely, how the United States put a man on the moon 8 years after President Kennedy issued the challenge.[2] It started with Alan Shepard's 15-minute, 28-second suborbital space flight in the *Mercury* capsule.[3] The *Mercury* platform, designed for only one astronaut, set the stage for the *Gemini* platform, designed for two astronauts. The *Gemini* platform, in turn, was transformed into the *Apollo* spaceship (platform) and constructed for the three astronauts needed for the lunar landing. Refinements were made to each platform before moving to the next one: 6 *Mercury* flights (platform 1.1–1.6), 10 *Gemini* flights (platform 2.1–2.10), and 5 *Apollo* flights (platform 3.1–3.5).[4] Valuable lessons were learned that were incorporated into the next platform. It ended with Neil Armstrong stepping on the lunar surface on July 20, 1969.

This historic tale demonstrates the power of the platforms to drive progress. Each mission series (platform) focused on different technological challenges and goals. The *Mercury* missions, for example, sought to "successfully orbit a human in space, explore aspects of tracking and control, and to learn about microgravity and other biomedical issues associated with spaceflight."[5] Once those lessons were mastered, the *Gemini* flights (platform) focused on issues we now take for granted such as space walking, maneuvering, and docking two spacecraft. NASA made progress both by refining existing platforms and exploring new ones. Note, however, that after all the major lessons were gleaned from a particular platform, it was time to move on to the next one. In other words, there are limits to the amount of progress that refining can generate. To paraphrase Picasso, "Every act of creation is first of all an act of destruction of existing platforms." Constructing the perfect *Mercury* space capsule would not have put a man on the moon. The mission was accomplished by embracing uncertainty and moving from one less-than-perfect platform to a better one. *The price of progress, then, is an abiding sense of incompleteness.* Years ago the Space Shuttle replaced the "ancient" *Apollo* spacecraft. In more recent years, the decision was made to scuttle the Space Shuttle program, as well. And so the wheels of progress grind forward.

SO WHAT?

We will examine many of the implications of the model in subsequent chapters. However, three issues warrant discussion at this stage.

No Platform Is Perfect

Platforms are constructed and maintained in a sea of uncertainty. Their primary function is to provide some stability amid the tumult. A platform does not have to be perfect to be successful; it just needs to solve the problems of today and those on the immediate horizon. For example, the slide ruler met the needs of its day. Yet "the slide ruler helped to design the very machines that would ultimately render it obsolete."[6] In essence, the slide ruler, like all platforms, provided enough utility to launch further inquiries. Sir Isaac Newton's theories, for instance, provided a platform of understanding that allowed Einstein to create an even more encompassing platform, and it is safe to say that someday, someone will use Einstein's platform to create another one.

Progress Occurs Under Conditions of "Dynamic Stability"

The *stability* of a platform arises from each successive refinement (1.1, 1.2, etc.). The *dynamism* of the system emerges from successive jumps between the platforms (1.7 to 2.1 and 2.7 to 3.1). The creative tension between the perceived certainty of the current platform and the uncertainty of a new platform allows progress to occur.

A *singular* focus on platform refining or platform jumping undermines progress. As we noted before, the platform refiner risks becoming irrelevant. Philosopher Robert Grudin put it this way: "The only thing forbidden should be to stand still and say, 'This is it.'"[7] On a similar note, Will Rogers once observed, "Even if you are on the right track, you'll get run over if you sit still."

The serial platform jumper can never consolidate enough gains to move forward. It's like the angst-ridden author who can't complete one book because his mind is flooded with ideas for a dozen other writing projects.

Visualizing progress as a wave-like rhythm of crests of uncertainty and troughs of certainty allows organizations to meet ever-changing challenges. Wise leaders understand how the relationship between the crests and troughs provides the essential tension for meaningful progress; in a dynamic climate, the seas are seldom flat.[8]

Perceptions of the Path Forward Vary Greatly Depending on Your Current and Projected Platform Position

In Figure 6.2, we highlight some of the perceptual issues facing progress makers. Let's reconsider the NASA mission to the moon using Figure 6.2. Clearly the move from version 1.5 to 1.6 is less traumatic than a jump to a new platform

Figure 6.2   Implications of the Progress Model

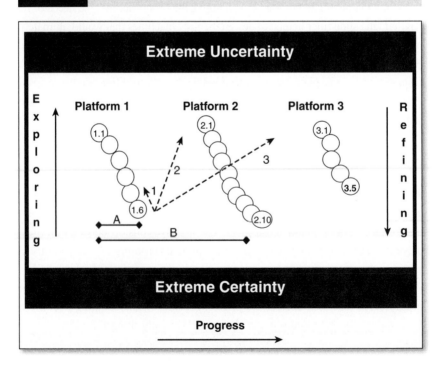

(compare the lengths of lines 1 and 2 in Figure 6.2). There was a great deal of uncertainty to conquer when looking at President Kennedy's challenge from the *Mercury* platform (see line 3 in Figure 6.2). Bounding across too many platforms too quickly appears to be a daunting task (see line 3 in Figure 6.2). In fact, it may be overwhelming and too risky.

The refinements to the existing platforms and the intervening platforms temper the natural anxiety associated with great enterprises. NASA did not jump from the first *Mercury* mission straight to the *Apollo* moon mission (1.1 to 3.5). The "one small step for a man, one giant leap for mankind" was made possible by (1) thoughtfully developing each platform and (2) stepping from platform to platform at the right time. Each iteration decreased the perceived uncertainty of the momentous undertaking.

Progress makers recognize the perceptual differences implied by different anchor points (start and stop points of the lines). They don't push their colleagues to embrace all the uncertainty at once (line 3); rather, they often focus on a psychologically manageable chunk (line 1 or 2). In this way, they enhance their colleagues' skills and confidence in dealing with progress-making challenges.

In short, progress makers learn to manage the perceptions of others by clearly identifying current platform positions and selecting the appropriate future platform position for their organization. They avoid being short-sided or overreaching. That requires a deep understanding of the follower's comfort and confidence levels. And it also requires a fundamental understanding of potential threats facing the organization. On the basis of those assessments, progress makers might emphasize progress through refining (1.5 to 1.6) or exploring (1.6 to 2.1). Yet, progress makers recognize that platform refining typically brings comparatively less progress than platform jumping (note that line A is shorter than line B in Figure 6.2).

CONCLUDING THOUGHTS

Leaders equipped with a basic understanding of the Progress Model can more clearly map out the challenges they face. Often they must manage multiple platforms at various stages of development. The U.S. Air Force, for example, now trains more pilots for unmanned drones than it does for manned jets and bombers.[9] Years ago, the unmanned drone program didn't exist. New initiatives like this one require a different progress orientation than more longstanding programs. In short, some organizational initiatives or processes under a leader's purview require platform refining while others call for platform jumping. This requires a deeper understanding of how refiners and explorers make progress. We discuss those issues in the following chapters.

NOTES

1. We gathered all quotes from two sources: (1) *The Big Book of Quotations* and (2) *Business 2.0.*

2. C. Nelson, *Rocket Men: The Epic Story of the First Men on the Moon.* New York: Viking, 2009.

3. http://www-pao.ksc.nasa.gov/history/mercury/flight-summary.htm (accessed June 15, 2009).

4. There were a total of 11 *Apollo* flights. It was on the fifth one that a man actually stepped on the moon. See "The Kennedy Space Center: Mission Factoids." http://www.nasa.gov/centers/kennedy/news/facts/hundred-toc.html (accessed June 14, 2009).

5. See "Project Apollo: A Retrospective Analysis." http://history.nasa.gov/Apollomon/Apollo.html (p. 14).

6. C. Stoll, "When Slide Rules Ruled." *Scientific American,* May 2006, 80–87, p. 87.

7. R. Grudin, *Time and the Art of Living.* New York: Ticknor & Fields, 1982, 2.

8. E. Abrahamson, "Change Without Pain." *Harvard Business Review* 78, no. 4 (2000): 75–82.

9. "Air Force Training More Drone Operators." http://www.upi.com/Top_News/2009/06/16/Air-Force-training-more-drone-operators/UPI-52341245153649/ (accessed June 16, 2009).

⊰ 7 ⊱

HOW EXPLORERS AND REFINERS MAKE PROGRESS

———◆———

Every day you may make progress. Every step may be fruitful. Yet there will stretch out before you an ever-lengthening, ever-ascending, ever-improving path. You know you will never get to the end of the journey. But this, so far from discouraging, only adds to the joy and glory of the climb.

—Sir Winston Churchill

Explorers and refiners make progress in distinctly different ways. However, they face many of the same challenges in moving away from the status quo. We discuss these issues in this chapter.

THE EXPLORERS' MODE OF MAKING PROGRESS

Explorers make progress by leaping from one platform to another. They bound into an unknown, searching for a new approach or idea that represents a significant departure from the existing platform. We depicted this in Figure 6.2 as a dotted line leading from version 1.6 to 2.1. All sorts of buzzwords get attached to this leap such as "radical innovation," "blue ocean strategy," or "paradigm shift."

For example, a few years ago, business leaders seized on the sexy sounding phrase "paradigm shift" and liberally sprinkled the notion throughout their public speeches and conversations. The heritage of the phrase, though, dates back to the early sixties, when Thomas Kuhn wrote an influential book titled the *Structure of Scientific Revolutions.*[1] In his historical study of scientific revolutions, he discerned a pattern that he labeled a "paradigm change or shift." A paradigm "is an accepted model or pattern" that has gained status because it is "more successful than [its] competitors in solving a few problems that the group of practitioners has come to recognize as acute."[2] A paradigm shift occurs when one prevailing scientific theory is displaced by another. Einstein's theory of relativity, for example, displaced the Newtonian scientific view. This paradigm shift restructured existing assumptions and defined a relatively new way of viewing our physical world. Newtonian physics was constantly refined by other scientists. In other words, if Newton represents 1.1, the other scientists who built on his idea represent 1.2, 1.3, and so on. In the world of physics, though, Einstein's theories represent a leap to 2.1.

A similar pattern emerges when examining business practices, models, or products. For example, videotapes (Platform 1.1) were displaced by DVDs (Platform 2.1), which are in the process of being superseded by Internet-based content (Platform 3.1).[3] Such jumps, while exhilarating, can be treacherous. We were reminded of the explorer's peaks and valleys in a moving tribute to an extreme skier who fell to his death in the French Alps:

> In our world, there will always be individuals who venture out of bounds, be they poets or painters, philosophers or scientists, explorers or skiers of the steeps. We need these individuals. They show us what is possible. They show us that our world of fences, rules, and conventions is a constantly negotiated boundary and that it is possible to move it. They show us what passion is required to explore new terrain, and sometimes, tragically, they show us the consequences.[4]

Such was the legacy of Doug Coombs, the extreme explorer. Everyday explorers may not take the kind of physical risks he did, but they push the boundaries of the conventional like he did. Explorers take greater chances than their refining counterparts in order to make progress. Einstein's theory was widely derided for many years. Even though he did win a Nobel Prize, he did not win it for his most famous theory—the general theory of relativity. At the time, it was considered too controversial.[5]

In fact, a new platform may move the organization backward, not forward. Motorola, for instance, pioneered cell phone technology but also invested and lost millions in the ill-fated Iridium satellite phone system.[6] There are no guarantees.

However, in many cases, after some initial pain, a new platform may usher in an entirely new wave of progress and growth. For example, the Saris Company began by marketing exquisitely designed bicycle racks for cars, ones that attached to the back of the vehicle. That platform remains viable today. But the company, led by Chris Fortune, needed to jump to other platforms to continue its growth pattern.[7] He recognized that many cyclists retreated to the indoors during the winter months, especially those living in the snowy regions of the company's headquarters in Wisconsin. Chris was also driven to find new sources for off-season revenue. For Chris, these were opportunities disguised as problems. So like a committed explorer, he seized on a business prospect and bought the CycleOps Company, which manufactured indoor cycle trainers. Now Saris had a four-season business; soon it became the leading seller of indoor cycle trainers in the United States.

In 1999, Chris engineered another strategic platform jump with the purchase of PowerTap, which brought further electronic expertise into Saris. With PowerTap, Chris's team further developed the basic technology, which allowed cyclists to easily track their speed, cadence, heart rate, distance, and power in watts. The cyclists trained, of course, on CycleOps equipment. Chris and his leadership team's latest platform jump involves a total off-season/in-season integrated electronic monitoring system for cyclists. Now cyclists can use a single display module for their indoor cycle trainer and outdoor riding. And all of the data can be downloaded on the cyclist's personal computer for analysis.

When Patrick Walters, the Director of New Ventures and Product Management, first heard about the platform notion, he immediately recognized how the Saris story fit the Progress Model. He remarked, "We started with bending and welding metal (bike racks), moved to soldering wires (electronics), then made another jump to writing software (PowerAgent) and are now adding education and services to the portfolio."[8] How has the company fared with all the platform jumping? When Chris became CEO in 1989, the company employed 25; today they're at 170 and growing. Saris has grown revenue at an average rate of 15% annually, even in difficult economic times.

THE REFINERS' MODE OF MAKING PROGRESS

The reengineering specialist asks, "How can we make this process simpler and more efficient?" The lean manufacturing expert asks, "How can we eliminate unnecessary steps in the process?" The Six Sigma black belt asks, "How can we remove variation from the process?" The marketing executive asks, "Could we tweak our existing products to offer consumers more choices?" While these are slightly different questions, the underlying attention is focused on improving existing practices and seizing latent opportunities.

Refiners make progress by incrementally improving a platform in a logical step-by-step manner. We depict this as a series of trailing nodes in the progress model. The nodes form a linked chain since they relate to the same, yet evolving, platform. Each version (1.1, 1.2 . . .) represents an improvement over the previous one.

Proponents of lean thinking have demonstrated that refining can "dramatically boost productivity—doubling to quadrupling it, depending on the activity—while dramatically reducing errors, inventories, on-the-job accidents, space requirements, time-to-market for new products, production lead times, the cost of extra product variety, and costs in general."[9]

Consider Air Products and Chemical, Inc., which generates over $7 billion in annual sales. Cost savings are a must because they compete in a commodity-based market. The company's manager of continuous improvement for global IT, Alan Jeffery, targeted software patching (e.g., updating software with new security and product upgrades) as an area for improving the company's efficiency. "The IT group each month patched Microsoft Windows running on more than 1,000 servers throughout the company—not exactly a value producing task."[10] In other words, every minute his IT group spent on patching took time away from other value-producing activities such as designing more specialized software. His team cut the amount of time needed for patching and other maintenance-like activities by one third, resulting in tens of millions of dollars in savings.

Refiners always embrace efficiency measures, but they also open their arms to incremental extensions of good ideas. Consider, for example, the wildly popular yellow Livestrong wristbands produced for Nike and the Lance Armstrong Foundation. Over 70 million have been sold, generating an equal number of dollars for cancer research. Other charities and businesses quickly recognized the possibilities for generating buzz, donations, and profits.[11] They hopped on the bandwagon. The Chicago Cubs baseball team, for example, produced over one-half million blue rubber bracelets with the words "Believe" emblazoned on them.[12]

We can find examples of similar evolutionary improvements when we move from the low-tech world of marketing knickknacks to the high-tech world of smart phones with all the bells and whistles. When Apple introduced the iPhone, it also heralded in the age of multitouch screens. Instead of using a single finger on a screen to interact with the device, users could use two fingers to make Charade-like motions to execute a command. Expand your fingers and the screen stretches, and so on. But this slick trick really only represents an incremental step forward from the old systems that restricted users to a single finger.[13] Neither the Cubs nor Apple made revolutionary moves. Rather, they simply took the next logical innovative step. Such are the opportunities that refiners seek out and exploit.

THE CHALLENGES FACED BY EXPLORERS AND REFINERS

Given all the wonderful benefits discussed above, it might appear that every organization would roll out the welcome mat to explorers and refiners. Some do. Others slam the door in their faces, if not literally, then figuratively. Why? Because explorers and refiners face four key challenges in helping their organizations make progress. We discuss these in this section.

Fighting the Status Quo

The greatest enemy of exploring and refining is the status quo. It lures, entices, and binds many employees with promises of comfort, stability, and even riches. The accepted way of doing a task or managing a process often has hidden and powerful allies. This challenge relates equally to explorers seeking to shift their organizations from one platform to another (1.6 to 2.1) as to refiners advocating a shift from node 1.5 to 1.6.

For example, lean protocols (refining) are designed to take out unnecessary or non-value-adding steps in critical processes. Anyone remotely familiar with such changes has heard some variant of these comments:

- "We've never done it that way before."
- "If we eliminate too many steps, what will happen to my job?"
- "Why change? It has worked so well in the past."

When these standard lines of argument don't work, you will often hear the other extreme. "If we modify this process, then everything has to change. And I just don't think everyone will be on board." During a lean planning session, an astute observer and a dedicated lean advocate said, "I believe in lean, but I just don't know if we can do it. We are supposed to be a tissue manufacturing company but we are really an accounting company that makes tissue on the side. We have systems in place to track and analyze everything but we can never seem to make a decision." What he meant is that the bureaucratic tracking systems required so much energy that accounting for time and materials became the focal point. What all these retorts have in common is the protection of the status quo.

Status quo protectors often have an "if it isn't broken, don't fix it" mindset. To be fair, sometimes that may be an appropriate stance. More often, though, it hinders progress making. Companies may not seize simple opportunities to extend on existing ideas. That's exactly the dilemma Todd Bashche encountered when he tried to interest lock companies in his simple improvement to the standard combination lock. The lock companies didn't see a problem that needed to be addressed. He did. He had trouble remembering the numbers to his combination. So, he thought, why not use letters? He patented the idea but couldn't find an interested party. It was not a credibility problem— after all, he worked "in product development for Hewlett-Packard and Apple, [and] has invented reams of stuff."[14] Eventually, he entered his idea into a consumer product competition at Staples and won the $25,000 prize. Now, of course, you can buy his lock at any number of stores (ironically, stores are known by their names, not by their federal tax ID number).

Perhaps the deepest difficulty the explorer and refiner faces is getting people away from their traditional modes of thinking. Our mind-sets are so deeply embedded, all-encompassing, and seemingly "real" that they are virtually invisible to us. For example, years ago telephone companies were providing all kinds of new features based on the landline platform: speed dialing, caller ID, voicemail boxes, and so on. And most baby boomers remember the 30-foot cords stretching from the phone to the handset. That was an attempt to make the phone more "mobile." All these bonus features provided new revenue streams for the companies. Yet, few executives vigorously lobbied for a radical platform shift to wireless telephone networks. In this case, the phone companies were making progress by innovating within the confines of an existing platform; in other words, they were refining. But that was not enough for long-term growth. With the exponential growth in mobile phones, the days of landline-based phones are numbered. In short, the telephone companies that failed to adapt were caught up in an existing mind-set about what constituted a "mobile phone."

Managing Fear

Like extreme skiers, platform jumpers often leap near the abyss. As we discussed in the second chapter, explorers know how to quell their own fears, but that only addresses part of the challenge. They must help others manage their fears, as well. After all, they are attempting to do something that no one has done before, and they need help. This goes beyond risk management and into the realm of uncertainty negotiation. Risks involve calculated odds of success. With uncertainty, you don't even have a way of calculating the odds. Instead, you are continually negotiating the path forward with limited and often inaccurate information. It's like the difference between playing poker (with known odds) and playing a game where the rules are always changing (with unknown odds).

Knowing the odds helps suppress fears and plot a path forward. But what happens if you don't know the odds of success? That's when debilitating fear grips many people. Under those circumstances, our courage wanes, creativity ebbs, and energy seeps away. Unfortunately, those are precisely the qualities needed to make progress in uncertain times.

Effective leaders intuitively grasp these psychological realities. Consider, for instance, a new president of the United States who faced a collapsing national banking system, debilitating unemployment levels, and demoralizing economic conditions. What did he say to get the country moving again?

> So first of all let me assert my firm belief that the only thing we have to fear is fear itself—nameless, unreasoning, unjustified terror which paralyzes needed efforts to convert retreat into advance. In every dark hour of our national life a leadership of frankness and vigor has met with that understanding and support of the people themselves which is essential to victory.[15]

Then he goes on to outline the specifics of his "New Deal." Note that the president starts by addressing the nation's fears. They must be tempered before divulging the grim facts and path forward. President Franklin Roosevelt instinctively recognized the necessity of mitigating fears before garnering support for his venture into an uncertain future.

Explorers relish the uncertain future. Yet, often their personal enthusiasm overwhelms their judgment about other people's ability to share in such adventures. Consequently, their challenge, like President Roosevelt's, resides in helping others manage their fears and then move forward.

While refiners might not face the same degree of fear as the explorer, they too must manage anxieties. They must be prepared to answer questions such as, Will I be able to learn the new skills associated with the improvement? Does the improvement threaten my job security? The refiners must reassure, as well, even as they mobilize toward action.

Battling Fatigue

Of course, not everyone defends the status quo. Some employees possess or develop a passion for crafting new platforms and continuously improving existing ones. However, the cumulative impact of these activities can be tiring and debilitating. The verbal commitment often endures while the mental, physical, and psychological energy start to wane.[16] Deep in their psyche, employees may say to themselves, "When will this ever end?" or "Is anything ever good enough?"

These comments reveal a fundamental misunderstanding about the nature of progress. Some people treat continuous improvement as a *goal* rather than a *mind-set*. What's the difference? A goal is something that, once it's accomplished, can be checked off the list.[17] A mind-set, like a lifestyle, lasts forever. For example, consider a government bureaucrat who trained for several years to run in the Boston Marathon. After successfully competing in several local marathons, he qualified to make the run in Boston. His hard work paid off; he ran the legendary race and finished well for his age group. He was tired, satisfied, and done for good. Soon after the event, he stopped running altogether. In a matter of months, his runner's physique and obsession gave way to other, less healthy passions.[18] What happened? In this case, it wasn't an injury. Rather, he treated the Boston Marathon like a goal. Check it off the list; on to the next goal. In contrast, people with a wellness or fitness mind-set never tire because that defines their essence. In the same way, creating a new platform or improving an existing one can be treated as an endpoint or a way of life. The person with the endpoint mentality resembles the now out-of-shape government bureaucrat. The person with the way-of-life mind-set keeps on running despite the fatigue, aches, and pains.

Knowing When to Resist

Innovative people love new ideas—particularly radical ones. They want to "put a ding in the universe," "make history," or "be disruptive."[19] But effective explorers learn to temper that emotion with reason. Apple CEO Steve Jobs is an explorer at heart. But he is also a skilled executive. While we hear about all the sexy new products he delights in introducing, he takes equal pride in the products he has chosen *not* to pursue. For instance, the company faced enormous pressure to produce a personal digital assistant (PDA). As one longtime Apple chronicler noted,

> Apple's labs are littered with prototype products that never made it out the door. The product Jobs is most proud of not doing is a PDA, a personal digital assistant, the successor to the Newton he discontinued in 1998.[20]

Investing energy in PDAs would have sucked up resources that were used on products of more enduring value. In Jobs's mind, the PDA represented a shaky and very tentative platform that did not advance his technological vision.

In short, abandoning a new platform idea may be the best alternative. Killing a project that many people believe in requires insight and emotional toughness. As one theorist put it, "The value of someone who is able to pull the plug on a project before it becomes a money sink hasn't generally been appreciated."[21] In fact, one study found that the "highest performers in the IT world . . . are those *most* likely to cancel projects—at a rate double that of their lower-performing counterparts."[22] Unfortunately, explorers have difficulty stopping questionable projects because the untried, unproven, and unknown entices them.

Refining has limits, as well. Products and processes often near an optimal state. For example, a company can show some dramatic increases in profits by eliminating personnel and pushing more responsibilities on those who remain. Yet, if the cuts are too deep, they will begin to impair company growth as service wanes and customers leave. At this point, products become commodities and prices stabilize across the industry. After you've squeezed every superfluous step out of the process, you cannot go any further without impairing performance.

Refiners need an intuitive sense of this point and stop just short of it. Otherwise, they risk falling into the classic business failure trap of "rigidly clinging to a formula for success" that has become increasingly irrelevant.[23] For instance, a *BusinessWeek* writer noted the following:

> The very factors that make Six Sigma effective in one context can make it ineffective in another. Traditionally, it uses rigorous statistical analysis to produce unambiguous data that help produce better quality, lower costs, and more efficiency (refining). That all sounds great when you know what outcomes you'd like to control. But what about when there are few facts to go on—or you don't even know the nature of the problem you're trying to define?[24]

He goes on to note several examples of the struggle between efficiency and creativity at 3M. The optimal amount of refining is difficult to specify, yet the danger signs are somewhat easier to detect. A mad rush toward perfection should send up a red flag, like trying to nail down every detail for an impending organizational change. Similarly, a concerted drive toward a single solution can signal that you are crossing the line.

In fact, highly adaptable or "refinable" platforms may become problematic. When do you stop making home improvements and decide that you need an entirely new home? These decisions are always tough ones, and people may, therefore, stay on the platform too long. As an executive with Hewlett Packard said, "The biggest single threat to our business today is staying with a previously successful business model one year too long."[25] A platform is not a retirement home.

CONCLUDING THOUGHTS

Explorers and refiners face similar challenges in moving their organizations forward. However, they possess a fundamentally different psyche. They make progress in different ways. They attack different kinds of issues. And they even approach similar problems in different ways. Someone needs to reduce their excesses while integrating their potential. That is the role of the progress maker and is the subject of the final chapter in this section.

NOTES

1. T. S. Kuhn, *The Structure of Scientific Revolutions.* Chicago: University of Chicago Press, 1962.

2. T. S. Kuhn, *The Structure of Scientific Revolutions*, 2nd ed. Chicago: University of Chicago Press, 1970, 23.

3. N. Wingfield, "Netflix Boss Plots Life After the DVD." *Wall Street Journal,* June 23, 2009, A1, A12.

4. P. Stark, "Doug Coombs: In Memoriam." *Men's Journal,* July 2006, 16.

5. W. Isaacson, *Einstein: His Life and Universe.* New York: Simon & Schuster, 2007.

6. S. Miller, "Motorola Executive Helped Spur Cellphone Revolution, Oversaw Ill-Fated Iridium Project." *Wall Street Journal,* June 20–21, 2009, A10.

7. Personal interview, Chris Fortune, June 14, 2009.

8. Phone interview, Patrick Walters, June 26, 2009.

9. J. P. Womack and D. T. Jones, *Lean Thinking: Banish Waste and Create Wealth in Your Corporation.* New York: Simon & Schuster, 1996, 295.

10. R. Whiting, "Air Products Strips Out Inefficiencies." *Information Week,* September 19, 2005, 95. See also http://www.informationweek.com/news/global-cio/showArticle.jhtml?articleID=170703590 (accessed June 28, 2009).

11. www.livestrong.org (accessed June 18, 2009).

12. J. Lieber, "Brace Yourself." *USA Today,* July 8, 2005, C1–C2.

13. S. Brown, "Hands-on Computing." *Scientific American,* July 2008, 64–67.

14. J. Boorstin, "Staples Lets Customers Do the Designing." *Fortune,* April 18, 2005, 48.

15. F. Roosevelt 1933 Inaugural Address in S. Montefiore, *Speeches That Changed the World.* London: Quercus, 2007, 101–102.

16. J. Lindsay, *Conquering Innovation Fatigue: Overcoming the Barriers to Personal and Corporate Success.* New York: John Wiley, 2009.

17. G. Moskowitz and H. Grant, *The Psychology of Goals.* New York: Guilford, 2009.

18. Apparently, this scenario is fairly commonplace. See K. Helliker, "The Fleeting Benefits of Marathons." *Wall Street Journal,* October 6, 2009, D3.

19. J. Dyer, H. Gregersen, and C. Christensen, "The Innovator's DNA." *Harvard Business Review* 87, no 12 (2009): 61–67, p. 66.

20. L. Kahney, *Inside Steve's Brain.* New York: Portfolio, 2008, 41.

21. I. Royer, "Why Bad Projects Are So Hard to Kill." *Harvard Business Review* 81, no. 2 (2003): 48–56, p. 50.

22. J. Feldman, "Victims of Success." *Information Week,* April 7, 2008, 43–46, p. 44.

23. G. Probst and S. Raisch, "Organizational Crisis: The Logic of Failure." *Academy of Management Executive* 19, no. 1 (2005): 90–105, p. 96.

24. B. Hindo, "At 3M, A Struggle Between Efficiency and Creativity." *Inside Innovation,* a special supplement published by *Business Week,* June 2007, 8–14, p. 10.

25. R. Hoff, "Hewlett Packard." *Business Week,* February 13, 1995, 67.

⚹ 8 ⚹

PROGRESS MAKERS

———•◦●◦•———

"Would you tell me, please, which way I ought to go from here?"

"That depends a good deal on where you want to get to," said the Cat.

"I don't much care where—" said Alice.

"Then it doesn't matter which way you go," said the Cat.

—"so long as I get somewhere," Alice added as an explanation.

"Oh, you're sure to do that," said the Cat, "if you only walk long enough."

—from *Alice's Adventures in Wonderland*

Can an explorer be a progress maker? Absolutely. Can a refiner be a progress maker? Definitely. In fact, we consider many of the leaders highlighted in previous chapters, such as Pat Summitt, Steven Jobs, and Chris Fortune, to be progress makers. These leaders have augmented their instinctive explorer or refiner tendencies. In fact, they have an ability best captured in writer F. Scott Fitzgerald's famous quip, "The true test of a first-rate mind is the ability to hold two contradictory ideas at the same time."[1] That's what sets the progress makers apart. Progress makers possess the talents of both the explorer and refiner. And some of those aptitudes seemingly contradict one another! No wonder progress makers are a rare breed.

Progress makers are superbly positioned to answer Alice's innocent question: "Would you tell me, please, which way I ought to go from here?"[2] In other words, every leader must address the exceedingly significant question, "What does it mean to make progress?" Remember we *are not* asking about inevitabilities, such as growing old or maintaining the status quo. We *are not* even discussing aimlessly wandering around Wonderland. We *are* talking about something far more difficult to determine. Why? Because leaders must successfully resolve the central dilemma of progress.

THE CENTRAL CONUNDRUM

We believe the fundamental quandary that leaders must thoughtfully address involves the tug-of-war between *exploration* (exploring) and *exploitation* (refining) implied by the Progress Model. Professor James March began his groundbreaking article on this tension with the following, almost benign, statement: "A central concern of studies of adaptive processes is the relation between the *exploration* of new possibilities and the *exploitation* of old certainties."[3] This plainly expressed notion set off a vigorous wave of debate, research, and commentary in business schools throughout the world. And it should be a central concern of every leader of every organization. Why? Because leaders, whether they acknowledge it or not, confront the tension between exploration and exploitation on a daily basis. How they resolve that dilemma profoundly influences the effectiveness and viability of their organizations.

How do these inherently incompatible approaches to progress stack up against each other? In the short run, exploitation trumps exploration. In the long run, it's just the opposite. Professor March put it this way: "Compared to returns from exploitation, returns from exploration are systematically less certain, more remote in time. . . . What is good in the long-term is not always good at another time."[4] For example, learning to make better, faster, and cheaper newsprint (exploitation) to the exclusion of other paper products makes perfect sense in a newspaper-crazy world. But this capability rapidly becomes irrelevant once the world shifts to the electronic transmission of news stories on Kindle, Nook, or iPad-like devices. In the long term, it makes more sense to pursue other paper-related products that will not be threatened by information technologies.

Unfortunately, most organizational leaders do a poor job managing the tension between the short term and long term, evolution and revolution, and exploitation and exploration. In fact, the editors of a special journal devoted to this dilemma noted,

> Exploration often leads to failure, which in turn promotes the search for even newer ideas and thus more exploration, thereby creating a "failure trap." In contrast, exploitation often leads to early success, which in turn reinforces further exploitation along the same trajectory, thereby creating a "success trap." In short exploration often leads to more exploration and exploitation to more exploitation.[5]

That's why in previous chapters, we have consistently warned about the excesses of both exploring and refining. It may also be why the CEO of Netflix, Reed Hastings, frets so much over a thriving business. Currently, the company rents DVDs to customers using a sophisticated Internet-based service model. Yet Hastings knows the days of the DVD are numbered and so he pushes for a new, totally online service. The company's current success is a trap waiting to be sprung. He knows he needs a new delivery platform even as he gleans revenue from the existing one. And he readily acknowledges that few companies have been successful exploring and refining simultaneously.[6]

THE PROGRESS MAKER'S RESPONSE

How do leaders wrestle this dilemma to the ground? They have two basic alternatives. First, they may seek to balance the exploring and refining forces in their organizations. Indeed, many thought leaders advocate this kind of ambidextrous organization.[7] Second, they may select a strategy of "long periods of exploitation (refining) and short bursts of explorations."[8] Both approaches have merit. But to be fair, trying to pin both exploration and exploitation to the ground proves exceedingly difficult.[9]

In fact, many organizations vigorously pursue the refining pathway while simultaneously proclaiming a commitment to innovation. Researchers examined the unintended consequences of that approach in a classic longitudinal study of the photography and paint industries. They concluded,

> Even as organizations are exhorted to innovate in times of rapid technological change, process management activities focused on mapping, incrementally improving, and adhering to organizational processes have been widely adopted. These activities aimed at refining and stabilizing processes may be in conflict with exploratory innovation required for adaptation as environments change.[10]

In sum, all the refining activities undercut efforts to explore a new path. Presumably, the opposite would also be true. Namely, a host of exploring activities would undermine attempts at refining. (There is a dearth of research on this issue because companies that fail to exploit existing platforms rarely survive.)

Both alternatives, though, gloss over the deep-seated quandary. That is, whether leaders select the ambidexterity strategy or the burst strategy, they still face the same core questions: When should we explore? When should we refine (exploit)? To be specific, progress makers grapple with the following questions:

- How long do we stay with platforms that are working?
- When should we start building a new platform?
- What should be the relationship between the old platforms and the new ones?

Progress makers in different industries answer these questions in different ways depending on circumstances.

Answering these questions may sound a lot like crafting an organizational strategy. If the word *strategy* conjures up some complex, onerous, detailed, step-by-step orderly process, then bury the association in a heap of other discarded management fads. If, on the other hand, you associate strategy with a robust, energetic, and thoughtful dialogue about how to define progress, then you are thinking like a progress maker. Former CEO of GE Jack Welch succinctly defined the idea: "Strategy means making clear-cut choices about how to compete. You cannot be everything to everybody, no matter what the size of your business or how deep its pockets."[11] The most important word in Welch's oft-quoted remark is *choices.*

MAKING THE RIGHT CHOICES

Progress makers, more often than not, make the right choices about which platforms to explore, refine, and even abandon. Let's consider two examples.

Chairman Mike Cowen of Sportable Scoreboards knows how to refine a platform and, when necessary, jump to a new one.[12] In 1986, he discovered a need for a portable scoreboard for youth sports. At that time, most facilities had no such scoring devices. His company developed a battery-powered scoreboard that used solid-state electromechanical number displays and was controlled by a wireless handheld electronic keyboard. His staff improved the reliability and performance of these products. But like a true progress maker, Mike realized that the company could continue to grow by developing new and larger permanent scoreboards for their school and park customers. These scoreboards used incandescent light bulbs to display the scores. They worked brilliantly, but the bulbs frequently burnt out and needed to be replaced. So his leadership team once again sought out a new platform. The result? They discovered how to replace the energy-hogging light bulbs with energy-saving LED lights. There was an added bonus: decreased maintenance costs. The company's latest platform jump involves wireless remote controls for scoreboards. Today, the multimillion dollar company provides scoreboards to many NFL and NBA teams "as well as major colleges and universities, high schools, park and recreation departments, youth leagues, corporate recreation leagues, military bases, and thousands of other organizations."[13] The company will soon be the largest in the market.

Perhaps the most dramatic example of the power and pain of strategic platform jumping involves Intel. During the early 1980s, Intel generated profits of over $100 million per year primarily from its memory chips.[14] By 1985, profits plummeted to less than $2 million. This was a platform crisis of immense proportions. Could Intel thrive in the increasingly competitive memory chip market? Or should the company focus on a new platform for success? CEO Gordon Moore along with Andy Grove made the decision to move out of memory chips to microprocessors. This momentous platform shift had enormous consequences—8,000 people were laid off, and the company posted a loss of over $170 million in 1986.[15] With that degree of pain and concomitant turmoil, few could see how the company could ever make any progress again. Yet, Intel thrived under Andy Grove's leadership. The evidence? During Grove's tenure as CEO (1987–1998), Intel experienced a 30% annualized growth rate.[16]

How do progress makers, such as Mike Cowen and Andy Grove, increase their odds of selecting the best path forward? How do they resolve the central conundrum between exploring and refining? How do they get others aligned with their visions of progress? These issues are the subject of the next section of the book.

In Section II, we introduce seven key strategies and related tactics that can transform leaders into progress makers. Some strategies you may already use; others may be entirely new to you. Either way, everyone can benefit by enhancing their understanding and further developing their progress-making aptitudes.

Here's a quick overview of these strategies:

1. Envision the future with calculated boldness

2. Cultivate a focused flexibility mind-set

3. Enlarge the circle of engagement

4. Foster the growth of investment-worthy employees

5. Seek, nurture, and evaluate actionable ideas

6. Select, detect, and correct the proper errors

7. Practice receiver-centric, strategy-based, feedback-driven communication

When Alice stumbled into Wonderland, she encountered a grinning Cheshire Cat who amused her but offered her no direction. Unlike the grinning cat, we provide well-tested strategies to move forward and life stories of real people who have used them. You will not run into any Mad Hatters in Section II. You will, though, encounter other progress makers who are profiled in various chapters throughout the book. When you synthesize the strategies and personal stories of progress makers, you should be well equipped to move your organization forward or, if necessary, out of Wonderland.

PROGRESS MAKER PROFILE

RON REED AND THE DISCOVERY CHANNEL

Which company generates more revenue: NBC or The Discovery Channel? Most people would answer NBC. And they would be wrong. In fact, Discovery is a $200 billion company built on a rock-solid reputation for delivering world-class educational materials for people of all ages. The story of one acquisition the company made provides an intriguing glimpse into its success.

United Learning, founded in 1969, created short video clips for teachers to use for instructional purposes. For example, if a teacher wanted her students to learn about mitosis (cell division), this company could provide a short video clip explanation of this process. A novel feature was that the

(Continued)

(Continued)

clips were specifically geared to grade levels. First graders would view a short and easy to understand clip, while 12th graders would see a more complex clip. In the parlance of the Progress Model, this unique collection of analog videos established the first platform for the company. Yet, it was an idea before its time because there really wasn't a powerful way to deliver the content to teachers. VHS tapes were fine, but they didn't really exploit the power of United Learning's wonderful teaching tools.

Intriguingly, United Learning's first platform had been built with an uncertain future in mind. They knew a better technology would emerge to more expediently and effectively deliver the content. They simply didn't know which one. So they built their library of material on the premise that someday the content would switch to a superior delivery mechanism. The movement from versions 1.1 to 1.3 (see Figure 6.1 in Chapter 6) was exhilarating and satisfying. Why? Most employees could see how the core product lines of United Learning were being enhanced. The quality was improving, and the breadth of the videos offered expanded from a handful to thousands. In short, United Learning was developing a full spectrum of quality products.

But the movement from 1.1 to 1.3 was also deceiving. How could this kind of progress be deceiving? Who wouldn't see that as real and meaningful progress? The CEO and president, Ron Reed, for one. He had guided the small company almost from its inception, and yet he had a nagging concern about sustaining the progress. He explained, "We were getting better at what we did . . . everyone was pretty excited about that. But I knew something was missing. Our content was fantastic. Teachers loved it. But we needed a quicker and more effective way to get it into the classroom." So Ron kept the team moving forward in the same direction while constantly scanning for the missing piece.

When Ron first saw the Progress Model, he studied it for a moment and then instantly pointed to the circle 1.7 of Platform 1 (see Figure 8.1). He explained, "That's exactly where we were as a company in the late 1990s. I knew it but I'm not sure many others recognized that we were teetering at the end of a platform." United Learning had made a lot of progress since its humble beginnings, and many people were looking back at past successes as a guarantee of future success. In fact, the company could have continued with business as usual for several years and probably maintained profitability.

Yet Ron saw it differently. He knew that the current business model was eventually doomed and the company had to "jump to a new platform." In particular, he realized long before others did that the analog video clips they used were going to be relegated to the same cyber burial ground as

Figure 8.1   **Ron Reed's Progress Model**

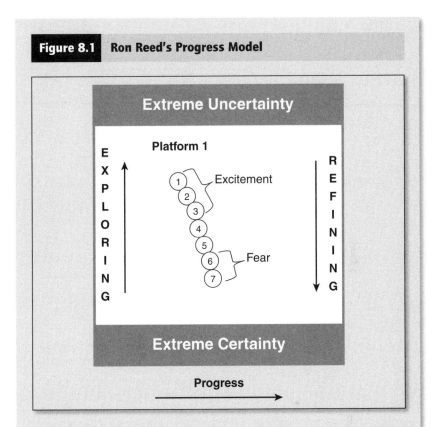

eight-track tapes and betamax video players. Then, the missing puzzle piece began to materialize. It was the almost magical delivery mechanism Ron had been searching for since the early days of the company. It was something we take for granted now, but at the time, it was in its infancy. It was the Internet, with all its potential, that put a grin on Ron's face.

Recall that flexibility was a key premise in the design and delivery of the content. But as the company got better at delivering its product on videotape, some employees unknowingly let that flexible mind-set slip away and became resistant to shifting to new delivery mechanisms. In fact, Ron came to the sad realization that some of the people who helped successfully build the first platform could not make the transition to the new digital streaming video technology via the Internet.[17] They either left willingly or were asked to do so by the management team.

Ron had the self-confidence, persistence, and fortitude to lead the organization through this platform shift. Soon United Learning was the

(Continued)

(Continued)

premier developer of educational materials that used digital streaming video. This second platform provided growth even more quickly than the first platform. Once again, Ron started scanning the horizon for potential opportunities and dangers. Yet, he also foresaw that other companies with greater resources could overwhelm their small but successful company. Here, again, they were facing another decision about the fate of an existing platform and, indeed, the company itself.

Around this time, The Discovery Channel started to court Ron and the owner of the company. Discovery Communications, Inc., with its commitment "to help satisfy natural curiosity," was a natural fit for United Learning. In 2002, The Discovery Channel bought the company and asked Ron to continue running it.

The successive jumps to new platforms were difficult but created a record of sustained progress. For example, in 2003 only 25% of the schools in the United States used the company's streaming videos. Today the clips are used in well over 70% of U.S. schools and in educational institutions in 12 foreign countries.

Ron also made personal progress. He stayed with Discovery for many years after the sale of United Learning and guided the acquisition of many other small educational companies. He is not your stereotypical, hyperkinetic, always-on-the-prowl-for-the-next-big-deal kind of executive. The only prowling he does is for fish in Lake Michigan. He is thoughtful, patient, and kind. He likes to describe himself as a servant-leader, a style he learned early in his career when he worked for the *Milwaukee Journal*. Perhaps his well-honed journalistic antennae picked up the signals about the need to shift platforms more quickly than others. Regardless, he embodies the qualities of a progress maker: tolerant of uncertainty, discerning, and passionate. His career allowed him to pursue his passion—education of others. So it is fitting that Discovery Education named him CEA—the Chief Education Advisor.

LESSONS LEARNED

- Sometimes the employees who helped create progress for one platform do not see the need to move to a new platform and cannot make the transition.

- Solid profit-generating platforms can be built without a crystal clear vision of the future.

- Shifting a platform does not necessarily entail developing new products; it could be developing new delivery mechanisms or processes.

NOTES

1. Quoted in *Leadership . . . With a Human Touch.* Chicago: Lawrence Ragan Communications, Inc., 2002, 6.

2. L. Carroll, *The Complete Illustrated Works of Lewis Carroll.* London: Chancellor Press, 1982, 62.

3. J. March, "Exploration and Exploitation in Organizational Learning." *Organizational Science* 2, no. 1 (1991): 71–86, p. 71.

4. Ibid., 73.

5. A. Gupta, K. Smith, and C. Shalley, "The Interplay Between Exploration and Exploitation." *Academy of Management Journal* 49, no. 4 (2006): 693–708, p. 695.

6. N. Wingfield, "Netflix Boss Plots Life After DVD." *Wall Street Journal,* June 23, 2009, A1, A12. See also U. Lichtenthaler, "Absorptive Capacity, Environmental Turbulence, and the Complementarity of Organizational Learning Processes." *Academy of Management Journal* 52, no. 4 (2009): 822–46.

7. M. Tushman and C. O'Reilly, "Ambidextrous Organizations: Managing Evolutionary and Revolutionary Change." *California Management Review* 38, no. 4 (1996): 8–30.

8. Gupta, Smith, and Shalley, "The Interplay Between Exploration and Exploitation," 698.

9. C. O'Reilly, B. Harreld, and M. Tushman, "Organizational Ambidexterity: IBM and Emerging Business Opportunities." *California Management Review* 51, no. 4 (2009): 75–99.

10. M. Benner and M. Tushman, "Process Management and Technological Innovation: A Longitudinal Study of the Photography and Paint Industries." *Administrative Science Quarterly* 47 (2002): 676–706, p. 702.

11. J. Welch, *Winning.* New York: Harper Business, 2005, 169.

12. Personal interview, Mike Cowen, June 22, 2009.

13. See http://www.sportablescoreboards.com/index.php?option=com_content&task=view&id=371&Itemid=159 (accessed June 24, 2009).

14. R. Tedlow, "The Education of Andy Grove." *Fortune,* December 12, 2005, 117–37.

15. R. Tedlow, *Andy Grove: The Life and Times of an American.* New York: Portfolio, 2006.

16. C. Edwards, "Inside Intel." *BusinessWeek,* January 9, 2006, 47–54, p. 47.

17. This is the primary technology used today to deliver video content on the Internet. At the time of the decision, video delivered via the Internet was in its infancy.

STRATEGIES
FOR PROGRESS MAKERS

❊ 9 ❊

ENVISION THE FUTURE WITH CALCULATED BOLDNESS

To try to be safe everywhere is to be strong nowhere.

—Sir Winston Churchill

When words such as *boldness, courage,* and *bravery* crop up in a conversation, often the stories involve military commanders, officers, and troops. Daring exploits against daunting odds usually provide the main storyline. Yet, the storytellers often neglect to mention an essential feature of most bold action—namely, *calculation,* which helps to minimize risk. In this chapter, we want to examine how progress makers act with both calculation and boldness. Clearly, there are times that too much calculation can lead to inaction (e.g., analysis paralysis). But progress makers rarely fall into that trap. In fact, progress makers see calculation as strengthening boldness.

So it seems fitting to start this chapter by examining how one of the toughest military units dealt with a largely administrative conundrum. In particular, let's study how the U.S. Navy SEALs (Sea, Air, & Land) approached the task of adding an additional 500 men to its ranks of 2,300 active servicemen.

That might not seem like a daunting task until you take into account some important facts:

- Fact 1: Navy SEALs are considered one of the most elite warriors in the world. They are tasked with the sensitive and difficult military missions like locating high-ranking Al Qaeda terrorists in the rugged mountains of Afghanistan.[1]
- Fact 2: They have plenty of applicants, but most can't make it through the grueling training process. Only one in four candidates survives BUD/S (Basic Underwater Demolition/SEAL training). [2]
- Fact 3: Compromising on quality is not an option.

Captain Duncan Smith dug into the data and discovered that triathletes were graduating from the program at over a 40% rate compared to others who graduated at a rate around 26%.[3] He decided to directly influence the system by altering the traditional recruitment methods that relied on the Navy sending the SEALs recruits. Captain Smith and his crew refocused the advertising and began to target athletes attending endurance events such as major triathlons and the Winter X Games. The strategy reaped benefits, as the graduation rates steadily climbed.[4]

Captain Smith demonstrates how progress makers think and behave. Elite warriors, like special leaders, know that *shooting* the target is easier than *locating* the target. *Progress makers zero in on the issues that need the most attention and then vigorously attack them.* In a nutshell, that's envisioning with calculated boldness.

DEFINING THE CONCEPT

The synonyms for *calculation* and *boldness* clash. Calculating leaders act with deliberation, design, and planning. Bold leaders act with audacity, courage, and daring. Overly calculating leaders hesitantly budge their organizations forward. Overly bold leaders impetuously jump to a new direction. Progress makers seek out the sweet spot between the overly timid and overtly brash (see Figure 9.1). They find the synergy between the two extremes by acting boldly when the right conditions prevail. They attack like cyclist Lance Armstrong does on the mountain stages of the Tour de France. He doesn't attack, attack,

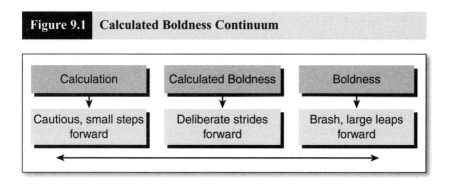

Figure 9.1   **Calculated Boldness Continuum**

attack. He realizes that this supreme athletic challenge is a "chess game" driven by simple truth: "It's easier to ride just behind someone than in front. A lot easier: At twenty-five miles per hour on the flats, the trailing rider uses 30 percent less power than the leader."[5] Consequently, he calculates the optimum time to stage an attack by sensing potentially decisive vulnerabilities of an opponent. Then he attacks with an astonishing degree of vigor and aggressiveness.[6] That's what it takes to win the yellow jersey of the Tour de France seven times.

Likewise, progress makers envision the future with calculated boldness by ascertaining the most timely and significant points of intervention. Why? BECAUSE THOSE IN LEADERSHIP POSITIONS WHO PUT A BOLD FACE ON EVERYTHING WIND UP EMPHASIZING NOTHING. Everything appears to be a top priority. And if the leaders will not make a choice, then the followers will choose whatever they wish as a priority. The intervention point may be refining a platform or creating a new one. Regardless, after progress makers make the determination, they forcefully and unrelentingly pursue their aims. In short, they shun both timidity and brashness.

Shun Timidity

Progress makers shun timidity by silencing their fears with three abiding convictions. First, they know that success is always temporary. Decline, growth, and change are inevitabilities that progress makers neither resist nor bemoan; rather, they embrace these inescapable realities with an eye toward the future. Second, they know that strategic opportunities are rare. Better to seize them than let them pass. For example, during recessions, companies such as Hewlett-Packard, Genentech, and Google jumped on opportunities to acquire strategic assets and buy small firms that propelled their growth for years.[7] Third, they know that sometimes you just have to ignore the economic headwinds and create your own opportunities. Such were the sentiments of the founders of CNN, Microsoft, and FedEx who started their companies during perilous economic times.[8] In fact, a Kaufmann Foundation study found that "well-over half of the companies on the 2009 *Fortune* 500 list, and just under half of the 2008 *Inc.* list began during a recession or bear market."[9]

Shun Brashness

Progress makers tend to be restless and can have a natural brashness. Yet, they temper these impulses with calculation. At the most basic level, calculation involves a thoughtful analysis of relative benefits and costs of a particular move. Calculations can be done on a paper napkin in the heat of battle as well as on a pristine sheet of flipchart paper in the friendly warmth of an executive retreat. For the progress maker, situational constraints matter little. Situational comforts matter less. Situational sensitivity, though, dominates all. Why? It allows the progress maker to envision thoughtfully WHAT issues to attack and WHEN to boldly move forward.

Calculated boldness does not materialize out of some inner feeling of power or omnipotence. You don't have to don Superman's cape to act with calculated boldness. In fact, feelings of anxiety and fear take a backseat to the cerebral activity of making a calculated determination of the odds of success. For the progress maker, bold thoughts precede action; the emotions will follow the mind's lead. It sounds simple in theory. In practice it is not. Why? Read on.

WHAT INHIBITS CALCULATED BOLDNESS?

Clearly, the timid and simple-minded cannot act with calculated boldness. But let's put those types of leaders aside for now. Instead, let's focus on those leaders who have the potential to become progress makers. There are often manageable issues that stand in the way of a leader's potential. We discuss three of the major ones in this section.

First, the Leader Overly Relies on Familiar Courses of Action

The "Law of the Hammer" declares that if you give child a hammer, she will start to see a lot of things that need hammering—even things that don't. People misuse and overuse tools all the time. Students, for example, routinely overuse the Internet for research. They often fail to take into account the credibility of the Web site, the motives of the content provider, and the bias of search engines. Moreover, they often fail to realize that some of the most valuable content lies outside the realm of the Internet in the aisles of the library and the in minds of experts. If you were to ask typical college students about problems with credibility, motives, and search biases, they would often say the right things. Unfortunately, many do not behave with those issues clearly in mind.[10] Why? Expediency and familiarity. In colloquial terms, it equates to the sentiment, "I've always done it that way before. Why change?" Consequently, inertia—rather than reason—sets organizational direction.

Let's turn to the sciences for a deeper perspective on inertia. It was Galileo Galilei who first advanced the principle of inertia that Isaac Newton eventually codified in his first law of thermodynamics. In the simplest terms, it means "a body in motion tends to remain in motion, a body at rest tends to remain at rest."[11] Translating the law from the physical to the organizational sciences proves revealing and enlightening, for the same law of inertia can apply to almost any organizational practice. Once certain processes or procedures are set in motion, they prove difficult to stop regardless of how dysfunctional they may actually be to organizational health. How else do we explain the seemingly mindless perpetuation of government subsidies to underperforming agencies and obsolete industries? Fighting against the forces of inertia may prove to be one of the most difficult battles that aspiring progress makers wage.[12]

Of course, few people hasten to defend "organizational inertia." More often, the progress maker encounters resistance couched in terms of "respect for tradition." One progress maker, Winston Churchill, growled a classic retort when faced with this type of resistance. Early in his career, he served as First Lord of the Admiralty. Unlike other government bureaucrats, he started pushing for major reforms. Near the end of a conference with his admirals, he was accused of "impugning the traditions of the Royal Navy."[13] His response: "'And what are they?' asked Winston. 'I shall tell you in three words. Rum, sodomy, and the lash. Good morning, gentleman.'"[14]

Second, the Leader Lacks Awareness
of All the Potential Points of Intervention

Imagine trying to develop a medical treatment for polio with no knowledge of viruses. Even Jonas Salk couldn't do that. Fortunately, he knew a great deal about diseases that occurred on the viral level and developed a vaccine that saved millions of lives. Likewise, how can leaders inspire progress without knowledge of the various levels at play in their organizations? They cannot.

Symptoms often appear at one level that are not the real source of the problem. Polio victims, for instance, can display symptoms of the malady on a variety of levels, including headaches (vascular or neurological level), nausea (gastrointestinal level), and, in some cases, paralysis (muscular level). But the disease cannot be effectively prevented or effectively treated at any of these levels.[15] Likewise, poor employee performance may be induced by inappropriate incentives, improper hiring practices, incompatible coworkers, or any number of other issues. Without an awareness of these levels, leaders may respond inappropriately to the situation.

The notion of levels implies nesting or layering. Planets nest within planetary systems, which nest within galaxies, which in turn comprise our universe. You can see a similar layering as we move between subatomic particles, atomic particles, atoms, molecules, and so on. Clearly, the idea of levels burrows deeply into our ways of thinking about the world.

As you change levels, you switch from the microscopic to the macroscopic (or vice versa), just as a photographer shifts between lenses of different magnification. And as any photographer will tell, you see different things with different levels of magnification. Although distinguishing between levels implies hierarchy, it does not necessarily suggest the superiority of one level over another. After all, which level of magnification should photographers use? That depends, of course, on how they intend to use the photo.

Unfortunately, leaders cannot shift to different levels of a system as easily as the photographer can switch a lens. Some people have special insight into one level of analysis, and they start to see *all* problems in life as occurring at that level. We might call it the "Law of the Level" because some people overly rely on one level of analysis out of desire for comfort, expediency, and familiarity. Motivational speakers, for instance, tend to see most organizational problems caused by varying degrees of employee motivation. They are not alone. This can happen to anyone with expertise ranging from communication and marketing to engineering and finance. In short, the lure of the familiar level can lead us to focus on the wrong one. Effective leaders operate on many levels, shifting rapidly as deemed necessary.

Third, the Leader Fails to Engage in Thoughtful and Spirited Debate

French philosopher Joseph Joubert may have captured the progress maker's sentiment best when he said, "It is better to debate a question without settling it than to settle a question without debating it." Unfortunately leaders often unwittingly opt for the second alternative. Why? They lack the appreciation, temperament, and/or education to glean actionable insight from debate.

Appreciation

Experience often breeds appreciation. Experienced debaters come to value how the intellectual clash can help evaluate evidence, clarify ideas, unearth hidden assumptions, and improve decision making. The good debate produces better understanding of precisely what issues require bold action. As one classic text put it, "In the highest tradition of debate, [the debater] is an investigator who co-operates with fellow investigators in searching out the truth or in selecting that course of common action which seems best for all concerned."[16] The object of the progress maker's debate is not to proclaim a winner and loser. Rather, it is to produce great decisions and an understanding of the evidence, values, assumptions, and arguments that led to the decision. The added bonus: The progress maker can more quickly adapt and seize the moment when the evidence changes, values shift, assumptions fail, or arguments wane.

Temperament

Some people in leadership positions personalize disagreements, viewing every counterargument as a threat to their power and credibility. Their fragile egos shatter like an eggshell when someone gently nudges forward a differing perspective. Other leaders possess such an inflated sense of their own intellectual or moral superiority that they simply cannot see the value of spirited debate. Instead, they value the affirmations of "yes-men." Their temperament stands in stark contrast to those on the Apple board of directors. Andrea Jung, Chairman and CEO of Avon and a member of the Apple board of directors, noted that "there's an extraordinary openness in the boardroom. Any board member (feels) free to challenge an idea or raise a concern."[17] The Apple board of directors, like the boards of most major companies, contains plenty of healthy egos brimming with confidence in their leadership abilities. So what? Clearly, even those with a healthy sense of self-worth can recognize the value of candid and energetic dialogue. It may not be their natural temperament, but they can learn to channel their spirit in a more productive direction.

Education

How do leaders learn to engage in a thoughtful clash of ideas? Where do they learn to properly

- Test the reliability and validity of evidence
- Weigh multiple pieces of evidence
- Connect evidence to claims
- Evaluate the soundness of an argument
- Respond to counterarguments
- Build a case for a particular course of action

Without these skills, leaders may act boldly, but they cannot act with *calculated* boldness.

WHAT TO DO?

Overcoming the inhibiters discussed above only gets the leader to the starting gate. Now what? In this section, we review the tactics that progress makers use to envision with calculated boldness.

Improve, Develop, or Acquire the Necessary
Tools to Monitor Organizational Health and Direction

A tool is any mechanism that extends on our natural abilities to perceive, monitor, or analyze issues. How could scientists explore cellular structures without a microscope? How could astronomers investigate the heavens without telescopes? Without these tools, they often dream up plausible but mistaken ideas. Prior to telescopes, for instance, many intelligent people believed that the Earth was the center of the universe. Even brilliant people, like

Aristotle, got it wrong. We have no doubt that with the proper tools, Aristotle would have amended his views.

Sadly, organizational leaders often find themselves in Aristotle's position. They have an incomplete set of tools at their disposal. They may, for instance, have some useful tools to evaluate the performance of employees, calculate employee turnover, analyze sales figures, and measure return on investment. But are these tools functioning properly? Does the organization need other tools? The central question is, Do leaders have well-functioning tools to direct their attention to the proper intervention points? This question resembles the challenge that fighter plane engineers face when designing a flying arsenal. It must project military power. It must respond to threats. It must be able to accomplish its mission. Ideally, an organization, like the fighter jet, has an array of tools available to monitor performance at all levels. That rarely happens. Why?

First, the tools may be broken

While most organizations have in-place performance appraisal systems, they are often poorly maintained and used.[18] Our multiyear research about organizational communication practices revealed that fully 60% of employees expressed dissatisfaction with their organization's performance appraisal system. Moreover, during employee interviews, we discovered that in many organizations, the appraisal was simply a sham. In several cases, supervisors never conducted formal appraisals of their employees and merely forwarded the appraisal forms to the personnel department.[19] How can an organization move forward without employees receiving candid feedback about their performance?

Second, the tools may be the wrong ones for the task

A carpenter wouldn't think of using a crowbar to pound in a nail. Unfortunately, something similar happens in organizations every day. In his book published in 2007, the former chairman and CEO of Citibank, Walter Wriston, made this eerily prescient observation:

> Measurement of knowledge workers' productivity is primitive at best and downright misleading at worst. . . . Does a productive loan officer make a lot of loans and have few defaults or does he or she make a few loans and have zero defaults? We have no agreed-upon measures. Indeed, there is a clear disconnect between what is traditionally measured and what is important.[20]

By late 2008, a tsunami of defaulted loans helped ignite a worldwide recession and a financial crisis at his former company.[21] Almost every investor in the world wished that their leaders had engaged in a serious thoughtful debate about the issues that Wriston raised. Such are the potential consequences of the using inadequate tools.

Third, the tools may be missing

For instance, we discovered at one Midwestern university that there was an overabundance of tools. The university routinely reviewed professor performance with departmental merit reviews, departmental retention reviews, departmental tenure reviews, personnel council reviews, and so forth. Yet, the university had no formal mechanism or tools to evaluate relationships it formed with local community members and organizations. Amazingly, the university prided itself on fostering "excellent community and inter-institutional relations." But how could they even know if they were being successful? In short, this particular organization resembles a carpenter with a toolbox full of hammers but nothing else. That's fine if you only plan on making progress by pounding on people. But the university had much bigger plans that required an entire assortment of tools.

Making progress means boldly attacking the right problem at the right time. You can't do that with wrong, broken, or missing tools. And your toolkit cannot be laden with too many tools of the same type. Progress makers know this and take active steps to get the right tools and toolkit in place. Then they build a progress-making machine.

Ponder and Debate the Gateway Questions Before Proceeding

Even with a great toolkit, leaders are often tempted to turn to their most trusty and reliable tool. That's often a mistake. Before progress makers decide important issues, they tend to spend a great deal of time—some may say excessive—on the gateway question. The gateway question is simple but profound: On what issue or level do I need to exert influence? Progress makers spend so much time on this question because they know if they get the answer wrong, the consequences can be severe. This is not like a singer missing a note; it is like a singer singing the wrong song. This is also an extremely difficult question to answer because it involves speculations and judgments about unknown variables. It requires deep discussion with thoughtful people and often some soul searching.

One of the best examples of this kind of thoughtfulness occurred during a press conference held by NBA Commissioner David Stern. He had the regrettable duty of publicly discussing the case of NBA referee, Tom Donaghy. The background: At the time of the press conference, Mr. Donaghy was accused of betting on NBA games, some of which he officiated. He later pled guilty to the charges. Clearly, this kind of scandal could undermine the fan base for the entire league. If not handled appropriately, we would be talking about regress instead of progress. Fortunately, the commissioner rose to the occasion and gave an extraordinary press conference. What we found particularly impressive was the internal review prompted by the scandal. He noted that his team examined the entire system for hiring, educating, monitoring, and evaluating referees as well as other security procedures. They even hired consultants in Las Vegas to see if there were any unusual betting patterns. While the NBA continued to actively look for security updates, Stern and his team concluded,

> I can stand here today and pledge that we will do every look back possible to analyze our processes and seek the best advice possible to see if there are changes that should be made and procedures that should be implemented to continue to assure fans that we are doing the best we possibly can. It's small consolation to me, but, you know, doing the best you can doesn't always mean that criminal activity by a determined person can be prevented. All you can do in many cases is deal with it as harshly as you can when you determine it and hope that that, in addition to all of your other processes and procedures, acts as a deterrent. But if there's anything that is possible, virtually regardless of the cost, we plan to pursue that and to, in effect, reaffirm our covenant with our fans; that the NBA is a product that will remain proud of its officiating staff, which we believe is the best in the world, and that our games are decided on their merits.[22]

This remarkable statement occurred only after he detailed all the other potential levels of inquiry that essentially led down a blind alley. And even in this official statement, he underscored the potential influence of unknown issues. That's exactly the way progress makers think. They dwell on and ponder the gateway question even when others want to move on to the specifics.

Identify System-Level Roadblocks to Progress

Progress makers realize the natural allure of analyzing a problem on the individual employee level. It is easier to blame a problem on the person than it is to address issues at other levels such as those identified in Figure 9.2. And it is simpler to solve: Just replace the person.

Figure 9.2   **Potential Levels and Types of Interventions**

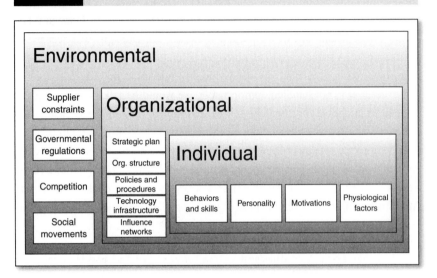

Progress makers slow this natural reflex by clearly identifying all the potential points of intervention. This even works on the individual employee level. If you perceive humans as a multileveled system, then you might address personnel problems in the way one executive did. He recognized the potential of one of his regional managers but realized this manager could never fill executive positions without being able to motivate more effectively. The executive pondered the issue for a while. He was trying to determine if the problem was something deeply based in the manager's personality or if it was simply a missing skill. He decided to hire a speaking coach for the manager to address this problem. It worked. The manager ultimately realized his potential and continued to move up in the organization. But that never would have happened without the executive viewing the employee as a multileveled system. Fortunately, he found the right level at which to exert influence.

Likewise, identifying the different intervention levels in your organization can lead to some breakthrough insights. We are not referring to the organizational chart. Instead, we are talking about the levels revealed in Figure 9.2. It may, for instance, involve seeking significant changes in the competitive environment by retooling supplier relationships, shaping new regulatory laws, or partnering with activist groups. It often involves thinking beyond the obvious and politically expedient. Consider, for example, the abuses and torture of detainees at the Abu Ghraib prison in Iraq during the second Gulf War. Some commentators quickly dismissed the sickening images by blaming the excesses on a few poorly trained rogue prison guards. Yet, two scholars from the traditional academic world and one from the U.S. Army War College could not so easily rinse the ethical stench down the moral drain. In their award-winning article, "Abu Ghraib, Administrative Evil, and Moral Inversion," they go beyond the politically expedient.[23] In fact, they raise provocative questions about how administrative philosophies, procedures, and policies can create conditions of "administrative evil." Progress makers raise such prickly and troubling system-level questions because they know how such issues can poison the culture of even the most gung ho organizations.

Calculate the Cost of Failing to Address Critical Issues

The complexity and difficulty of addressing issues does not deter progress makers. Why? They know that failure to do so can halt progress. That is a hidden cost that progress makers will *not* incur.

Consider the tough decision that a relatively new athletic director at a mid-sized university had to make. Traditionally, the athletic department raised scholarship funds from an annual festival complete with carnival rides, area bands, and lots of food. Over its 20-year history, the festival had raised hundreds of thousands of dollars. But over the years, the trend line started heading south. What to do? Convincing arguments were made from a variety of perspectives: charge higher admission prices, change the dates, and recruit alternative musical acts, to name a few. The athletic director took a different tact by asking a simple but profound question: Could the energy the team invested in the festival be directed more wisely at other fundraising efforts?

Staff members' light bulbs started to click on. They soon realized the enormous amount of time, energy, and resources tied up in a festival with a dwindling rate of return. And they realized the enormous potential of redirecting that energy to other activities. Viewed in that light, the athletic director decided to stop sponsoring the festival. This was not an easy decision because so many people had a vested interest in the festival platform. But it was the correct one because of the high cost of *not* seeking a more lucrative fundraising platform. Note how the athletic director skillfully jumped up a level and asked a system-level question about the viability of the entire festival enterprise. He listened to the voices within the existing system but concluded that the system needed to change. That's exactly how progress makers think and make decisions.

Use the Power of Self-Fulfilling Expectations

If you suffered from osteoarthritis of the knee, how would you like your malady treated? Choice one: undergo arthroscopic surgery, which involves cutting out and flushing away bad cartilage, or choice two: undergo a "make-believe" surgery in which a skin incision is made but the surgeon doesn't touch the cartilage. Choice one is the real deal and choice two is sham surgery—it only looks like the real deal.

Most patients would opt for the "real deal." But it turns out that the "real deal" was no better than the "fake deal." The research reported in the *New England Journal of Medicine* involved 165 patients randomly placed in groups, one receiving the actual surgery and the other only the scar from the surgery. In this double-blind experiment (the gold standard for researchers), both groups experienced almost identical improvements in range of movement and pain relief. In essence, the placebo effect—thinking you got treatment—was just as effective as the actual surgery.[24] Were the study results a fluke? Not by a long shot. The power of the placebo effect, self-fulfilling prophecies, or "subject expectancy effects" has been well documented in numerous scientific studies.[25]

Progress makers make use of this psychological phenomenon by encouraging employees to form robust expectations about the possibilities for refining an existing platform or building a new one. Long ago, the Greeks recounted a tale about a king of Cyprus who fell in love with a gorgeous statue. It was Aphrodite, the Goddess of Love, who eventually infused the statue with life to the great pleasure of the king. Such was the inspiration for George Bernard Shaw's play *Pygmalion,* which was brought to life in the much loved movie, *My Fair Lady.* Myths can be transformed into reality.[26] In some ways, you almost have to believe or expect to see something before you find it. In a twist on the "seeing is believing" conventional wisdom, thoughtful scholars have come to the conclusion that "believing is seeing."[27] In other words, we can't see it until we expect to see it. The project team, for example, can't see the way to incrementally refine a process until it expects to do so. Albert Einstein put it this way:

> It seems that the human mind has first to construct forms independently before we can find them in things. Kepler's marvelous achievement is a particularly fine example of the truth that knowledge cannot spring from experience alone, but only from the comparison of the inventions of the mind with observed fact.[28]

Einstein's insight resonates with the research about the placebo effect. Once we believe something, we tend to seek out confirmatory evidence. The progress maker knows that creating expectations of things unseen—the incremental improvement, the breakthrough idea, or vision of the future—often results in flashes of brilliance.

Learn to Tolerate Setbacks and Recover

Envisioning with calculated boldness starts the quest, but sustaining it requires something more. Progress makers inevitably encounter setbacks, delays, and disappointments. They need to have the mental toughness to handle this and still seek an alternative way to advance toward the objective or, in some cases, retreat. Reading the tales of great explorers such as Ernest Shackleton in the riveting book *Endurance: Shackleton's Incredible Voyage* gives one a sense of the resiliency a team needs to respond to adversity. Gaze at the images of these courageous men facing unspeakable odds when trekking across ice floes, enduring subzero temperatures, and rowing their way across the raging seas near the South Pole. Unimaginable hardships yielded to resiliency. Daunting odds gave way to resiliency. And despair was held at bay by resiliency. Even those reading the tale warmed by a fire will be chilled to the bone as they replay the harrowing adventure.[29] Contemplate the pictures. Read the book. See the movie. Then you will get a sense of what a team needs to do to endure literally against all odds. And sometimes that's exactly what progress makers must endure to realize their bold but calculated visions.

CONCLUDING THOUGHTS

How does the son of a poor bookseller with poor eyesight and poor hearing rise to become one of England's greatest literary figures? He was acclaimed as a poet, biographer, essayist, literary critic, and the lexicographer responsible for the enormously influential *Dictionary of the English Language*. As you might expect, his own words supply the best explanation: "Great works are performed not by strength but by perseverance."

True, but Sir Samuel Johnson's adage should be tempered a bit. In particular, think about people who act with misplaced perseverance—the friend who holds a losing stock too long, a business partner who sticks with a venture when it makes more sense to cut his losses, or an inventor who continues to "perfect" an idea even as competitors enter the marketplace. Behavioral economists have a lovely name for this phenomenon—the sunk cost heuristic.

In essence, we have sunk so much energy and resources into something that we persevere well past the optimal payoff point. Psychologically, cutting our losses means admitting that we erred. As the wonderfully insightful economist John Kenneth Galbraith said, "In the choice between changing one's mind and proving there's no need to do so, most people get busy on the proof."

This means that perseverance, while admirable, can be fatal as well. We hail the admonitions of great progress makers such as Leonardo da Vinci who said, "Every obstacle yields to stern resolve." Yet, we need to be aware of the dangers of exercising misplaced resolve. That's why we end this chapter with a cautionary note about *pragmatic perseverance* and not simply *perseverance*. Before deciding to persist, it is important to take stock and determine whether it is worth it. Progress makers know when to cut their losses and move on. They also know when it is important to stay the course. That is putting calculated boldness into practice. And that idea provides the foundation for the strategy we discuss in the next chapter, focused flexibility.

PROGRESS MAKER PROFILE

BRIGADIER GENERAL H. R. McMASTER

If you asked your typical career counselor about how to move up the corporate ladder, then you probably would not receive the following advice: (1) write a highly critical review of the decisions and decision-making process of those in charge, (2) publish the review in a book titled *Dereliction of Duty,* and (3) watch the book become a critically acclaimed bestseller. Then again, there is nothing typical about Brigadier General H. R. McMaster, who did just that. He does not fit the stereotypical image of a military general. After all, he earned a Ph.D. in American history at the University of North Carolina at Chapel Hill. And despite the burdens of military command, he has amassed a scholarly record of articles and speeches that would be the envy of most college professors.

He breaks the Hollywood typecast in other ways. When you talk with him, his voice relays a sense of tentativeness and confidence. The *tentativeness* arises from an experienced conviction that his facts, analyses, and conclusions may be in error. He invites you to challenge them. One key tenet of his leadership philosophy is "don't be afraid to change your thinking. Sometimes we get caught up in flawed ideas and we just can't let them go."[30] The *confidence,* though, emerges from a deep-seated belief that he can take in all the contradictory facts and analyses and synthesize them into a workable path forward. After all, another one of his key tenets of leadership is to "make sure your objectives are clear and you know what your mission is."[31] In essence, he believes that "confidence should not equate with certainty."[32]

He has a passion for passing on lessons learned to others. That's why he wrote *Dereliction of Duty.*[33] As a young soldier and scholar, he realized there were profound lessons to be learned from the Vietnam War. He wanted to unearth them, deeply understand them, and teach them to a new genera-tion of military professionals. It is the spirit of a learner and teacher that pervades his treatises. Unlike some investigative reporters, he does not seek to embarrass people or stoke the flames of a scandal. Instead, he reflects, contemplates, synthesizes, and seeks out underlying patterns.

Many academic historians pride themselves on being dispassionate chron-iclers of the past. They are the educated bystanders who tell the stories of oth-ers, ones they rarely experienced firsthand. Consequently, few historians would fit our criteria as progress makers. Here again, General McMaster breaks with the conventional wisdom. He can tell the story of warfare firsthand. And he can describe it with passion, precision, and perspective. The *passion* emerges from the firsthand experience of the vagaries, pressures, and bru-talities of armed combat. The *precision* materializes from a keen eye for the telling detail. And the *perspective* emerges from an ability to put the con-flict in the deep historical context of both friend and foe. This rare elixir of qualities provides a glimpse into how he has been able to build new plat-forms, abandon them, and construct new ones at precisely the right time. We can illustrate this progress-making ability by examining two of his seem-ingly different command experiences in the first and second Gulf Wars.

In late February 1991, then Captain McMaster led the Second Armored Cavalry Regiment into one of the first Gulf War battles with the notorious Republican Guard. In what is known as the Battle of 73 Easting, he com-manded a brigade of nine tanks into an encounter with a superior force of Iraqi tanks under the command of Major Mohammed. (The Iraqi major actu-ally trained in the United States at the Infantry Officer Advanced Course at Fort Benning, Georgia.) A hard rain the day before produced a heavy fog, which gave way to a blinding sandstorm. Nevertheless, the order to engage the enemy went forward. And with Captain McMaster's tank at the tip of the V-shaped wedge, the regiment executed the command with astonishing velocity and ferocity. Something far deadlier than a sandstorm soon slammed down on General Mohammed's well-positioned

(Continued)

(Continued)

tanks and troops; it was McMaster's mortars and artillery. Within minutes, the enemies' first and second lines of defense were overwhelmed by McMaster's unit. The pace was so aggressive, quick, and disciplined that General Mohammed barely reached his command bunker before his entire force was demolished. The superior training, discipline, and element of surprise were the key factors leading to the astonishing results: 50 T-72 enemy tanks destroyed, 40 trucks and other vehicles disabled, while U.S forces suffered no casualties.[34] And Captain McMaster won the U.S. Army's third highest medal, the Silver Star, for "gallantry in action against an enemy of the United States."

A superficial analysis of the Battle of 73 Easting might glean the lesson that lightning quick aggressive action is the key to winning wars. But there is nothing superficial about General McMaster. Years later, when writing about the battle in a memorandum for his platoon leaders, he notes, "The Battle of 73 Easting may not at all be relevant to the way you fight a platoon in combat."[35]

In fact, his intellectual dexterity can be best illustrated by comparing the Battle of 73 Easting with his leadership 14 years later during the second Gulf War in the remote Iraq town of Tal Afar. Same country. Different mission. Different strategy.

First, some history. Prior to the McMaster's posting in Tal Afar in 2005, Shia extremists, Al Qaeda, and other terrorist groups were ripping apart the country in the power vacuum left by the demise of Saddam Hussein's government.[36] The surge of U.S. troops allowed a major shift in military action toward a counterinsurgency strategy advocated by McMaster. His strategy, developed with others under the leadership of General Petraeus, was exactly the opposite of swift and aggressive action that worked so well in other conflicts. In fact, it required patience, not speed. And restraint, not bold aggression. It took patience to work with the civilian population to build trust and the infrastructure to root out the insurgents. It took restraint to use force only when necessary.[37]

Making such a "clear, hold, and build" strategy work in practice proved enormously challenging even for the best military minds.[38] But it was necessary if the mission was to defeat the insurgency, create a capable and trusted Iraqi military force, build a legitimate government, and cultivate the right conditions for economic renewal.

What to do? McMaster helped build a new platform to meet these mission goals. It was unconventional war, and it required an unconventional platform. It was unconventional to extensively train U.S. soldiers in Iraqi and

Islamic history. It was unconventional to immerse some of the frontline troops in the basics of the Arabic language. It was unconventional to bring in professors with regional expertise to lecture the troops about the cultural mores, history, and people of the region where they were going to be posted. And it resulted in unequivocal success in the region because the troops used their unique capabilities to execute the strategy. By the end of 2007, the military operations and counterinsurgency campaign drove Al Qaeda and other insurgents out of much of Iraq. By 2008, "violence in Iraq decreased dramatically" and paved the way for a drawdown of troops in subsequent years.[39]

Why did it work? Because General McMaster believes you must build deep understanding of the culture where you wage counterinsurgency efforts. It goes beyond respecting another culture's traditions; it involves seeing the world from the perspective of the civilian population. This is not some kind of feel-good incantation. Rather, McMaster's commanders translated that idea into a work-a-day rule: "Every time you treat a civilian disrespectfully, you are working for the enemy."[40] If the troops can see how their actions might be used in the hands of insurgent propagandists, then the training has built the mind-set necessary for a counterinsurgent war. That's when the success of a mission turns less on the number of enemy killed and more on the number of tips received from civilians about insurgent activities. It requires that troops get out of their large, well-defended bases and live in the neighborhoods, building relationships with the local sheiks and political leaders. It requires, in other words, a profound sense about the human beings involved in the conflict.

And that is exactly the connection that General McMaster sees between the tank Battle of 73 Easting and his counterinsurgency campaign in Tal Afar. We can glimpse into General McMaster's mind by quoting one of his favorite passages from the great military historian John Keegan:

> What battles have in common is human: the behavior of men struggling to reconcile their instinct for self-preservation, their sense of honour and the achievement of some aim over which other men are ready to kill them. The study of battle is therefore always a study of fear and usually of courage; always of leadership, usually of obedience; always of compulsion, sometime insubordination; always of anxiety, sometimes of elation or catharsis; always of uncertainty and doubt, misinformation and misapprehension, usually also of faith and sometimes of vision.[41]

(Continued)

(Continued)

General McMaster embraces the inevitable uncertainties of war even as he clings to the certainties of the human condition such as fear, honor, and self-preservation. By understanding the contours of the enemy's history, terrain, and mind-set, General McMaster can craft ever-shifting but effective strategies. He favors this kind of complex but unquantifiable knowledge over the more conventional number-crunching and bullet-point approach that characterizes so many of the military mistakes he has chronicled. He put it well in a paper he wrote at the U.S. Army War College:

> PowerPoint slides seem to lull what otherwise might be (critically thinking) audiences into passivity. PowerPoint's "bulletizing" of ideas leads to shallow analysis. Color graphics and contrived charts substitute for thought and logic, yet create a façade of analytical credibility. The briefing dynamic often betrays an unspoken agreement between presenter and audience to give a higher priority to getting through the slides than examining the ideas and proposals that those slides represent.[42]

No wonder he implores his commanders to "visit the front leaders," "avoid receiving guidance uncritically," and "keep asking basic questions about opportunities and threats." Those are the sentiments of a critical thinker, thought leader, and progress maker.[43]

LESSONS LEARNED

- **Be wary of frozen, orthodox quantitative measures and methods of thinking.** Why? Seeking out less tangible, ambiguous information allows you to better understand complex and shifting environments.

- **Seek out deep and broad understanding of the culture or industry in which you are working.** This allows your followers to quickly adapt to new opportunities and threats.

- **Act with confidence but avoid certainties.** Why? Leaders should always be ready to revise plans as the situation warrants. They should seek to scrutinize decisions rather than validate them. Effective leaders may chuckle at the Queen's declaration in *Alice in Wonderland:* "First the verdict, then the trial." But they also heed Lewis Carroll's implicit warning.[44]

NOTES

1. M. Luttrel, *Lone Survivor: The Eyewitness Account of Operation Redwing and the Lost Heroes of SEAL Team.* Boston: Little, Brown, 2007.

2. "BUDS: Navy Seal Training at Its Best." www.usmilitary.com/9711/buds-navy-scal-training-at-its-best (accessed July 2, 2009).

3. T. Sohn, "Swim. Bike. Shoot. Kill." *Outside Magazine,* September 2007. See also http://outside.away.com/outside/culture/200709/navy-seals-1.html.

4. Ibid.

5. D. Coyle, *Lance Armstrong's War.* New York: HarperCollins, 2005, 319.

6. P. Liggett, Television Commentary on Tour de France, July 22, 2009, 9:30 CST.

7. S. Ante, "Creative Beginnings in a Downturn." *BusinessWeek,* July 27, 2009, 52.

8. "Schumpeter: Thriving on Adversity." *The Economist,* October 3, 2009, 82.

9. D. Stangler, *The Economic Future Just Happened.* Kansas City: The Kaufmann Foundation, June 9, 2009, 1.

10. K. Heyboer, "New Test Finds Students' Cyber Attitude Wanting." *Chicago Tribune,* February 18, 2007, Section 1, p. 5.

11. R. Feynman, R. Leighton, and M. Sands, *The Feynman Lectures on Physics: Volume 1.* Reading, MA: Addison-Wesley, 1963, 9–1; J. Gleick, *Isaac Newton.* New York: Pantheon, 2003.

12. D. Kelly and T. Amburgey, "Organizational Inertia and Momentum: A Dynamic Model of Strategic Change." *Academy of Management Journal* 34 (1991): 591–612.

13. As cited in W. Manchester, *The Last Lion: Winston Spencer Churchill.* Boston: Little, Brown, 1983, 443.

14. Ibid., 443.

15. J. Kluger, *Splendid Solution: Jonas Salk and the Conquest of Polio.* New York: Putnam, 2004.

16. D. Ehniger and W. Brockriede, *Decision by Debate.* New York: Dodd, Mead & Company, 1972, vii.

17. A. Jung, "All About Steve." Interview by P. Sellers. *Fortune,* November 23, 2009, 124.

18. R. Connors and T. Smith, *How Did That Happen? Holding People Accountable for Results the Positive Principled Way.* New York: Portfolio, 2009.

19. P. Clampitt, *Communicating for Managerial Effectiveness.* 4th ed. Thousand Oaks, CA: Sage, 2010.

20. W. Wriston, *Bits, Bytes, and Balance Sheets: The New Economic Rules of Engagement in a Wireless World.* Stanford, CA: Hoover Press, 2007, 95.

21. L. McDonald and P. Robinson, *A Colossal Failure of Common Sense: The Inside Story of the Collapse of Lehman Brothers.* New York: Crown Business, 2009.

22. D. Stern, "NBA Commissioner David Stern Press Conference." http://www.nba.com/news/sternpc_070724.html (accessed May 15, 2009).

23. G. Adams, D. Balfour, and G. Reed, "Abu Ghraib, Administrative Evil, and Moral Inversion: The Value of 'Putting Cruelty First.'" *Public Administration Review* 66, no. 5 (2006): 680–93.

24. B. Mosely, K. O'Malley, N. Peterson, T. Menke, B. Brody, D. Kuykendall, J. Hollingsworth, C. Ashton, and N. Wray, "A Controlled Trial of Arthroscopic Surgery for Osteoarthritis of the Knee." *New England Journal of Medicine* 347, no. 2 (2002): 81–88.

25. S. Birch, "A Review and Analysis of Placebo Treatments, Placebo Effects, and Placebo Controls in Trials of Medical Procedures When Sham Is Not Inert." *Journal of Alternative and Complementary Medicine* 12, no. 3 (2006): 303–10.

26. D. Eden, "Leadership and Expectations: Pygmalion Effects and Other Self-Fulfilling Prophecies in Organizations." *Leadership Quarterly* 3, no. 4 (1992): 271–305.

27. K. Weick and K. Sutcliffe, *Managing the Unexpected; Resilient Performance in an Age of Uncertainty.* San Francisco: Jossey-Bass, 2007, 54.

28. A. Einstein, *Ideas and Opinions.* New York: Crown, 1954, 266.

29. A. Lansing, *Endurance: Shackleton's Incredible Voyage.* 2nd ed. New York: Basic Books, 1999.

30. H. R. McMaster, *Top 10 Lessons From the Battlefield* (excerpt from presentation at the Chairmen's Roundtable, San Diego, June 2, 2009).

31. Ibid.

32. H. R. McMaster, *Crack in the Foundation: Defense Transformation and the Underlying Assumption of Dominant Knowledge in Future War* (Student Issue Paper, Volume S03–03). Carlisle Barracks, PA: Center for Strategic Leadership, U.S. Army War College, November 2003, 43.

33. H. R. McMaster, *Dereliction of Duty: Lyndon Johnson, Robert McNamara, and the Joint Chiefs of Staff, and the Lies That Lies to Vietnam.* New York: HarperCollins, 1997.

34. H. R. McMaster, Internal Memo to Brave Rifles Platoon Leaders, September 2004.

35. Ibid., 1.

36. K. Kagan, *The Surge: A Military History.* New York: Encounter Books, 2009.

37. D. Finkel, *The Good Soldiers.* New York: Sarah Crichton Books, 2009.

38. G. Packer, "The Lessons of Tal Afar," *New Yorker,* April 10, 2006.

39. Kagan, *The Surge,* 196.

40. H. R. McMaster, "Preserving Soldiers' Moral Character in Counterinsurgency Operations." In *Ethics Education for Irregular Warfare,* edited by D. Carrick, J. Connelly, and P. Robinson. Surrey, England: Ashgate, 2009, 15–39, p. 15.

41. J. Keegan, *The Face of Battle.* London: Penguin, 1976, 303.

42. McMaster, *Crack in the Foundation,* 10.

43. McMaster, *Top 10 Lessons From the Battlefield.*

44. McMaster, *Crack in the Foundation,* 80–81.

✧ 10 ✧

CULTIVATE A FOCUSED
FLEXIBILITY MIND-SET

———◆◆◆———

*Let him who boasts the knowledge of actually existing things, first
tell us of the nature of the ant.*

—St. Basil

King Solomon admonished us to "Go to the ant, you lazybones; consider
its ways, and be wise."[1] Are we to pay attention to the ant's work ethic?
Definitely. Are we to emulate the management structure of the ant hill?
Perhaps. But the wise king may be asking us to look at something even deeper.
As two scientists observed, "By maintaining pheromone trails and continuously
exploring new paths, the ants serendipitously set up a backup plan and thus are
prepared to respond to changes in their environment."[2] Ants have a remarkable
ability to quickly forget old pathways and switch roles as the needs of the
swarm change. In other words, ants practice "focused flexibility"; they *focus* on
present needs while maintaining the *flexibility* to meet future ones.

Some companies are now beginning to recognize the wisdom of such an
approach when responding to uncertainties in the business environment. Two
organizational strategy scholars observed,

> Managers of (successful) companies know that the greatest opportunities for
> competitive advantage lie in market confusion, so they jump into chaotic

markets, probe for opportunities, build on successful forays, and shift flexibly among opportunities as circumstances dictate. But they recognize the need for a few key strategic processes and a few simple rules to guide them through the chaos.[3]

Sounds just like the ants! Focus provides the motivation, resources, and direction needed to accomplish ever-changing goals. Flexibility allows companies to respond more quickly to marketplace changes while decreasing development costs. Researchers found that product designers who use flexible strategies can complete their projects in half the time of those using more conventional design processes.[4]

Maintaining both focus and flexibility tests the progress-making abilities of even the most skilled leaders. It means developing an ability to quickly inspire others to shift focus with little loss in productivity. It means redefining "the problem from one of improving forecasting to one of reducing the need for accurate long-term forecasts."[5] It means teaching employees to partially forget the old ways of doing things while maintaining those memories in case they are needed in the future. Above all, it means artfully reconciling the trade-offs between focus and flexibility. Too much focus destroys your flexibility, while too much flexibility crushes your capacity for focus. This is the wisdom gleaned from pondering the ways of the ant.

A DEEPER LOOK AT FOCUS AND FLEXIBILITY

Let's step back and take a deeper look at these seemingly contradictory notions. Consider, for a moment, the extraordinary degree of focus that a professional baseball player, like Mike, needs to have to make contact with the ball, much less hit it to the right place. Mike must block out all the physical distractions: the screaming fans, the crying babies, the scoreboard lights, the players moving around on the field, and the catcher's mitt posed inches away from him, just to name a few. There are also the psychological distractions that he must suppress: his disappointment over being asked to shift from the center to right-field position, his current batting average, his contract renegotiations, his family obligations, and so on. Then, of course, he must not think about the pitcher, who is throwing a spherical object with the hardness of a granite rock at close to 100 mph, just inches from his head. And he can only see this rocket thrown at him for the first two thirds of the distance to the plate.

In that time, he has a few milliseconds before making a decision whether to swing at the ball, let it pass, or jump out of the way.

In those fleeting moments, micro adjustments occur in Mike's eyes: The tiny dime-shaped ciliary muscles flex the lens in Mike's eyes, changing shape to bring the ball into optimal acuity. By necessity, his natural blind spot slightly moves, obscuring parts of the visual field and blurring other parts. These are unavoidable, unchangeable, and nonnegotiable consequences of the physical act of focusing.[6] Psychologically, much the same happens. When we concentrate on a task, by necessity, we ignore much of what is around us and have only a vague awareness of other issues. You better be able to do this when managing a fast-moving crisis or trying to hit a 100-mph fastball.

But this kind of focus can be problematic, even on the baseball field. Let's assume that Mike plays his new right-field position with the same degree of tenacity and concentration as he exhibits in the batter's box. Joining him on the field is another great player, Carlos, with similar abilities. Then an opposing player—we'll call him David—hits a long fly ball directly in the gap between the players. They both charge toward the ball, yelling, "I've got it, I've got it."

Now what happens? Is focus friend or foe? In this case, it's foe. Both players focus on the ball, ignoring the crowd and even their teammate. Mike and Carlos collide in a bloody horrible mess. The ball squirts between them, and their opponents end up winning the game. How do we explain this? We could attribute it to poor communication. Or lack of field awareness. Or the fact that both players were trained as center fielders. Perhaps. But at the core are the focusing abilities of these extraordinary athletes: The very ability that served them so well in the batter's box becomes their nemesis in the outfield. Regrettably, this is not a hypothetical case. Baseball aficionados no doubt will remember the particularly brutal collision between Met's outfielders Mike Cameron and Carlos Bettran during a game with the San Diego Padres.[7]

Unfortunately, this is not all that rare of an occurrence in professional baseball. Indeed, it may be more likely on the professional rather than on the amateur ball field. Why? Professional baseball players are far more likely to have similar, highly developed focusing skills than their counterparts in the amateur leagues. Yet focus not only poses a threat to baseball players but can potentially destroy any organization. Concentrating on building the world's best buggy whip, double-winged airplane, or cassette tape recorder may bring rewards for a short time, but that fixation will ultimately destroy the company. In fact, the fixation may morph into an uncontrollable passion much like a gambler's addiction. Recent psychiatric research confirms conventional wisdom about gambling addicts. They suffer from a type of "cognitive rigidity" that inhibits mental flexibility and explains why "gamblers on a losing streak keep playing till they go bust."[8]

Flexibility provides the counterpoint to focus. In the physiological realm, flexibility improves our range of motion, enhances our circulation, and helps prevent injury to our muscles. What could possibly be the downside to flexibility? To gain perspective on that question, let's examine the professional record of Edward Arnold "Eddie" Chapman, also known as Edward Simpson, Arnold Thompson, and Edward Edwards, among other aliases. He is the only British Secret Service or MI5 agent to receive the Nazi's highest military award, the Iron Cross. How did he do it? He was a double agent, serving both the Third Reich and British Intelligence in the 1940s. That's flexibility of the highest order under the most stressful conditions imaginable. To fool the Nazis, he had to convince his handlers that he was providing them valuable information and sabotaging British airplane factories while simultaneously collecting valuable intelligence for the British. It required an ability to convincingly switch identities at a moment's notice under intense and often brutal interrogation. In fact, he was extraordinarily adept at zigzagging between facades. After all, he maintained fiancés in both England and occupied Norway. The British dubbed Eddie as Agent Zigzag. He certainly lived up to the name, adroitly zigzagging between personas as well as his Norwegian and British fiancés.

The ability to crisscross personas, loyalties, and ethical boundaries served him well during World War II but not so well before and after the war. Before the war, he was a notorious thief, blackmailer, and safecracker. In fact, the Nazis recruited him when they found him languishing in a British prison in the Channel Islands for one of his crime sprees. After the war, he resorted to his earlier roots of smuggling, passing forged currency and the like. His biographer observed that "his vices were as extreme as his virtues, and to the end of his life, it was never clear whether he was on the side of the angels or the devils, whether he deceived the deceivers, or whether he made a pact with his German spymaster."[9] Agent Zigzag never went straight.

Agent Zigzag represents flexibility taken to the extreme: flexible allegiances, morals, and personal loyalties. Who could trust him? British officials, sometimes. The Nazis, but they were deceived at times, as well. The Norwegian fiancé? The British fiancé? You always wonder whether the highly flexible person will deliver. Today he may, but what about tomorrow? Reliability. Credibility. Loyalty. These are not the words that come to mind when thinking about Agent Zigzag or others who are highly flexible. Moreover, if you are constantly adapting, shifting, and morphing, you may not develop the capacity to excel. It's like the university students who have such a wide range of interests that they cannot settle on a major. As a result, they end up never graduating. Intellectually flexible, yes. Useful to society, sometimes.

Our discussion underscores the importance of maintaining the dynamic tension between focus and flexibility. In fact, researchers confirmed that leaders who create dynamic working climates tend to produce greater job satisfaction, employee commitment, and less cynicism than their counterparts (see Appendix B). Too much focus obscures your vision of potential threats and opportunities. Too much flexibility inhibits your ability to master the challenges, get over the hills, and achieve the objectives.

WHAT INHIBITS FOCUSED FLEXIBILITY?

If you ask those in leadership positions about the *idea* of focused flexibility, you will rarely encounter resistance. The struggle usually takes place over the day-to-day *practice* of focused flexibility. Why? Practicing focused flexibility rubs against the natural tendencies of the explorer and refiner. As seen in Figure 10.1, refiners are most comfortable in a high-focus, low-flexibility situation. Explorers naturally gravitate toward high-flexibility and low-focus situations.

Figure 10.1   **Focused Flexibility Matrix**

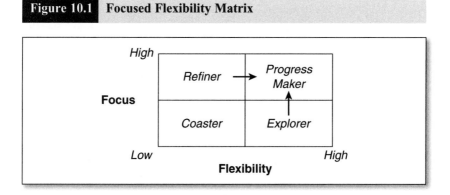

For the moment, we leave aside the "coasters" who have limited inclinations either way. Instead, we direct our attention to the underlying sources of *excessive focus* and *disproportionate flexibility*. Our research revealed that both problems spring from the following three factors.

Unexamined Success

Consider the cold hard facts about organizational success and failure:

- "[Slightly] over 10% of all the companies in the United States, the largest and most successful economy in the history of the world, fail every year."[10] And larger firms are only slightly less likely to fail.

- Even large companies that endure over time rarely stay in the same core business. After all, 3M was founded in 1902 as Minnesota Mining and Manufacturing Company. They don't do much mining these days. Nokia started operations in 1865 as a wood pulp mill in Finland. Today the company uses paper to package its high-tech phones.

- Figures widely vary, but most experts believe that while over 80% of small businesses survive their first year, only 50% will still be in business 5 years later.[11]

Clearly, present success provides no guarantee of future success. However, organizations often *act* like it does. Why?

Consider the case of a paper mill that generated higher profitability by focusing a lot of energy, resources, and people around continuously improving (refining). Would any mill manager in her right mind fail to seize the opportunity to replicate these successes in other parts of the mill? Of course not. Employees are gaining confidence in their abilities. Expertise grows. Results are virtually assured. This kind of focus is a "no-brainer."

It's not, though. In fact, this is precisely the time organizational leaders need to do some serious thinking. Why? Well-earned confidence may lead to overconfidence. Resource allocations tend to freeze in place. Organizational expertise may create vested interests in particular programs that inhibit future growth. And the results that came so easily with the first round of refining become more difficult with the next round as new competitors appear on the horizon with entirely new manufacturing processes (platforms).

This can happen in any size of organization. Why, for instance, didn't Sears become the Amazon.com? During the 1960s, Sears was a *Fortune* 100 company.

In fact, you could find a Sears catalogue in virtually every U.S. household. Today, of course, its fortunes have changed dramatically.[12] *Somebody* in the organization had to know about the Internet and its potential power. *Somebody* had to see that making the leap from a paper catalogue to an online version would be difficult but doable. And *somebody* had to know that Sears already had many of the pieces in place, such as distribution centers and purchasing agents. Wouldn't it have been easier to simply start shifting resources to an online venture than building all that from scratch? In a word, no. Why? *Nobody* could successfully champion the idea because everybody was focused on essentially exploiting and preserving the status quo. The leaders lacked the flexibility to move to a new platform because success silently morphed into inertia.

Celebrate success, if you will, but don't count on it. Stealthy attackers, like termites, silently nibble away at the foundations even as storm clouds of competitors gather for a more visible assault on your structures. Either can be toxic.

Unmanaged Stress

Any horticulturist will tell you that stressing flowering plants actually induces blossoming. However, when a plant faces prolonged stress induced by a lack of water or essential nutrients, it retreats into itself by shedding new growth, losing flowers, and drooping. This protects the plant from danger until conditions change. Humans respond in a similar manner. Up to a point, stress spurs on performance by sharpening senses, releasing adrenalin, and improving cognitive functions. After a certain point, the deterioration can be dramatic and may include depression, eating disorders, fatigue, confusion, memory failures, skin problems, repetitive thoughts, anger, and inability to concentrate.[13]

How else can we explain world-class mountaineers who violate their self-made rules about when to turn back from a final assault on Mount Everest? Under low-stress conditions, every professional climber would agree with the motto, "Safety is first; fun is second, success is third."[14] Yet, too many world-class climbers have reversed the order of this dictum when confronting the high-stress conditions in the thin air of the "Death Zone" on the world's tallest mountain. And they have paid the ultimate and tragic price.[15] Stress has a way of narrowing attention to only the task at hand. If we are refining, we ignore potential dangers on the horizon and get blindsided. If we are exploring, we fail to exploit a fruitful alternative and collapse in a heap of indecision. In short, stress can rob us of our mental faculties at the time we need them most.

Organizations may experience stressors in much the same way that humans do. However, leaders rarely talk about it that way. Consider the following potential organizational stressors: loss of a major client, major lawsuits, departure of a key leader, new government regulations, a new competitor, or an old competitor introduces new products or services, just to name a few. What happens to organizations encountering wave after wave of internal and external stressors? They respond just like any other complex organism: They retreat to protect what they consider vital and ignore the rest. If their core competencies reside in focusing on present customer needs, they will do that. Consequently, they will ignore new potential customers. If their core competencies reside in flexibly responding to day-to-day emergencies, then they will do that. And they will forgo building high value-adding services. Think about a medical clinic that does a great job of responding to patients' day-to-day needs but fails to seize opportunities that have longer term impacts, such as programs to promote healthy living lifestyles.

Dysfunctional Sensory Mechanisms

Could a human function with eyes that could not see, ears that could not hear, and fingers that could not feel? Or, could a person function with eyes, ears, and fingers that constantly flood the consciousness with signals? Either alternative represents a horrifying scenario. All too often we take for granted our sensing mechanisms. But consider the reaction of a husband whose wife encourages him to see an audiologist after her repeated requests to "turn down the TV." He doesn't see a problem. Indeed, hearing loss usually happens in almost imperceptibly small steps as if slowly descending into a long, low, and quiet valley. We naturally trust the integrity of the signals sent by our ears, eyes, and fingers. The undiagnosed hearing-impaired person usually makes an instinctive but mistaken assumption.

Leaders can lose their senses in much the same way—in barely discernable steps on a slow march toward inadvertent detachment. Progress makers recognize this danger. Consequently, they carefully consider the structure of sensory mechanisms in their organizations. In particular, they thoughtfully consider who serves as the eyes, ears, and fingertips of the organization. Will they sense subtle changes in the marketplace? Do they have appropriate access to key decision makers? Without proper sensing mechanisms, the company cannot exploit opportunities and avoid dangers.[16] After all, most companies would want to fast-track a wonderful innovation. Unfortunately, sensory mechanisms often get clogged up and the company continues to focus on "what it *does* best" at the expense of "what it *might* do well."

On the other hand, hypersensitive organizations jump on opportunities too quickly. The overly flexible response to changing conditions often results in failures to *exploit* opportunities. These businesses are, in essence, overly tuned in to the signals. They need to learn to ignore some of the signals or at least not react too hastily. The former CEO of Intel, Andy Grove, for instance, received much adulation in the business press for his painful decision to move away from the computer memory business to microprocessors. What receives little publicity was his decision to continue to exploit Intel's CISC (Complex Instruction Set Computing) chip technology when he was personally enamored with a new RISC (Reduced Instruction Set Computing) chip technology. In fact, he had recorded a rap video promoting RISC. But two executives persuaded him to reverse direction and continue to focus on CISC. It was not the right time to be flexible. In essence, Grove resisted the lure of all high-tech companies to chase the next great innovation. Instead, he rightly chose to focus at that time and exploited the existing technology.[17]

Sometimes hypersensitivity occurs because leaders pay too much attention to one particularly articulate voice inside or outside their organization. Think of it this way: Your body would not function very well if you only attended to the sensations from your itchy nose. Likewise, always attending to only one sensor can destroy an organization's capacity for focused flexibility. The other sensors—or voices in the organization—just stop sending signals.

WHAT TO DO?

Organizations that cultivate a focused flexibility mind-set use a wide variety of strategies to confront the potential problems posed by success, stress, and sensing mechanisms. We discuss below the more salient ones.

Build Frequent Iterative Loops

We were working with a very astute Web site designer who had an unusual career path. He worked for years as a highly successful executive in the entertainment industry, rising to second-in-command. But he made an abrupt move, deciding to unleash his inner artistic desire. He went back to school to get an art degree and stumbled across Web design. He fell in love with the possibilities and started an entirely new career. Yet, unconsciously, he still used his managerial talents when working with clients. When working on one long-term design project, he insisted on meeting every week with the client to get feedback about the direction he was going with the Web site. Although some meetings would last only 5 minutes, he used the time to tweak the site and gauge the client's reactions. The result was a wonderfully inventive and effective site.

What would happen if the feedback loops were longer? A refiner might pick up on an idea and "run with it" all the way down the wrong path. She might develop a wonderfully intricate site with all kinds of bells and whistles that simply did not meet the client's needs. So, 2 months down the road, the client might end up with a beautifully designed "flop" and a lot of lost time and money that can never be recovered. Quick feedback loops build flexibility into the final design by ensuring the refiner avoids prematurely focusing on the wrong task. On the other hand, an explorer would probably use the 2 months to sketch a wide array of different kinds of possible Web sites. None would be fully developed or close to implementation. In this case, quick feedback loops temper the explorer's flexibility and cultivate the focus to move toward implementation.

This example illustrates the power of selecting the right timing for a feedback loop. Progress makers actively manage iterative loops by determining the optimal timing for discussions about incremental adjustments.[18]

Search for the Optimal Environments

When talking to people who have mastered focused flexibility, you will often notice a seemingly curious technique they use to channel their natural tendencies. For example, one particular professor and best-selling author is a notorious explorer, traveling all over the world, meeting new people. Great way to develop a wide repertoire of ideas; not such a good way to buckle down to the difficult task of intense writing. What he needed was "a cage" to stop his flights of mind and body. That's exactly what he found. He secured a secret cage in the university library. Yes, it was literally a cage made of steel fencing, and it housed all his research and writing materials. He would disappear on selected days without telling anyone—not even his research assistants—where his "cage" was located. In essence, he had a particular location designed to create the focus needed to complete his books.

On the other hand, one refiner took just the opposite approach. She was great at getting things done and focusing on the task at hand. She had difficulties allowing her mind to creatively wander to think of new approaches and ideas. By happenstance, she found that taking hikes freed her mind and imagination, providing the kind of cognitive and emotional agility to jump to new platforms.

Progress makers employ similar techniques with groups of employees. Sometimes, for example, moving to an off-site meeting location can create the kind of focus necessary to dig deeply into a particular opportunity. Another company built a "brainstorming room" outfitted with sketch pads, white boards, hundreds of magazines, and even bean bag chairs. We could heap example upon example and still not reveal an underlying pattern for selecting the optimal setting. We found that discovering the right setting often falls into the category of "whatever works for you."

Improve Peripheral Vision

Far more natural species suffer extinction than gets commonly recognized. We all know about dinosaurs, but what about 90% of the marine species that simply disappeared 250 million years ago?[19] It gets worse. Paleobiologists, who study such events, discovered that the underlying species extinction patterns tend to be erratic, making prediction enormously difficult. Scientists simply don't know enough to predict what predator, event, or conditions will send a species into extinction. And we don't even know when it is most vulnerable. After all, if you compared dinosaurs and large mammals on strength, agility, and sheer ferocity, you would be hard pressed to argue that mammals would win the evolutionary contest. But that's exactly what happened.

What does all this have to do with peripheral vision? A great deal, as it turns out. Often organizations focus attention only on their direct competitors (within the species). Just as the T-Rex kept close tabs on rival T-Rexes, Sears warily observed Wards. But clearly, Amazon.com wasn't on the right leaders' radar screens (attack from another species). Threats often emerge from the periphery and simply go undetected.

Professors George Day and Paul Schoemaker studied the issue and noted,

> Good peripheral vision is much more than sensing, it is also knowing where to look more carefully, knowing how to interpret the weak signals, and knowing how to act when the signals are still ambiguous.[20]

They go on to note that the human eye devotes the majority of its retinal cells to peripheral vision at a ratio of almost 20 to 1. Most organizations flip that ratio on its head by focusing most resources on the task at hand—a great recipe to provide focus at the expense of flexibility. No wonder the extinction threat looms so large.

Yet any organization can improve peripheral vision by altering organizational structures, scanning the environment, and creating sense-making opportunities. IBM, for example, institutionalized a scanning function appropriately named the Crow's Nest, which devoted resources to searching for vague threats or opportunities. Insights gleaned from the scanning were discussed with senior management and used to set the future agenda.

Manage the Amount of Stress the Organization Places on Employees

Progress makers may have limited influence on the personal stressors in employees' lives. They do, however, have a great deal to say about the stresses imposed on their organizations. Like any bridge, there is only so much stress an organization can bear at any given point in time without destroying its focus or flexibility.

How do progress makers learn to do this? In the ideal world, we could accurately measure organizational stressors and the organization's capacity to bear the stress. Then we would plug in the numbers and determine when the organization nears the breaking point. Unfortunately, that magic formula proves to be as elusive as determining which snowflake on the mountaintop will cause the avalanche. Instead, progress makers rely on more rudimentary measures such as organizational climate questionnaires, pulse surveys, and employee focus groups to provide indications about the stress points in the organization.[21] In the end, progress makers must make a judgment that takes into account a number of factors:

- How much stress is the organization currently experiencing?
- What is the likelihood that external stressors will emerge (e.g., new government regulations, new competitor, etc.)?
- How much stress will new organizational initiatives put on the organization?
- How much stress can the organization effectively manage?

Progress makers ponder these questions in order to decide what actions to take. That means making some tough choices such as deferring worthwhile projects until the organization can handle it. Or, maybe leaders decide to forgo a market opportunity in order to preserve focus on a key issue.

Declare War on the Terrible Triad:
Excessive Planning, Overconfidence, and Cognitive Bias

This terrible triad locks in a thinking routine that destroys any glimmers of focused flexibility (see Figure 10.2). But it gets worse. Without aggressive, war-like measures, the triangle grows in strength and influence as each element reinforces the other. Progress makers forcefully attack the harmful triangle by clearly understanding the three enemies discussed below.

Figure 10.2   Terrible Triad

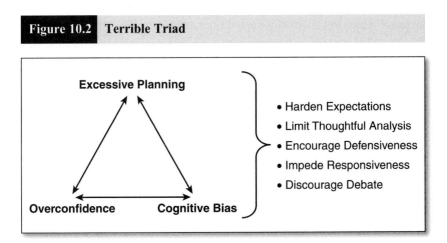

Excessive Planning

Proper planning clearly benefits organizations. However, few people address the potential dangers of excessive planning. The former CEO of the Southwest Airlines, Herb Kelleher, is one exception. He explains,

> Reality is chaotic; planning is ordered and logical. The two don't square with one another. . . . The meticulous nit-picking that goes on in most strategic planning processes creates a mental straightjacket that becomes disabling in an industry where things change radically from one day to the next.[22]

Because Southwest was one of the few financially successful airlines during tumultuous times, we ought to pay attention to his admonitions. In essence, he argues that a company can become a *victim* of its planning processes.

Traditionally, the management planning process follows a standard, well-defined series of steps. It typically works like this:

Step 1: Endpoint objectives are developed.

Step 2: Gaps between current positions and the objectives are identified.

Step 3: Action plans, timetables, and outcome measures are created to close the gaps and drive toward the desired results.

The process usually works well. But taken to extremes, managers often drive out even more uncertainty by making the plans more specific and detailed. This quest can turn into a single-minded crusade that builds momentum but blinds the organization to opportunities and dangers. It creates focus at the expense of flexibility. Managers may become less open to input from others along the way and more blind to new information that might suggest a needed change in direction. Ironically, *the more they attempt to drive out the uncertainty, the more unpredictable the results really are.* Why? Because they systematically avoid information that might alter or change their plans. And this tendency becomes heightened by the other two elements of the terrible triad.

Overconfidence

Excessive planning often leads to overconfidence in the ability to control events. In contrast, former CEO of Intel, Andy Grove, once quipped that "only the paranoid survive." But it was more than a quip; it became an organizational mantra and hedge against overconfidence.[23] Paranoids are mistrustful and suspicious. They embrace doubt; most people don't.

In fact, researchers have found that most people overestimate the accuracy of their judgment. In a clever way to test for overconfidence, people were asked a series of factual questions such as, "How many patents were issued by the U.S. Patent and Trademark Office this year?" Then they were asked to provide a low and high estimate that they are 90% certain the correct answer will fall within these limits (e.g., 3000–5000). In one study of over 2,000 people, a whopping 99% of them failed this test; almost all were overly confident of their estimates.[24] Apparently, this is a natural human tendency. Of course, "overconfidence isn't all bad!"[25] It is a close relative to positive thinking. Yet overconfidence can lead to unrealistic expectations, overly aggressive goals, and a host of other miscalculations.[26] It is one reason "why smart executives fail," as Professor Finkelstein explains in his wonderful book by that title. They end up thinking they have all the answers and may "ruthlessly eliminate anyone who isn't 100 percent behind them."[27]

Wise leaders clearly distinguish what they know from what they don't know. This is not as easy as it sounds. The Nobel Prize–winning physicist Richard Feynman put it best: "The first principle is that you must not fool yourself and you are the easiest person to fool."[28] A case in point: Prior to World War II, the French generals defiantly insisted that the series of fortifications along the northeast border of France—the infamous Maginot Line— would protect the country from any Nazi attack. They were terribly mistaken. Perhaps if those in power had been a little less certain, the tragic and almost inexplicable human toll could have been diminished. Approximately 55 million people were killed; 25 million were military causalties and 30 million were civilian. This does not include the 6 million Jews who perished in the Holocaust.

But French generals are not alone. Leaders of any organization can suffer from overconfidence. Success is usually the culprit. For example, one scholar's investigation of corporate failure concluded that

> there is something about the way decisions get made in successful organizations that sows the seeds of eventual failure . . . "good" management was the most powerful reason they failed to stay atop their industries. Precisely because these firms listened to their customers . . . carefully studied market trends and systematically allocated investment capital to innovations that promised the best returns, they lost their positions of leadership.[29]

The "something" lurking behind their decisions is overconfidence in established methodologies, markets, and modes of operation. Of course, companies need to listen to their customers. But not too closely. As former Chrysler CEO Lee Iacocca once said, "No focus group ever told us to build a minivan."[30] Of course, companies need to watch market trends, but not too carefully because they can obscure new opportunities.

If overconfidence is the disease, then feedback provides the cure. Only when people test their beliefs, often through trial and error, can they discern the difference between what they *think* they know and what they *really do* know. As two scholars aptly put it, "Experience is inevitable; learning is not. Overconfidence persists in spite of experience because we often fail to learn from experience. In order to learn, we need feedback about the accuracy of our opinions and doubts."[31] Unfortunately, that too becomes problematic because of persistent and entirely human cognitive biases that form the third element of the terrible triad.

Cognitive Biases

There is abundant and growing evidence that thinking errors lie behind most visible mistakes in organizations. For example, research into medical errors revealed that 80% of the misdiagnoses "could be accounted for by a cascade of cognitive errors."[32] The two most prevalent errors are discussed below.

Sunk cost fallacy—Imagine that your best friend is an avid baseball fan and that he attended two different local baseball games during one week. The first game was a local college game for which he paid $10 for a nonrefundable ticket. It was dismal to watch. After the third inning, his team was losing 15–0. The second game was the professional team for which he paid $125 for a nonrefundable ticket. Unfortunately, this was not a good week for hometown baseball. It was the same situation as the college team. After the third inning, his team was losing 15–0, and it was a miserable game for any aficionado to watch. Which game would your friend be more likely to leave? Most people would say the college game—after all, it cost less. That would seem reasonable, but it's not. With either game, the costs are sunk—he can't recover the ticket price.

Why won't he cut his losses and leave the second game? Because he invested more money and expects more of a return on his investment, he is more willing to endure the second awful game of the week. But the likelihood of a "good return" is the same. Logically, the amount of money paid is irrelevant. Psychologically, though, it glows with relevancy. The discrepancy between the logic and the "psycho-logic" can lead to significant errors when judging evidence. It destroys your flexibility because you can end up over-committing to a losing cause or proposition.

Confirmation bias—Humans tend to seek out evidence to confirm—not disconfirm—their preconceived notions. If a student has a strong expectation that her professor will be tough and demanding, she can usually find something—a test, a comment, an assignment—that will confirm this expectation. She won't be very motivated to find evidence to the contrary. Nassim Taleb further explains this principle in his wonderful book, *The Black Swan:*

> Alas, with tools and fools, anything can be easy to find. You take past evidence that corroborate your theories and you treat them as evidence. For instance, a diplomat will show you his "accomplishments," not what he failed to do . . . I can find confirmation for just about anything, the way a skilled London cabbie can find traffic to increase the fare, even on a holiday.[33]

Until you look for evidence to the contrary, you can't be sure of anything. In short, if I expect the new idea or process to work, then I can usually find evidence to support my expectation. Consequently, the confirmation bias tends to reinforce preexisting modes of operation.

Think about how all three elements in the terrible triad could work in tandem to reinforce one another (see Figure 10.2). Those trapped in this iron triangle harden their expectations, limit thoughtful analysis, respond with defensiveness, and impede responsiveness to shifting conditions. Consider, for example, the employee or team that has devoted an enormous amount of energy in planning, creating, and producing the world's greatest widget. What will the team do when the marketing report comes back that there is no market for its revolutionary new widget? Take your pick: (a) discredit the marketing report, (b) "villainize" the marketing manager, (c) conduct its own marketing study, or (d) all of the above. Any of these actions can be explained by the terrible triad. The team's planning process created overconfidence. Then, when faced with counterevidence, the sunk cost and desire to seek confirmatory "evidence" influenced the team to reject the feedback.

Note that we did not say whether the marketing team or widget wizards were correct. Why? The widget wizard's planning process and confidence may be entirely justified. While it's true that sunk costs may lead the wizards astray, the costs can also spur the kind of persistence needed for progress. Likewise, seeking out confirmatory evidence can demonstrate (but not prove) that the wizards are honing in on something important. In fact, if you contemplate the flipside of sunk cost and confirmation biases, you will discover two essential human qualities: determination and hope.

So what does this all mean? In short, the progress maker's team would actively analyze the report and make a conscious decision about whether to continue or cut its losses. That's declaring war on the terrible triad while still picking the battles worth winning. Leaders who do so build "learning organizations" that are "continually expanding [the organization's] capacity to create its future."[34]

Legitimize Strategic Forgetfulness

Song writers tend to romanticize memories. They encourage us to "Walk Down Memory Lane," "Hold on to Memories," and even consult the Internet at "www.memory." And don't forget to say "Thanks for the Memories." Forgetting doesn't get quite the airplay and positive vibe. That's unfortunate. While you may lament forgetting where you put your car keys, you might appreciate not recalling all the details of certain traumatic events. Indeed, our brains actually have mechanisms that inhibit memory formation during shocking events.[35]

Remembering the wrong lessons can imperil an organization's ability to embrace focused flexibility. An international team of researchers explains,

> Organizational learning frequently depends upon processes of organizational forgetting. That is, companies that want to transform themselves not only must acquire new capabilities, but they also must often forget old knowledge that traps them in the past. Furthermore, businesses must purposefully forget other types of knowledge, such as bad habits learned from a partner.[36]

Leaders are more likely to lament "knowledge loss" than they are to praise purposeful forgetting. Memories get embedded in organizational processes, procedures, and systems. That makes them all the more difficult to forget.

Consider one manufacturing plant that was attempting to dramatically improve safety. During our research, we interviewed one union worker who said, "The problem is that these guys think that just because they didn't get hurt in the past, they won't get hurt tomorrow. What they don't realize is that they are getting older. The average worker is over 50 years old! These guys can't lift and twist like they could in their 20s. That's why ergonomics is a big deal for me." He put his finger on a deeply entrenched problem. Indeed, many of the plant's "safe" procedures and standards were written by the 20- and 30-year-old workers. Before safety could improve, the workers would have to forget and unlearn formerly "safe" ways to perform tasks. This is a classic case of getting stuck with old, inferior, and unexamined memories that deprive the organization of the flexibility to respond to the changing dynamics of the workforce. Unfortunately, no one composed a song that workers could hum about the dangers of these memories.

Designate "Project Pruners" and Elevate Their Status

Even those employees attuned to the "terrible triad" and the importance of "strategic forgetfulness" may not know when it is prudent to "cut their losses" and move on. Therefore, progress makers build that function into their organizations. "Irrational exuberance," the concept popularized by former Federal Reserve Board Chairman Alan Greenspan, best captures the essence of what project pruners are seeking to control. Employees involved in exploring or refining efforts should be intellectually and emotionally committed to project success. Sometimes, however, the exuberance overwhelms rational inclinations. Unconsciously, their irrational exuberance persists because project champions often select team members who share their enthusiasm. The team's internal discussions tend to drive out dissenting opinion in a self-perpetuating and self-reinforcing brew of overly eager optimism.

   Project pruners or "exit champions" recognize the necessity of optimism but also value dispassionate analysis. A University of Paris professor put it this way:

> Exit champions: managers with the temperament and credibility to question the prevailing belief, demand hard data on the viability of the project, and if necessary, forcefully make the case that it should be killed.[37]

We chose the term *pruner* to emphasize the positive role played by those who make such hard decisions. All too often, the linguistic underground labels these people "hatchet men." That is unfair. Actually, these people can promote organizational progress by directing resources to the right projects. Any master gardener will tell you that pruning out the dying branches and overly exuberant growth actually promotes more robust and healthy growth. Progress makers set employee expectations about pruning by building those roles into their organizations.

CONCLUDING THOUGHTS

To some, the notion of focused flexibility implies seemingly contradictory counsel such as "listen to your customers, but not too much"; "be confident, but not overconfident"; and "watch for trends, but not too closely." Fair enough. Focused flexibility is about creating a mind-set about the dangers of the extremes and being able to lean in the right direction at the proper time. Recall our discussion in Chapter 8 about the tendency for *exploitation* to undermine *exploration* and vice versa. A focused and flexible mind-set addresses this problem even though it requires an intellectual and emotional agility that challenges even the greatest leaders.

Nevertheless, the quest is a worthy one. Why? Because creating a focused and flexible organization is one of the most powerful ways of creating sustainable growth. Consider, for example, the case of Google. The original business plan did not include advertising as a revenue source. Yet when the co-founders first coupled text ads with searches, they discovered something unexpected—a new unanticipated revenue stream. And they were flexible enough to seize on this unplanned, almost serendipitous discovery.[38]

They took the lesson to the next step and hardwired focused flexibility into the Google culture. When co-founder Sergey Brin was asked about the type of people who fail at Google, he said,

> I think you have to be flexible. For example, we don't usually tell people what they're working on until they show up, because our priorities might change. So somebody who's really obsessed and needs to know, "I'm going to be working on X" probably wouldn't enjoy it.[39]

Focused flexibility requires that organizations celebrate present success but not be overly influenced by it, remember the right things and forget others, and quickly stabilize even as they continue to innovate. In short, it requires a set of seemingly contradictory qualities that a super-organism, such as an ant hill, displays.[40] No wonder many scientists believe that the ants will survive on earth long after humans become extinct.

NOTES

1. Proverbs 6.6 (New Revised Standard Version).

2. E. Bonabeau and G. Théraulaz, "Swarm Smarts." *Scientific American,* March 2000, 73–79, p. 76.

3. K. M. Eisenhardt and D. N. Sull, "Strategy as Simple Rules." *Harvard Business Review* 79, no. 1 (2001): 106–19, p. 108.

4. S. Thomke and D. Reinertsen, "Agile Product Development: Managing Development Flexibility in Uncertain Environments." *California Management Review* 41, no. 1 (1998): 8–30, p. 17.

5. Ibid., 11.

6. W. Martinez-Conde and S. Marcknick, "Windows on the Mind." *Scientific American,* August 2007, 56–63.

7. M. Noble, "Cameron Suffers Fractures in Collision." August 12, 2005. http://outfield.mlb.com/news/article.jsp?ymd=20050811&content_id=1166603&vkey= news_nym&fext=.jsp&c_id=nym) (accessed January 5, 2009). Thanks to Rick Fantini for providing this example.

8. C. Hodlen, "Gamblers Bad at Cards." *Science,* April 4, 2008, 27.

9. B. Macintyre, *Agent Zigzag: A True Story of Nazi Espionage, Love, and Betrayal.* New York: Harmony Books, 2007, 298.

10. P. Ormerod, *Why Most Things Fail: Evolution, Extinction, and Economics.* New York: Pantheon, 2006, 18.

11. R. Abrams, "Focus on Success, Not Failure." *USA Today,* May 6, 2004. http://www.usatoday.com/money/smallbusiness/columnist/abrams/2004–05–06-success_x.htm (accessed January 4, 2009).

12. Meir Russ, Professor of Entrepreneurship at the University of Wisconsin–Green Bay, pointed out that much the same argument could be made about Wal-Mart. Sears was a weak competitor by the time Amazon.com came along. Wal-Mart, on the other hand, was thriving. Why didn't Wal-Mart innovate and become the first major e-retailer?

13. U. Kraft, "Burned Out." *Scientific American Mind,* June/July 2006, 29–33.

14. E. Viesturs, *No Shortcuts to the Top: Climbing the World's 14 Highest Peaks.* New York: Broadway Books, 2007, 66.

15. J. Krakauer, *Into Thin Air: A Personal Account of the Mount Everest Disaster.* Topeka, KS: Topeka Bindery, 2003.

16. See L. McDonald and P. Robinson, *A Colossal Failure of Common Sense: The Inside Story of the Collapse of Lehman Brothers.* New York: Crown Business, 2009.

17. R. Tedlow, "The Education of Andy Grove." *Fortune,* December 12, 2005, 117–38; R. Tedlow, *Andy Grove: The Life and Times.* New York: Portfolio, 2006.

18. A. De Meyer, C. Loch, and M. Pich, "Managing Project Uncertainty: From Variation to Chaos." *MIT Sloan Management Review* 43, no. 2 (2002): 60–67.

19. Ormerod, *Why Most Things Fail,* 161.

20. G. Day and P. Schoemaker, *Peripheral Vision: Detecting the Weak Signals That Will Make or Break Your Company.* Boston: Harvard Business School Press, 2006, 2.

21. O. Hargie and D. Tourish, *Auditing Organizational Communication.* London: Routledge, 2008.

22. K. Freiberg and J. Freiberg, *Nuts! Southwest Airline's Crazy Recipe for Business and Personal Success.* Austin, TX: Bard Press, 1996, 85–86.

23. Tedlow, *Andy Grove: The Life and Times.*

24. J. E. Russo and P. J. Schoemaker, "Managing Overconfidence." *Sloan Management Review* 33, no. 2 (1992): 7–17.

25. Ibid., 16.

26. M. Gladwell, "Cocksure." *New Yorker,* July 27, 2009, 24–28.

27. S. Finkelstein, *Why Smart Executives Fail and What You Can Learn From Their Mistakes.* New York: Portfolio, 2003, 226.

28. R. Feynman, *"Surely You're Joking, Mr. Feynman!"* New York: W. W. Norton, 1985, 343.

29. C. M. Christensen, *The Innovator's Dilemma.* Boston: Harvard Business School Press, 1997, xii.

30. Cite by J. O'Boyle, *The Unconscious Drivers of Choice,* presented at IDFA Smart Marketing Conference, March 17, 2005, Atlanta, GA. See http://www.idfa.org/meetings/presentations/sm2005_choice.pdf

31. Russo and Schoemaker, "Managing Overconfidence," 10.

32. J. Gropman, *How Doctors Think.* New York: Houghton Mifflin, 2007, 24.

33. N. Taleb, *The Black Swan: The Impact of the Highly Improbable.* New York: Random House, 2007, 55–56.

34. P. Senge, *The Fifth Discipline: The Art & Practice of the Learning Organization.* New York: Doubleday, 1990, 14.

35. D. Schacter, *The Seven Sins of Memory: How the Mind Forgets and Remembers.* New York: Houghton Mifflin Harcourt, 2002.

36. P. Martin de Holan, N. Phillips, and T. Lawrence, "Managing Organizational Forgetting." *MIT Sloan Management Review* 45, no. 2 (2004): 45–51, pp. 45–46.

37. I. Royer, "Why Bad Projects Are So Hard to Kill." *Harvard Business Review* 81, no. 2 (2003): 48–57, p. 50.

38. R. Stross, *Planet Google: One Company's Audacious Plan to Organize Everything We Know.* New York: Free Press, 2008.

39. A. Lashinsky, "Google Is No. 1: Search and Enjoy." *Fortune,* January 22, 2007, 70–82, p. 82.

40. B. Hölldobler and E. O. Wilson, *The Superorganism: The Beauty, Elegance, and Strangeness of Insect Societies.* New York: W.W. Norton, 2009.

⚛ 11 ⚛

ENLARGE THE CIRCLE OF
ENGAGEMENT

———•◦•———

There are many objects of great value to man, which cannot be
attained by unconnected individuals, but must be attained, if at all,
by association.

—Daniel Webster

A historian called it the "greatest act of statesmanship in the nation's history." A statesman said it was "one of the greatest and most honorable adventures in history." A scholar wrote that it "was conceived of in U.S. interests; but those interests were pursued with a policy that reflected the best in national ideals: freedom, generosity, humility, partnership and service. [It] offered those who worked on it, or those who supported it, the opportunity to be part of something transcendent."[1] And it is the quintessential example of enlarging the circle of engagement.

It started inauspiciously enough with a barely audible speech delivered in Harvard Yard by the then U.S. Secretary of State. By default, the plan—the Marshall Plan—would be named after him because as the "organizer of victory" during World War II, he had more credibility than President Truman. Indeed, Americans were not in the mood for helping Europe get back on its feet after a horrific war that claimed 300,000 American lives and over $300 billion of the U.S. government's budget. Dean Acheson, the Assistant

Secretary of State, succinctly summed up the American mood: "I can state in three sentences what the 'popular' attitude is toward foreign policy: 1) Bring the boys home; 2) Don't be Santa Claus; 3) Don't be pushed around."[2] That was the backdrop for this audacious plan to assist and rebuild Europe after the war. The American public was dubious, senators skeptical, and congressmen apprehensive.

There was one man, though, who pondered the long-term interests of the United States. It was George C. Marshall, who realized that without aid, Europe would fall under the spell of something almost as sinister as Nazism—namely, Communism. And he knew that would ultimately pose a grave threat to American security.[3] Yet, he was not a naturally blessed orator (he spoke in a monotone), nor was he much of a salesman. But he possessed another, even more important, skill: He knew how to engage others who would provide essential support and expertise.

His speech at Harvard received scant publicity but provided the moral, practical, and conceptual underpinning of the plan. And as all change agents must, he declared an enemy. But it was not the usual one; as he said, "Our policy is directed not against any country or doctrine but against hunger, poverty, and chaos."[4] From there he sought to enlist the aid, support, and ideas of significant persons all around the world. But he paid particular attention to congressmen and senators from both sides of the aisle. He engaged the doubters, skeptics, and naysayers. He listened to their concerns, sought their input, and allowed others to reshape the plan. He encouraged congressmen to travel to Europe to see the need for themselves. As one said afterwards, the question had turned from "What would it cost us?" to "What would it cost us *not* to aid Europe?"[5]

Others would follow, including the deeply skeptical Republican Senator Arthur Vandenberg, who was a committed isolationist. Marshall wooed him, and in the end, Senator Vandenberg would become a staunch ally. Vandenberg perhaps best summed the skeptic's embrace of the plan (or of any new platform):

> I understand and share the anxieties involved. The greatest nation on earth either justifies or surrenders its leadership. We must choose. There are no blueprints to guarantee results . . . I have no quarrel with those who disagree because we are dealing with imponderables. But I am bound to say to those who disagree that they have not escaped to safety by rejecting or subverting this plan. They have simply fled to other risks, and I fear greater ones.[6]

The senator, along with others who shared his sentiments, widened the circle of supporters by recruiting top businesspeople from around the country to administer the aid. The odd collection of supporters included a former Studebaker car salesman who turned into the Marshall Plan's chief administrator and public spokesperson. He smartly summed up the program: "The idea is to get Europe on its feet and off our back."[7] And that is almost exactly what happened. During the almost 4-year history, roughly $13 billion ($100 billion in today's dollars) were distributed to help rebuild Western Europe and get the economies up and growing. Europe became largely self-reliant, communism was held at bay, and World War III was averted.

Most observers who look back on the Marshall Plan see it as an almost unequivocal success story. But it was not always seen in this light. Progress makers such as General Marshall have the wisdom to recognize that viewpoints shift over time and the skill to bring about that change. General Marshall realized the importance of a compelling platform, but he also knew that was not enough. He had to bring together people of all political persuasions, biases, and skills. He had to build a critical mass of advocates that included the indifferent, skeptical, and fearful. In short, he had to enlarge the circle of engagement. That's the focal point of this chapter.

THE CONCEPT

This momentous achievement of the Marshall Plan underscores the possibilities of enlarging the circle. On the surface it might appear like a simple notion akin to "participative management." We have a more nuanced view than simply "getting people involved." We are not seeking mere acquiescence or a nod of approval but something more profound and engaging. This strategy hinges on three key words—*enlarge, circle,* and *engagement.*

First, note that the term *enlarge* suggests that progress makers formulate an artistic judgment about who to include in the circle and, by necessity, who to exclude

Artists use their imagination and talents to create works of aesthetic value. Progress makers use a similar talent to uniquely combine the talents and skills of those selected to include in the circle. They know those choices cannot be strictly driven by the numbers; "We need one marketing expert, another expert on finance, etc." Why? Because we are talking about something more than just adding up the skill set to produce a product. What artist would start with a quota of colors? Rather, she would focus on putting together the appropriate combination of colors to create a particular effect. Likewise, progress makers are intent on assembling the right combination of people in order to create synergies. They "think about their teams in their own highly personalized ways."[8]

Clearly, progress makers surround themselves with team members who possess the right values, aptitudes, skills, knowledge, and style.[9] Similar values are important. But similar aptitudes, skills, and style? Maybe not. In particular, progress makers realize that a team composed of all first-class refiners would be as dysfunctional as one dominated by first-class explorers. Avoiding this dynamic requires some deep insight into each potential team member's fundamental orientation. As we have previously suggested, every person tends to lean more toward the explorer or refiner orientation (see Figure 11.1). Discerning leaders look for a variety of clues and behaviors to make a judgment about each person's predisposition. Then, of course, the really tough question emerges: What is the right mix? 80% refiners, 20% explorers? Or, vice versa? That's the key judgment call that progress makers make as they enlarge the circle.

Figure 11.1	Explorer and Refiner Tendencies

Explorers *Gravitate Toward the:*	**Refiners** *Gravitate Toward the:*
• Latest development • General • Basic approach • Unknown • Unproven	• Best possible • Specific • Detailed plans • Known • Proven

**Second, notice the word *circle* denotes
a self-contained completeness or wholeness**

While a circle includes, it also excludes. Biologist Tyler Volk notes that "borders function as bulwarks against forces of disruption. They cloak creatures and their internal parts against the ravages of the exterior world—the ionizing, rotting, eating, and crushing world. Borders hold at bay all that would destroy the difference between being and environment; they prevent universal homogenization."[10] Progress makers heed the biologist's insight. They are not trying to include everyone, at least in the early phases. Instead, they bring together the *right* people in the *right* order to fully realize the potential of an existing platform or create a new one.

Finally, note the presence of the noun *engagement* suggests the importance of cultivating commitment

How many major organizational initiatives can be sustained by a small group of people? To be sure, major initiatives may be conceived of by one employee or a small group, but this is not enough to nourish and grow the idea. The father and mother create an infant, but the parents need caring relatives, wise teachers, and skilled coaches for the child to thrive. Progress makers recognize this and are constantly looking to expand the circle to nurture further growth. Yet, they are cautious about how they do it.

That's exactly the lesson Jonathan Abrams learned. Who is he? He's the founder of the first online social network, Friendster. At one time, his company was considered one of the hottest entrepreneurial ventures in the world and received glowing profiles in *Time* and *Entertainment Weekly*. Predictably, venture capitalist jumped on the opportunity by investing large sums of money and installing a blue-chip board of directors. But along the way, something unfortunate happened. Friendster never became the premier social networking site that Facebook and MySpace became, which were based on similar notions. Abrams's explanation: He was "naive" and believes he brought in the "big guns" too early in the process. It put the wrong kind of pressures on the developers, and the site's problems went largely unaddressed. The competition seized on some of those underlying management and software problems.[11] The broader lesson: The circle needs to maintain its completeness even as it expands. And that's where the artistry comes into play.

WHY DON'T WE ENLARGE THE CIRCLE?

Most leaders intuitively recognize the need to enlarge the circle of engagement. Often they create the illusion of broadening the circle in the hopes of creating that elusive element they call "buy-in." Why do so many leaders settle for a mere fantasy? There are, no doubt, many explanations, but three issues in particular pop up again and again in our research.

Expediency

Let's face it, getting people to truly "buy in" and become agents for progress requires a lot of energy, effort, and time. Many organizational leaders feel that events in their industry move much too fast to truly build employee commitment. On one level, this appears to be a perfectly reasonable point of view. On another level, the logic falls apart. As one executive explained to us, "You either pay me now or you pay me later, but you are going to pay me." Translation: Either leaders invest the time in the early stages of an initiative or they will spend a lot more time cleaning up the messes from sloppy implementation. Establishing a new platform or improving an existing one exacts a cost. The only question is *when* those costs show up on the organization's psyche balance sheet. In this seasoned executive's view, the costs are far less if you invest time in proper "circle enlargement" up front. In particular, a proper up-front investment smoothes the transition by improving understanding and execution of critical tasks. And in some cases, it provides an early warning about pursuing a potentially dangerous project or initiative.

Ego

Sometimes leaders fail to widen the circle of engagement because they are too heavily and personally invested in their own ideas.[12] Broadening the circle means reducing their personal ownership of ideas even as the notions are shaped and interpreted by others. Let's first provide some perspective: In one sense, hearty egos can be healthy, particularly for those who establish new platforms. Why? Leaders are rightly proud of their ideas, which motivate them to overcome the inevitable objections, obstacles, and the obstinacy of others. Just as homeowners will fight to preserve their neighborhoods, idea owners will fight for their ideas. But at a certain point, ownership can slip into arrogance, inhibiting progress.

On the flipside, a leader's overly inflated ego can strike at the central nervous system of an organization. Why? Because employees begin to sense that only those in leadership positions have the progressive ideas. Consequently, employees retreat to their day-to-day responsibilities and focus on daily survival. They rarely propose new ideas and fail to send signals to the leadership about emerging shifts in the workplace or market. It's as if the organizational sensing mechanisms simply shut down.

Consider, for example, the case of a chancellor at a Midwestern university. When faculty or other administrators offered opinions or ideas that differed from his, he often trotted out his favorite phrase, "That dog don't hunt." Translation: Your idea won't work. It didn't take long for most people to recognize that they should put a strong leash on all their "dogs." This, of course, delighted the chancellor because he could claim that he had "full endorsement" of his initiatives. After all, no one objected. That provided sufficient evidence of "buy-in." In his rare moments of candid reflection, he would complain, "Why do I have to do all the thinking around here?" A wiser leader would have viewed that sentiment as a bright red warning flag. He did not. That's the way overconfidence ruins careers. It moves from self-absorption to self-deception and ultimately to self-destruction.

Along the way, many good employees move on, some initiatives stall, and the organization stagnates. All this happened under this chancellor's tenure. When he moved on to another job, most employees silently cheered. The story does not end there; excessive pride reached its sad, if inevitable, conclusion. He had moved on as chancellor at a larger university, but within 6 months the board had fired him for misleading them about how funds were appropriated. Most people at his former institution were not surprised by this almost unprecedented action by the board. Why? They knew about how he silenced critics, and they were heartened to know that his dog would not be hunting again. To this day, the ex-chancellor feels he did nothing wrong.

This tale may seem extreme, but it is not uncommon. The situation resembles the arc of Enron scandals along with others. In all these cases, the overconfidence of the appointed leader inhibits enlarging the circle. Clearly, most leaders do not exhibit this level of arrogance, but even a moderate level may slow organizational progress.

Anxiety

Enlarging the circle requires embracing diverse people, ideas, and perspectives. Few leaders would openly admit they fear entertaining new ideas or bringing others on board. Yet often lurking behind the veneer of civil discourse with colleagues lurks anxiety, uneasiness, and apprehension. Why? Truly exposing our ideas to others invites the possibility of conflict, disagreement, and, potentially, rejection. Suppressing emotions raised by these very real possibilities can prove particularly challenging. Think, for example, about the reluctance of many managers to have candid discussions with average performers. They often smooth over differences and sidestep tough questioning in order to quell their own fears of conflict. A similar reluctance can sully a leader's desire to enlarge the circle.

As one commentator notes, "fear is the most electric of emotions" and "almost always plays upon some real threat—it seldom, if ever is created out of nothing."[13] The threat a leader may fixate on—often subliminally—is loss of face. This manifests itself in an "us vs. them" mentality. To be sure, leaders may temporarily appear to lose face when confronted with objections to their ideas. That's a realistic but temporary concern. The long-term threat lies in not building enough support to sustain initiatives. Anyone who has seen an old Western movie has watched the settlers "circle the wagons" when they feared attack. The small and tight circle is designed to protect and defend. Necessary? At times. Progress making? Never. Circled wagons can never make progress. They stall progress. And that's why great leaders *expand,* not constrict, the circle.

HOW DO YOU ENLARGE THE CIRCLE OF ENGAGEMENT?

Our history books focus a great deal of attention on individual progress makers praising the exploits of Ferdinand Magellan, Daniel Boone, and Madame Curie. Yet a more mature analysis would highlight the fact that most progress-making events were a collective, rather than an individual, experience. Think, for example, of the thousands of engineers, specialists, and technicians it took to put Neil Armstrong on the moon. He might well have amended his famous utterance to "One small step for a man, one giant leap for *our technical team.*"

So how do effective organizations go about thoughtfully enlarging the circle? During our interviews with progress makers, we discovered seven notions that undergirded their approach:

Assemble a Diverse but Collaborative Team

Research in the physical as well as the behavioral sciences indicates that the emergent properties of "the collective" or "the system" are often quite different from the characteristics of the individual components.[14] An atom of hydrogen, for example, behaves quite differently in the presence of chlorine than it does in the presence of two parts of oxygen. One yields the toxic substance hydrochloric acid; the other, water. Likewise, the composition of the team can yield either toxic results or a free-flowing, innovative endeavor. Putting together the right team for progress is far more difficult than selecting the right combinations of elements from the periodic table. Why? Frankly, we simply do not know enough about classifying the elements of human personality, and we know even less about the behavior of different combinations.

Nevertheless, progress makers recognize that they cannot make progress without bringing on board others with diverse viewpoints. Authors, for example, are often stereotyped as lonely recluses writing in some isolated cabin deep in the woods. The image overly romanticizes the reality. The author of *The Chronicles of Narnia,* C. S. Lewis, perceptively noted that "two heads are better than one, not because either is infallible, but because they are unlikely to go wrong in the same direction."[15] He heeded his own advice. He was part of a group known as the Inklings, who regularly gathered in Oxford to read the first drafts of each other's works.[16] It was in this gathering of authors and other Oxford dons that Lewis first read aloud many of his works and that J. R. R. Tolkien previewed the *Lord of the Rings.* It was in this setting that these gifted authors honed their great works, which eventually became blockbuster movies over 40 years later. Even though they were exploring imaginary worlds, they wanted to be on solid intellectual footing.

In a similar way, progress making requires this kind of invigorating, affirming, and stimulating give-and-take that occurred in those wonderful meetings of the Inklings. The group needs a diversity of talents, skills, and viewpoints. But that is not enough. In fact, researchers have determined that "left unmanaged, employee diversity is more likely to damage morale, increase turnover, and cause significant communication problems and conflict in the organization."[17] Successful circle enlargers know this. Consequently, they seek to integrate the individuals into a working team that uses the differences in a meaningful way. It requires special team members who are skilled communicators, great listeners comfortable with debate, and proficient conflict resolvers. Every specialist may not be properly equipped to work in such an environment. Indeed, researchers have determined that human beings viscerally respond to people of another race as they do to a snake or spider.[18]

Fortunately, we don't need to become a snake charmer or entomologist to overcome our qualms, but it does require some training and experience. Deft leaders and skilled team members overcome their natural misgivings and use their collective inklings to make progress.

Communicate in a Collaborative Manner

Translating collaborative potential into actual collaboration requires proper communication and transparency. Progress makers communicate to build critical relationships and enrich ideas. Both skills are essential to progress. Yet, all too often, groups unconsciously choose one at the expense of the other. For instance, some people build relationships by essentially turning off their critical thinking skills. They gloss over important differences with soothing words and equivocal agreements. In essence, they value relational harmony over all else. Chris Argyris of Harvard University explained the problem:

> The ability to get along with others is always an asset, right? Wrong. By adeptly avoiding conflict with co-workers, some executives eventually wreak havoc. And it's their very adeptness that's the problem. The explanation for this lies in what I call skilled incompetence, whereby managers use practiced routine behavior (skill) to produce what they do not intend (incompetence).[19]

At the other extreme are the very bright and perceptive individuals who lack the requisite interpersonal and relationship-building skills. In essence, they value the mission over all else. They drive toward the best, most efficient solutions. And they often believe that they alone know the optimum solution. When working on teams, their overbearing style may cause others to dismiss, marginalize, or ignore their opinions and insights. When in leadership positions, they can enforce a degree of compliance but fail to engender commitment from others. In either situation, these intellectually gifted but relationally challenged people fail to realize that even the most brilliant insights cannot prevail without support from others.

Fortunately, those with natural proclivities toward one extreme or the other can learn how to collaborate. It starts with a desire to seek both harmony and efficiency in their discussions. Progress makers recognize the danger signs of either extreme (see Figure 11.2). The absence of disagreement or serious debate, for example, often signals an overemphasis on relational harmony. Yet groups that

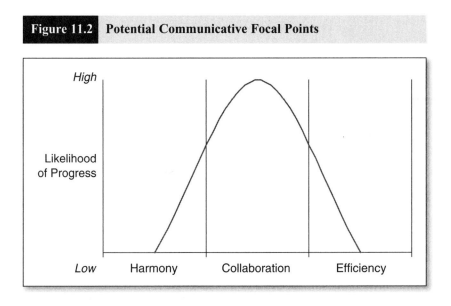

Figure 11.2 **Potential Communicative Focal Points**

constantly bicker and argue may have descended into a struggle for intellectual dominance. Neither extreme engenders lasting progress.

Effective collaboration centers on three interrelated skills:

• *Exploring and respecting differences.* When Hewlett-Packard and Microsoft collaborated on a software project, tensions arose because of "differences in the two companies' business models, cultures and expertise."[20] The impasse was eventually breached by documenting and discussing perceived differences between the cultures. One result was a statement about the respective strengths of both companies.

Another technique we've used is to ask team members to prepare personal "Instruction Manuals."[21] When you buy a new product, you get an instruction manual detailing how to work the product and alerting you to a list of warnings. Why not do the same thing when working with a new person? The "manual" can take almost any form, but typically it consists of listing key personal characteristics, underlying motivations, and pet peeves (e.g., starting meetings late). It takes an employee's resume to the next level by encouraging team members to make candid self-assessments and then share those with others. It is a way to help a group navigate around potential roadblocks and avoid misunderstanding (see Figure 11.3).

Figure 11.3   **Example of Professor's Instruction Manual**

Almost every new product you buy has an instruction manual. Why doesn't someone issue a similar manual for the people we work with most frequently? In an attempt to bridge the gap, I've constructed a manual of tips for working with me.

Characteristics	So What?
I'm a thinker. ("T" on the Myers-Briggs scale)	• I like to hear both sides of an issue before making a decision. • Link your rationale to enduring principles.
I'm an innovator. ("P" on the Myers-Briggs scale)	• Show me new ideas based on sound principles. • Expand on preexisting ideas and avoid repeating exactly what I say in a lecture or article.
I focus on the big picture. ("N" on the Myers-Briggs scale)	• Talk to me about strategy and then discuss your tactics. • Show me the links between your main points (e.g., illustrations, diagrams). • Occasionally I get impatient with too many details.
I'm a former debater.	• Show me a clear organizational structure. • Give me evidence to back up your claims. • Don't assume that because I make a counterargument that I disagree with you. • Don't assume that if I push you to defend your ideas, I disagree with them.
I read a lot.	• Be ready to answer questions about links to current events and ideas (e.g., *BusinessWeek*, *Wall Street Journal*, *Fortune*, *Forbes*, *Harvard Business Review*). • I appreciate well-written papers and clever phrases.
I have some introvert characteristics.	• Give me some time to get to know you. • Sometimes I may seem standoffish but that will disappear in time.
I'm busy.	• Come prepared to meetings. • Focus your communication on high-value items. • If the matter can be handled through lean channels, then use them. • E-mail is often the best way to make initial contact with me. • Don't assume that time constraints mean I'm uninterested.
I like to have fun and be challenged.	• Sometimes I'll spontaneously veer off-track, for a moment, in a lecture. • I get bored quickly. • I'll often "joke around" with people.

• *Promoting a spirit of inquiry.* Successful platform refiners and creators encourage people to ask penetrating questions.[22] Like all other forms of discourse, questions can be used for good or ill. As philosopher Kenneth Burke once wrote, "All questions are leading. . . . Every question selects a field of battle, and in this selection it forms the nature of the answers."[23] Progress makers select "battlefields" arrayed for constructive conflict. For instance, when a problem occurs, leaders can ask, "Who was at fault?" Or they can inquire about "What went wrong?" The first question promotes blaming and "cover-your-butt" type of culture. The second one can engender inquiry, learning, and prevention. In short, progress makers are as thoughtful about the questions they ask as they are about the answers they evaluate.

Questions promoting inquiry are carefully crafted to release the collective critical thinking of a team. For example, asking, "What assumptions are we making?" often provokes a more thoughtful discussion about key decisions. Likewise, inquiring about underlying patterns can often help ferret out an important trend. The other questions in Figure 11.4 also spur on a critical thinking perspective.[24] In short, progress makers know the often subtle difference between asking questions that prompt posturing and those that promote inquiry.

Figure 11.4   Critical Thinking Checklist

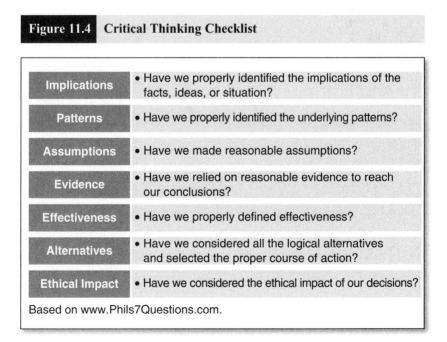

Implications	• Have we properly identified the implications of the facts, ideas, or situation?
Patterns	• Have we properly identified the underlying patterns?
Assumptions	• Have we made reasonable assumptions?
Evidence	• Have we relied on reasonable evidence to reach our conclusions?
Effectiveness	• Have we properly defined effectiveness?
Alternatives	• Have we considered all the logical alternatives and selected the proper course of action?
Ethical Impact	• Have we considered the ethical impact of our decisions?

Based on www.Phils7Questions.com.

- *Encouraging people to express doubt.* Research involving over 1,000 employees has determined that organizations that embrace doubt and uncertainty engender more employee satisfaction, commitment, and buy-in to organizational decisions. Employees in uncertainty-embracing organizations are better able to cope with change than their counterparts in uncertainty-suppressing organizations. This pattern emerged regardless of how employees rated their personal abilities to manage doubt and uncertainty.[25] A collaborative team creates an uncertainty-embracing climate by allowing employees to freely express concerns and challenge decisions.

Let's be more specific. Would it be safe for a team member to say, "I don't know"? Would he be marginalized or even ridiculed? How would the team react to someone who said, "I know everyone thinks we are on the right track but I don't"? Would others seek to dissuade him or even bully him into agreement? The answers to these questions can serve as a collaborative barometer. In a collaborative climate, everyone can say, "We don't know but that's okay" or "We don't agree but that could set us free to seek a better solution." These sentiments become the springboard for further exploration and consensus seeking.

In essence, a collaborative communication style means that leaders have the ability to look at issues from different perspectives. They seek consensus before deciding what to do and make sure most people are comfortable with the solution. Even when some irresolvable conflict emerges, they might say something like, "Most of us agree. Can the rest of you live with this decision?"[26] Queries like this demonstrate the desire for collaboration and respect for others while signaling a need to move forward. In essence, it reconciles the healthy tension between a quest for harmony and efficiency.

Seek and Discover the Unifying Point of Commitment

Noble missions cultivate the resiliency, determination, flexibility, and creative "oomph" to make progress. The quest to put a man on the moon motivated the engineers and technicians for decades. The dread of a Nazi military victory spurred on scientists of all political persuasions, national origins, and specialties to be the first to produce an atomic bomb. Even the pacifist Einstein spurred on the quest.[27]

This is where leaders provide the most value. They are the ones who engender the quest with nobility and purpose. They frame it, promote it, and personalize its relevance. It doesn't have to be something as earth shattering as a moon walk or a kiloton bomb. It can be something as "mundane" as Jeff Bezo's quest to build the "earth's most customer centric company; a place where people can come to find and discover anything they might want to buy online." The quest draws on the imagery of the world's largest river and hence the name Amazon.com. The noble mission helps people move beyond their egos and ambitions and believe in something bigger than themselves.

Think, for instance, about the challenges of executing a merger of four large hospitals and seven other facilities, each with a unique organizational culture. One scholar studied such a scenario. She concluded that effective leaders "recognize how existing cultural differences can be reconciled under a broader umbrella of cultural unity."[28] What was the storm-resistant umbrella? Better patient care. That was a point of commitment that all parties agreed on. Successful leaders would seize on that point to shape expectations and set in motion needed changes. Every goal, initiative, and even disappointment would be linked to that core point of commitment.

Moderate the Influence of Status and Roles

Let's assume that you knew of a simple method—one that involves nothing more than some clipboards, paper, and pencils—to save hospitals millions of dollars and prevent the deaths of many patients. Let's take the thought experiment one step further and assume that you have empirical evidence (e.g., case studies, statistics) to back up your claims. You might expect that hospital administrators from New York City to New Delhi would beat a path your door. Unfortunately, you would be mistaken.

This is not a mere academic thought experiment. It is, in fact, a real and seemingly inexplicable dilemma. Here's the background: In 2001, a critical care specialist, Peter Pronovost, wrote down a simple five-step checklist to use in the intensive care unit (ICU) when placing the lines or catheters into patients to deliver medicines or other fluids. He suspected and later confirmed that the simple instructions known to most doctors and nurses were not routinely followed. In fact, he determined that one or more of these steps were not followed for over 30% of patients. That's frightening enough. What really sent tremors through the hospital, though, was the discovery that bacteria spread through line infections resulted in extended ICU patient stays (the most expensive type of care) and, in some cases, patient deaths.

This problem appears important and simple to resolve. Important, yes. Simple, not exactly. Developing, printing, and distributing the checklist *is* simple. But getting the right people to use it proved more challenging. Why? Two issues surfaced: First, how do you convince the medical staff that this is not just another piece of mindless administrative paperwork? Second, how do you empower nurses to correct a physician who inadvertently misses an item on the checklist?

The first issue was addressed in refresher training. The second proved more vexing because status discrepancies are deeply ingrained in medical culture; nurses rarely correct or question physicians. Fortunately, Dr. Pronovost and his staff were able to persuade administrators to empower their nurses to stop a physician who skipped a step on the checklist. Indeed, the administration vowed to back up any nurse who confronted a physician about an item on the checklist. The result: This hospital saved $2 million and prevented at least eight deaths.[29] A similar project, launched in Michigan hospitals under the name of the Keystone Initiative, achieved similar spectacular results: An estimated cost savings of $75 million and prevention of over 1,500 patient deaths during an 18-month period.[30]

Some commentators point to the checklist as the magic potion. We beg to differ; the checklist was critical but not the difference maker. After all, almost everyone already knew the proper procedure. The real magic elixir was that Dr. Pronovost enlarged the circle by shifting the culture enough to let the nurses challenge physicians. The checklist provided an agreed-upon standard around which conflict could be managed while not significantly challenging the traditional authority and judgment of hospital physicians. In this case, shifting the roles meant expanding the authority of the nurses. In short, these case studies suggest that anyone who is serious about gaining acceptance of a new platform or moderating an existing one often needs to address the issue of organizational roles and status. Initiatives such as Keystone work because status differences were acknowledged and skillfully managed in a nonthreatening way.

Sense and Seize Moments of Acceleration

Progress makers have an intuitive sense about when a team is ready to move beyond the status quo. Sometimes the team is stuck in a rut and needs new blood to move on. At other times, the team has an uptick in energy as members sense some vague but significant turning point. Progress makers seize these moments by asking probing questions, providing thoughtful advice, allocating new resources, shifting personnel, or adding new team members. It is a quest to prod the group beyond the tipping point into genuine value-adding endeavors.

Likewise, progress makers discern when their organizations are ready to take the next step. This may be the point when they shift the organizational structure, develop a new business alliance, or reallocate resources, to name a few. Building employee understanding of the rationale for these changes often proves crucial to the acceleration. That's the point at which progress makers make skillful use of networks to inform, influence, and educate others in the organization.

To fully understand the import of the relationship between networks and acceleration, let's examine one of the most practical and influential theoretical models ever developed by social scientists. The name of the model, diffusion of innovation, may sound imposing to some people, but the key concepts are quite easy to understand. As one of the pivotal scholars explains,

> *Diffusion* is the process by which an innovation is communicated through certain channels over time among the members of a social system. It is a special type of communication, in that the messages are concerned with new ideas. *Communication* is the process in which participants create and share information with one another in order to reach a mutual understanding.[31]

Substitute the word *platform* for *innovation* and useful parallels emerge.

One seminal point of the research concerns how people adopt innovations or new platforms. Scholars divide those who adopt new innovations into five groups: innovators, early adopters, early majority, late majority, and laggards. Let's use the mobile phone as an example. The innovators (approximately 3% of those in the social system) are the adventurous ones who quickly adopt new ideas. They like to live on the cutting edge. They were the first ones to adopt the cell or mobile phone. The second group, the early adopters (13% of the social system), listen to reviews of the early adopters. If they like the innovation or platform, then they will, in turn, adopt it. Next comes the early majority (34%), followed by the late majority (34%). The laggards (16%) tend to be oriented around the historical, stable, and proven. They are the people still clinging to their landline phone service. They are deeply suspicious of new platforms and only adopt the innovation if they can see tangible personal benefits. This almost perfect bell-shaped curve helps explain how networks embrace or resist platform improvements or replacements.

So what? Seizing moments of acceleration requires quickly identifying the innovators, early adopters, early majority, late majority, and laggards. Wise leaders should not expect a laggard, regardless of title, to get on board until the very end. Conversely, it is not enough to have a few committed zealots or innovators. Progress makers position the innovators to educate and influence the early adopters, who then, in turn, influence their more skeptical colleagues in the early and late majorities. Progress makers sense these often silent ripples as they swell across their organizational waters. And they take active steps to amplify the natural currents as they encourage the circle to naturally swell.

Add Talent to the Team in a Thoughtful Sequence

Enlarging the circle is NOT merely about securing people's nod of acceptance. Rather, it means building support by allowing people to make a difference. As others are added to the platform team, they shape, mold, and add to the ideas. Progress makers do not cobble together a group of supporters; they build a group of owners.

Consider, for example, the iPod platform developed by Apple. When critics seek to explain these enormously successful "hand-held entertainment-playing devices," they often point to the wonderfully intuitive user interface. Rightly so. But what often goes unnoticed were the agreements reached with music producers, artists, and their companies to legally sell songs over the Internet through the iTunes store established in 2003. Indeed, in the long run, the legal unbundling of the traditional CD may prove to be one Apple's most important innovations. While the technology dazzles users, it's the legal, intuitive, and simple access to music hits that propelled Apple to be the number one provider of digital music in the world. The genius of CEO Steve Jobs was to recognize that the technical characteristics of the devices were only half of the problem.[32] He needed to create partnerships in the music industry.

In essence, he recognized that the team that can win the Super Bowl is not the same team that can win the World Series. His solution: add "A-players not Bozos" to his personally screened team by forging partnerships with others that possessed a different and valued skill set.[33]

Apple demonstrated the principle in another way through the company's enormously successful Applications (Apps, for short) program for the iTouch, iPhone, and iPad devices. There are thousands of free and low-priced tools that allow users to play their favorite games, access weather conditions, and find their current location, to name a few. The real genius, though, resides in how the Apps are developed. The basic architecture and core Apps were developed by Apple. Yet, third-party developers can submit their novel Apps to Apple for consideration. If the App meets the necessary benchmarks, then it will be offered to the public through the iTunes store. This unleashes a tidal wave of innovations that benefit users as well as Apple.

The Apple Apps case demonstrates one seemingly simple way to add talent to the core team. But we want to emphasize the word *thoughtful* in this tactic. Apple executives carefully considered this atypical move.[34] Adding talent through an "innovation community" works in certain circumstances. In other situations, perhaps a consortium or business alliance makes sense. The choice really comes down to the leadership group's assumptions about the industry and their business model. Once these issues are thoroughly understood, leaders can make wise choices about how they wish to govern an expanding circle of collaborators.[35]

Routinely Take Stock and Evaluate Progress

No matter how noble the mission, a team needs to routinely stand back and assess progress. Rocketing humans into space clearly is a wondrously noble task. Yet, the *Challenger* and *Columbia* Space Shuttle disasters provide stark evidence that heroic missions alone cannot guarantee success. Indeed, two scholars noted,

> Organizational barriers prevented effective communication of critical safety information and stifled professional differences of opinion. Management was insufficiently integrated across program elements. An informal chain of command evolved, together with decision-making processes that operated outside the organization's rules.[36]

Clearly something was missing in the collaborative environment. Without routine evaluation, no one can say for sure that progress is being made. In fact, that is why we've highlighted the relationship between collaboration and progress. Too often, people see collaboration as an end in itself. Consequently, they focus their energy on maintaining relationships rather than achieving important goals. In this environment, the group inevitably suppresses dissent, discourages candor, and settles for hollow displays of agreement. This apparently happened at NASA.

In contrast, teams of progress-driven collaborators engage in at least three levels of evaluation:

- *They assess the role structure: Do they have the right people in the right roles?* For example, the executive team at a *Fortune* 100 company recognized that their union negotiating team lacked specific expertise in communicating contract provisions to their members. Consequently, they hired some outside communication specialists who became part of their team.

- *They assess the performance of employees in their roles.* This can be as simple as informally letting team members know when they provide useful suggestions or fail to live up to standards. It may also involve a more extensive and routine discussion about every team member's level of contribution.

- *They regularly assess their progress: Are we really making progress on our key success factors?* Investigators into the *Columbia* disaster found that quite a number of employees felt that NASA was not making progress on safety issues. In essence, many of the lessons from the first shuttle tragedy, *Challenger,* were ignored in subsequent years.

This brings us full circle back to the progress model. A progress-driven collaboration always focuses on the tough questions: Have we further developed the platform? Are we moving to a progress-enhancing platform? Are we doing the right amount of exploring? Refining? Asking the questions is far easier than answering them. Yet, leaders who grapple with these issues have the greatest probability of making sustainable progress. And by doing so, progress makers ensure that the circle has been genuinely enlarged with owners vested in the outcome.

CONCLUDING THOUGHTS

Progress makers enlarge the circle by resisting initial judgment and integrating diverse ideas. That commitment leads them to embrace uncertainty rather than seek to eliminate it. When faced with something new, a person's first words often prove revealing. Progress makers do not immediately dismiss a new concept with a tart, "what a ridiculous idea." Instead, they are intrigued and say, "How fascinating" (see Figure 11.5).

In short, progress makers have thick skin and sensitive ears: Thick skin because as they enlarge the circle, they will encounter criticism, often directed at their most cherished ideas. Sensitive ears because as they enlarge the circle, they need to be attentive to underlying issues that can impede progress while being able to seize on notions that can propel their organizations forward. Such was the character of one remarkable man who served as Secretary of State after the carnage of World War II. He was the first professional soldier to ever be awarded the Nobel Peace Prize.[37] Because he extended the circle of engagement, the entire Western world owes a debt of gratitude to George Marshall.

Figure 11.5   **Potential Responses to Uncertainty**

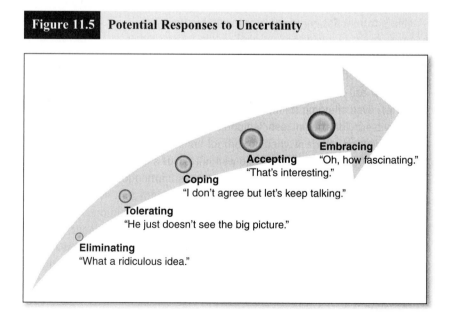

PROGRESS MAKER PROFILE

VICKI WILSON AND DOOR COUNTY COFFEE & TEA

The aroma envelops you before you jump out of your car, hop off your bicycle, or dismount your snowmobile. You don't need to look at the sign; your senses announce that you've arrived at Door County Coffee & Tea. But don't let the charming café and shop fool you. This is more than a quaint little coffee shop tucked away in a Midwestern resort village. It is, in fact, a thriving small business that creates, produces, and sells its own blends of coffees to thousands of clients, including major grocery store chains and coffee houses.

How did this all happen? It all started when Vicki Wilson and her husband Doug decided that something was missing in one of their favorite vacation spots: Where could they satisfy their coffee fix? They realized that Door County was a premiere vacation spot, and a specialty coffee producer would nicely complement the ambience of the county's natural beauty. They did their homework about locating the specialized equipment, finding the premiere suppliers, engineering an efficient process, and lining up financing. Then they faced the big decision: Should Vicki abandon her 23-year career in retail to devote herself full-time to her dream? The dream won. And Doug kept his day job as a process engineer, as a backup.

Vicki and Doug realized that all would not go smoothly. We discussed this issue with her as she savored the warmth of her favorite cinnamon hazelnut–flavored coffee. She reflected on her experiences starting up a business: "Failure was not an option. We had everything riding on this business and no matter what obstacle presented itself, we were confident that we could get through it. Was it blind faith? Stupidity? Stubborn determination? A 'never say die attitude'? Perhaps it was all of the above." Did Vicki and Doug make mistakes? Her response: "You bet, and a lot of them! As a business partner, Doug was always supportive. We had an understanding that we'd have to stub our toes, even fall down at times, but we'd learn from those mistakes. You really never learn when times are good."

As the dream became a reality, Vicki instilled in her staff the value of refining practices and processes. She believes "organizations are dynamic, not static, and if you're not changing (hopefully improving), you're left in the dust. Progress is what we strive to do each day, with each and every initiative or task. Each process is examined and refined . . . all of which propel us forward.

When everyone knows they can make a positive difference by doing something better than was done yesterday, it is progress and it's to be celebrated! In fact, we celebrate each and every upgrade—no matter the impact. The best organizations create a culture where everyone wants to improve for the sake of improvement!" Vicki not only empowers her employees to make these upgrades, but she also expects them to make these contributions.

She also pushes to strategically explore new platforms. The company has a long history of launching new initiatives, new products, and new programs. Their customers are always looking for new items. Over the years, the Door County Coffee & Tea team has served up new flavors, seasonal packaging, free freight programs, and a host of other significant innovations. Vicki's approach to innovation differs from conventional wisdom. She explained, "I'd like to tell you that there was a collection of market data, focus groups and the like prior to launching new initiatives. But the truth is 'speed to market' is far more important to us than getting it perfectly right. The pursuit of perfection can cause paralysis." Study it, launch it, and see what happens. Have all the initiatives been successful? With a twinkle in her eyes, she responded, "Are you kidding? And when they are not, we are quick to recognize it, make changes or abandon. No egos get in the way when something isn't profitable." That's exactly what the "prophet of innovation," Joseph Schumpeter, envisioned when he coined the concept "creative destruction."[38]

Often, though, her intuition guides her in the right direction. For example, she realized how much her district sales managers (DMs) valued the time they spent meeting and greeting clients face-to-face. In the early years, the DMs made cold calls and physically visited existing clients to generate more business in their territories. Nothing wrong with that. Except as gas prices soared, economic conditions toughened, and the company's geographic reach expanded, relying primarily on the face-to-face model became increasingly difficult to justify from a business perspective.

What to do? She explained, "We strategized as the sales team and asked the district sales managers to shift the balance away from face-to-face visits to more phone and e-mail contacts. After many discussions and meetings, we'd get heads that were shaking 'yes, we'll try it.' They, however, will be the first to tell you that the minute they left the conference room, the 'no, it will never work mentality took over.'" But it did. Within 12 to 18 months, they started seeing results of the new strategy. Then the emotional "buy-in" was complete.

(Continued)

(Continued)

She cited another example of platform jumping that paid off. She knew that coffee sales dipped during the spring and early summer months. For 3 years, her team worked on coffee blends and packaging designed for those months. She explained what happened next: "We had made a major investment in design, plates and materials for the new packaging. We were as ready as we could be to build a new platform. Then during the last quarters of 2008, the economic meltdown hit." Doubts surfaced in the team. They wondered if this was the right time to launch the new coffees and "Daisy" packaging. They knew their coffees were popularly priced, and after a thorough discussion, the team concluded that coffee sales would remain stable during the recession. They decided to take the risk and roll out the new brew with innovative packaging. And they felt customers deserved something new—particularly during a recession. They were right. The new coffees and Daisy packaging accounted for about 25% of their coffee revenues in early 2009.

Vicki pauses and smiles when recalling such decisions. You don't see Vicki pause very often. She has that "full-speed ahead" zest for life that bubbles over to everybody and everything. She loves people. She adores coffee. Yet she practices "enlarging the circle of engagement" and embodies the "focused flexibility" mind-set. Full-speed ahead, yes. That's the focus part. But she readily steers in a new direction if necessary. That's the flexibility part. And then she zooms off at full speed. If she spills a little coffee during the shift in direction, she mops it up and keeps on going. That's a progress maker working at full tilt.

LESSONS LEARNED

- **"Check egos at the door" when evaluating results.** That provides flexibility to optimize results.

- **Adjust, experiment, and be willing to try different approaches to reach more important aims.** If one approach doesn't work, then simply try another.

- **Expect bumps in the road but have faith in your own abilities to flexibly respond while focusing on the task at hand.** Be confident even as you as you embrace a provisional mind-set about specific initiatives.

NOTES

1. G. Behrman, *The Most Noble Adventure: The Marshall Plan and How America Helped Rebuild Europe.* New York: Free Press, 2007, 329.

2. As quoted in Behrman, *The Most Noble Adventure*, 15.

3. M. Stoler, *George C. Marshall: Soldier-Statesman of the American Century.* New York: Twayne Publishers, 1989.

4. As quoted in Behrman, *The Most Noble Adventure*, 69.

5. Ibid., 117.

6. Ibid., 158–59.

7. Ibid., 181.

8. D. C. Hambrick, "The Top Management Team: Key to Strategic Success." *California Management Review* 30, no. 1 (1987): 88–108, p. 102.

9. Ibid.

10. T. Volk, *Metapatterns: Across Space, Time and Mind.* New York: Columbia University Press, 1995, 52.

11. M. Chafkin, "How to Kill a Great Idea." *Inc. Magazine,* June 2007, 85–91.

12. S. Finkelstein, *Why Smart Executives Fail and What You Can Learn From Their Mistakes.* New York: Portfolio, 2003.

13. C. Robin, *Fear: The History of a Political Idea.* New York: Oxford University Press, 2004, 1, 16.

14. J. Casti, *Complexification: Explaining a Paradoxical World Through the Science of Surprise.* New York: HarperCollins, 1994.

15. C. S. Lewis, *God in the Dock: Essays on Theology and Ethics.* Grand Rapids, MI: William B. Eerdmans Publishing, 1970, 202.

16. H. Carpenter, *The Inklings: C. S. Lewis, J. R. R. Tolkien, Charles Williams, and Their Friends.* New York: Ballantine, 1981.

17. L. Roberson and C. Kulik, "Stereotype Threat at Work." *Academy of Management Perspectives* 21, no. 2 (2007): 24–40, p. 24.

18. A. Ohman, "Conditioned Fear of a Face: A Prelude to Ethnic Enmity?" *Science* 29, no. 309 (2005): 711–13.

19. C. Argyris, "Skilled Incompetence." *Harvard Business Review* 64, no. 5 (1986): 74–79, p. 74.

20. J. Hughes and J. Weiss, "Simple Rules for Making Alliances Work." *Harvard Business Review* 85, no. 11 (2007): 122–31, p. 126.

21. J. S. Lublin, "Job Candidates Get a Manual From Boss: 'How to Handle Me.'" *The Wall Street Journal Online,* January 7, 2003. http://online.wsj.com/article/0,,SB104188161556302106400.html (accessed December 30, 2008).

22. Hughes and Weiss, "Simple Rules."

23. K. Burke, *The Philosophy of Literary Form.* Berkeley: University of California Press, 1973, 67.

24. See Phils7Questions.com for further insight into critical thinking issues.

25. P. Clampitt and M. L. Williams, "Conceptualizing and Measuring How Employees and Organizations Manage Uncertainty." *Communication Research Reports* 22 (2005): 315–24; K. Sweetman, "Embracing Uncertainty." *MIT Sloan Management Review* 43, no. 1 (2001): 8–9. See also Appendix B.

26. K. Lovelace, D. L. Shapiro, and L. R. Weingart, "Maximizing Cross-Functional New Product Teams' Innovativeness and Constraint Adherence: A Conflict Communications Perspective." *Academy of Management Journal* 44, no. 4 (2001): 779–93, p. 784.

27. W. Isaacson, *Einstein: His Life and Universe.* New York: Simon & Schuster, 2007.

28. M. Bligh, "Surviving Post-Merger 'Culture Clash': Can Cultural Leadership Lessen Casualties?" *Leadership* 2, no. 4 (2006): 395–426, p. 405.

29. A. Gawande, "The Checklist." *The New Yorker,* December 10, 2007, 86–95.

30. P. Pronovost, D. Needham, S. Berenholtz, D. Sinopoli, H. Chu, S. Cosgrove, B. Sexton, R. Hyzy, R. Welsh, G. Roth, J. Bander, J. Kepros, and C. Goeschel, "An Intervention to Decrease Catheter-Related Bloodstream Infections in the ICU." *New England Journal of Medicine* 355, no. 26 (2006): 2725–32.

31. E. Rogers, *Diffusion of Innovation.* 4th ed. New York: Free Press, 1995, 5–6.

32. A. Lashinsky, "The Decade of Steve." *Fortune,* November 23, 2009, 93–114.

33. L. Kahney, *Inside Steve's Brain.* New York: Portfolio, 2008.

34. Ibid.

35. G. Pisano and R. Verganti, "Which Kind of Collaboration Is Right for You?" *Harvard Business Review* 86, no. 12 (2008): 78–86.

36. M. Farjoun and W. Starbuck, "Synopsis: NASA, the CAIB Report and the *Columbia* Disaster." In *Organization at the Limit: Lessons From the Columbia Disaster,* edited by W. Starbuck and M. Farjoun. Malden, MA: Blackwell, 2005, 16–17.

37. Stoler, *George C. Marshall.*

38. T. McCraw, *Prophet of Innovation: Joseph Schumpeter and Creative Destruction.* Cambridge, MA: Belknap, 2007.

⊰ 12 ⊱

FOSTER THE GROWTH OF
INVESTMENT-WORTHY EMPLOYEES

———•◆•———

*The common wisdom is that . . . managers have to learn to moti-
vate people. Nonsense. Employees bring their own motivation.*

—Tom Peters

If you came face-to-face with world-class talent, would you recognize it?
Over 1,000 people had the opportunity to answer the question in a
Washington, D.C., subway station.

Here's how to conduct the test. Step one: Find a world-class musician.
The Grammy Award–winning classical violinist Joshua Bell comes to mind.
Step two: Convince the musician to exchange his formal concert attire for a
pair of jeans, T-shirt, and baseball cap. Step three: Ask him to play a few sig-
nature pieces during morning rush hour at a local subway station. Step four:
See what happens. Some enterprising social scientists did just that.[1]

Did people stop and listen? Not many. Did they drop any money into his vio-
lin case? A few. He earned a little over $30 in 40 minutes. That's quite a salary cut
for a musician who commands over $100 a ticket for a concert. Did they even
seem to notice the world-class talent on display? In a word, no.[2]

What happened? Perhaps this delightful urban experiment proves once again
how context exerts significant power over our perceptions. Maybe we just need to
see people in the proper context to identify their talent. Fair enough. But it also

illustrates how difficult it really is to recognize talent. And if *recognizing* talent proves so difficult, then properly *investing* in it may prove as challenging as hitting the high C note on a fiddle. But that is exactly the task that progress makers relish. Why? Because they know that their organization's ability to make progress directly depends on spotting the right talent, nurturing it, and mobilizing it.

The progress maker recognizes the downside of investing in the wrong people. Studies suggest that "the average hiring mistake costs fifteen times an employee's base salary in hard costs and productivity loss."[3] That means "a single hiring blunder on a $100,000 employee can cost a company $1.5 million or more."[4] As executive recruiter Nancy Thompson put it, "In my business I'm looking for just the right fit for both parties: for the organization with a position to fill and a person who desires a special role. In my experience the chasm between the *poor fit* and *adequate fit* is wide as the gulf between the *adequate fit* and the *right fit*. But detecting the second often proves more challenging."[5] Getting the right fit requires a special perspective on finding and developing talent. We discuss this in the following sections.

DEFINING THE CONCEPT

This strategy revolves around two shared responsibilities. Leaders shoulder one of the obligations—creating a growth-fostering environment. Employees shoulder the other—becoming and remaining investment worthy.[6] When leaders cultivate a growth-fostering environment, they are making an investment that has high potential to yield progress (see Figure 12.1). Let's look at both sets of responsibilities in more depth.

Growth-Fostering Environment

Progress makers assume the responsibility of surrounding employees with the tools, experiences, and challenges to fulfill their potential amid the storms of everyday life. They buffer their employees from inclement organizational elements. Clearly, this requires financial resources, but it also suggests something more. It requires, for instance, that progress makers allocate their time to provide people with competency-building tasks and developmental feedback.

Researchers over the past 50 years have investigated what motivates employees to stay with an organization. At the top of the list is "exciting,

Figure 12.1   **Formula for Fostering Progress-Making Potential**

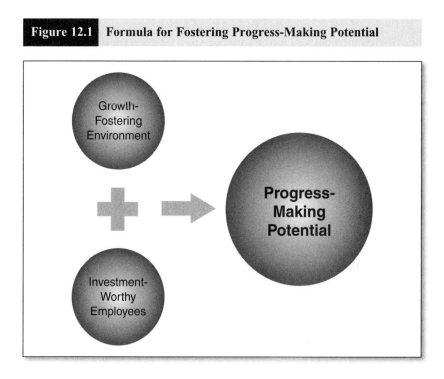

challenging work" and "career growth, learning and development."[7] While fair pay and benefits are on the list, they are by no means the sole determinant of retaining talent. Note that what you might find "exciting and challenging" may not be what others do. Too often managers make the naive assumption that because they find something stimulating, others will as well. A natural explorer must recognize that some people gain greater joy from perfecting than they do from discovering something new. A natural refiner freezes up at the thought of inventing a new platform. A wiser leader recognizes the innate differences in motivation and uses them to achieve progress.

At The Boldt Company, for instance, employees are required to write out their own career development plans for the upcoming year when preparing for their annual performance appraisals. In particular, they must answer three critical questions:

- What are your most significant learnings during the past year? How have you applied them to your business responsibilities?
- What are your learning/training plans for the coming year?
- How have your updated your career path aspirations?

Thoughtfulness gets rewarded; inattentiveness does not. Senior executives review all plans and seek to discover creative developmental opportunities in employees' plans that match company needs. The deep, enduring talent development happens in the one-on-one discussions of the employee's career plan. In one case, a manager realized that after 6 years of running a small business unit, he had mastered the major job challenges and that his learning opportunities were diminishing. In a candid discussion with his executive manager, he shared these concerns. The executive agreed with him. In due course, they worked out a plan to move him into a position with greater responsibility, opportunity, and growth potential. Now he runs the entire West Coast operations.

Serious discussions like those at Boldt send powerful signals to employees about the importance of personal growth. Here's where the insightful inquiry, provocative probe, and nuanced nudge conjure up opportunities to enhance employee performance. Done well, it is a magical and transformative experience for all involved. Two colonels at the U.S. Army War College describe the conditions necessary for this kind of discussion to yield lasting results:

> By providing opportunities to experiment and fail, effective stewards set the conditions for high-quality collaborative inquiry into divergent knowledge. Accepting thoughtful, open, and honest feedback, they encourage and share a passion for creativity among professionals. . . . The steward's role is to help set conditions for *action research* with other professionals in the absence of the clarity, accuracy and precision so appealing to the technically rational mind-set.[8]

Candid conversations within the context of experimentation may well be the most important way to craft a growth-fostering environment.

Investment-Worthy Employees

Authors have devoted a lot of pixel power to motivating employees. But the responsibilities of the followers often get lost in the white space between the glowing electronic letters. It is as if motivation was some wonder drug that leaders inject into followers. Progress makers reject that view. Instead, they believe employees have a responsibility to *engage in self-development and advance the best interests of their organizations.* A Chinese proverb put it best: "Teachers open the door, but you must enter by yourself."

The former CEO of Procter & Gamble, A. G. Lafley, captured the sentiment when reflecting on his initial years at the helm:

> I always talk about this hierarchy of commitment. On the high end it's disciples—people who really believe in what you're doing and in you. And on the low end it's saboteurs. And there's everything in between. So I had to make sure that we got rid of the saboteurs, built a strong cadre of disciples, and moved all the fence sitters to the positive side.[9]

Such a perspective partially explains P & G's success under his leadership. At the core of his comments we see discernment and a willingness to act on those insights. In fact, all progress makers seek to separate those people incapable or unwilling of advancing the best interests of the organization from the others.

How do progress makers discern whether employees are "investment worthy"? In a perfect world, leaders might wish to have a detailed checklist to sort out those who possess the potential to be engaged and those who do not. Alas, no such gizmo exists. The specific tests of "investment worthiness" will differ from business to business. Yet we can paint some broad brush strokes of the test. Employees should be willing, capable, and committed to

- Adapting

  Investment-worthy employees waste little time studying their job descriptions. They realize events change far more quickly than job descriptions and eagerly embrace necessary changes.

- Continuously learning

  Investment-worthy employees are always looking for better and more efficient ways to do existing tasks. They are the last ones to justify an action because "we've always done it that way."

- Embracing the organizational direction

  Alignment requires, of course, an understanding of where the organization is heading. Investment-worthy employees seek out information about the issues shaping their organization's future. They orient their day-to-day activities around their organization's direction.

To be investment worthy requires a certain level of connection and commitment. To be specific, progress makers limit their investments in people deemed disconnected from the tasks at hand, whether that be refining an existing platform or building a new one. Yet, they foster the growth of all others who will help the organization move forward.

BARRIERS

Managing the balance between building a growth-fostering environment and retaining investment-worthy employees proves tricky for several reasons that we address in this section.

Leaders Lack the Disposition to Invest in Others

Some people in leadership positions lack the temperament to meaningfully invest in talent. They may be too self-absorbed. They may secretly fear the success of others. Or, they may rigidly hold to a sink-or-swim mentality regarding personal development. Regardless of the reason, those leaders eventually undermine their own success. Why? Talented people will seek other growth opportunities, leaving only the less talented to execute the plans.

Leonard Bernstein, famed composer and conductor of the New York Philharmonic, eloquently described an alternative temperament:

> I believe that man's noblest endowment is his capacity to change . . . I believe in the potential of people. I cannot rest passively with those who give up in the name of "human nature." Human nature must, by definition, include among its elements the element of metamorphosis. Human nature is only animal nature if it is obliged to remain static. Without growth there is no godhead. If we believe that man can never achieve a society without wars, then we are condemned to wars forever. This is again the easy way. But the laborious, loving way, the way of dignity and divinity, presupposes a belief in people and in their capacity to change, grow, communicate, and love.[10]

Such sentiments provide some insight into one of his most baffling and debated conducting decisions.

The background: The famed conductor rarely spoke before a concert. But he made an exception on the night that legendary pianist Glenn Gould was scheduled to perform the Brahms D Minor Concerto, Op. 15. Why? The conductor and soloist disagreed on how the music should be played. What to do? Bernstein chose to preface the performance with these revealing comments:

> You are about to hear a rather, shall we say, unorthodox performance . . . I cannot say I am in total agreement with Mr. Gould's conception, and this raises the interesting question: "What am I doing conducting it?" (Mild laughter from the audience). I'm conducting it because Mr. Gould is so valid and serious an artist that I must take seriously anything he conceives in good faith, and his conception is interesting enough that I feel you should hear it, too. . . . Because I am fascinated, glad to have the chance for a new look at this much-played work; because, what's more, there are moments in Mr. Gould's performance that emerge with astonishing freshness and conviction . . . we can all learn something from this extraordinary artist who is a thinking performer, and finally because there is in music what Dimitri Mitropoulos used to call "the sportive element" (mild audience laughter)—that factor of curiosity, adventure, experiment—and I can assure you that it has been an adventure this week (audience laughter) collaborating with Mr. Gould on this Brahms concerto, and it's in this spirit of adventure that we now present it to you.[11]

Music critics moaned; they were not pleased with Bernstein's decision. But the progress makers in the audience would have applauded; they would have understood the logic. Progress makers recognize the value of such investments in extraordinary talent.

Leaders Lack the Discernment to Properly Judge Talent

Young leaders often struggle with the discernment issue. They avoid seeing differences between employees. It rubs against their egalitarian sensibilities, smacking of discrimination. After all, "we are all created equal." They don't want to "give up" on anybody. Fair enough. But we are not talking about creation, treatment under the law, or even a humanitarian axiom. Instead, we are talking about where to invest resources. Only foolish investors place all their bets on highly risky stocks.

This does not mean that deciding on whom to invest in is easy, natural, or risk free. Indeed, distinguishing between those who merit investment and those who do not often proves tricky. After all, every professional sports team has traded away a high-impact player. The Atlanta Falcons football team, for instance, traded away three-time MVP quarterback Brett Favre for the soon to be forgotten running back Tony Smith. On the flipside, teams have made similar mistakes paying big dollars to players who never fulfilled their potential. But this "damned if you do, damned if you don't" dilemma need not lead to paralysis. Rather, the progress makers seek to maximize their odds of success. In particular, they are aware of three potential talents that often slip under the radar screen.

First are the *happy cynics.* Few businesses tolerate them, but universities and other government bureaucracies are full of them. These employees merrily go about their business—often with quiet efficiency and effectiveness. Yet, they disengage from larger organizational efforts because of frustrations often encountered years ago.[12] Their ideas—often quite innovative ones—fell on deaf ears. So, they learn to love their job by restricting their scope of ownership, narrowing their footprint in organization life to as small as possible. This frees them to be the insightful critic regarding everything else in the organization. Satisfied within the narrow confines of their self-defined "job," smug in their cynical perspective, they disengage from the rest of the organization. But they are not necessarily a hopeless cause. If properly identified and challenged, their talents may be exactly what the organization needs to step forward. The novice leader overlooks or ignores them; the progress maker does not.

Second are the *visionaries,* such as Mary Kay Ash, who worked for over 10 years at a direct sales company, World Gift. She envisioned marketing opportunities for the company that others did not recognize. When a man she trained was promoted ahead of her, she quit. And the rest, as they say, is history. She went on to build one of the most innovative and admired companies in the world, Mary Kay Cosmetics. Leaders from the former company must envy the business she built with over two million consultants and over two billion dollars in annual sales using a similar direct marketing technique.[13] In the strictest sense, she may have failed the "embracing organizational direction" test discussed above. But leaders with good judgment would have invested in her and her ideas. Instead, they squandered an opportunity. Novice leaders are tempted to disinvest because an employee takes a slightly different tact to achieve organizational goals. Progress makers double down on people like this.

Third are the *busy bees,* who may or may not add value. Progress makers realize that activity does not equate with accomplishment. Fans of the *Dilbert* cartoon snigger at the fictional cubicle politics because they recognize how closely it mirrors reality. Often the plot lines center on all the energy invested in creating the *impression* but not the *reality* of meaningful work. *Dilbert* creator, Scott Adams, explains,

> For every boss who wants to make you work harder, there are a dozen employees who want to prevent it. Naturally, most of the new goofing off technology will be disguised as productivity tools, just as the current ones are. Employees today goof off with the telephone, e-mail, Internet connections, and their computers. It all looks like work to the unsuspecting employer.[14]

Does he exaggerate for comic relief? Of course. Does he accurately describe some people? Definitely. Can the busy bees stop buzzing about and add value to the hive's enterprise? Absolutely. But only when progress makers provide them with the right directional signals.

Leaders' Investments Are Small, Narrow, or Misguided

Even with the proper outlook and the right people, something can go awry. Feeble investments result in meager development and less progress. For instance, a single performance appraisal a year, no matter how thoughtful, rarely provides the proper degree of direction or incentive to develop talent. That's too *small and narrow* of investment to do much good.

Talent investments, like financial ones, can also be *misguided.* Consider a situation in which a leader must choose between only two books for employee development: (1) *How to Be Your Own Best Friend* and (2) *The Art of Conversation.* The first builds self-esteem, the second a skill. Arguably, both are useful. However, progress makers know where the real value lies in this trade-off: Skills trump self-esteem every time. In fact, raising self-esteem rarely improves job performance. Indeed, a team of psychologists concluded,

> We have found little to indicate that indiscriminately promoting self-esteem in today's children or adults, just for being themselves, offers society any compensatory benefits beyond the seductive pleasure it brings to those engaged in the pleasure.[15]

In short, investing in appraisals, assignments, or associations designed to merely build self-esteem is akin to purchasing fool's gold.

WHAT TO DO?

The basic principles of personal finance management provide a useful framework for crafting actionable ideas to implement the strategy we have outlined. We look at these issues from the perspective of progress makers: how they select and develop investment-worthy employees and create a growth-fostering environment. We use most of these principles on two levels. First, we examine how to apply the principles on a team basis. For example, what does it mean to "diversify your portfolio" for the *team*? Second, we consider how the principle relates to an *individual* employee. For instance, how can a progress maker "diversify the investment" for a particular employee?

Craft a Talent Investment Approach

One of the first questions a skillful financial adviser would ask a client is, "What are your investment goals?" The logical follow-up questions would include such things as "What is your ideal retirement date? What major purchases and investments do you want to make?" Then the questions turn to assets on hand. Now the financial strategy can emerge at the intersection of current allocations and future aspirations. After that, it becomes a matter of executing the plan (e.g., saving a certain amount of dollars a month), monitoring performance, and tweaking the portfolio.

Progress makers employ a similar approach. They start with these questions: "Where is the organization headed?" "What are the key objectives?" Then they turn to the strategic assets: "What kind of people talent does the team (or organization) already possess?" Finally, they start crafting the investment approach by asking if the current team consists of the right talents for the tasks and objectives envisioned. "Do we need younger people? More seasoned ones? More financial analysts? More engineers? Fewer explorers? More refiners?" And so on. One executive at Wachovia Corporation may have put it best when he said, "Business people typically look at problems from the revenue or risk angle first, but I've yet to see a business problem or strategy that doesn't have people at its core."[16] That's exactly the perspective a progress maker brings to this key investment decision.

Other important decisions flow from the basic investment approach. Three particular issues should be considered.

Talent Proposition

What should be the talent proposition for recruiting and retaining top employees? A talent proposition is the statement about the tangible (e.g., financial) and intangible (e.g., prestige) benefits the organization offers to potential and existing employees. Consider, for example, the challenge of attracting young technical talent at the world's largest private energy service provider, E.ON. In an age when politicians, activists, and high-profile artists rail against global warming and other eco-evils, energy companies often are cast as the villains. What kind of talent proposition could attract the right people in this business climate? After careful research and thoughtful discussion, E.ON developed a wonderfully actionable talent proposition: "Your energy shapes the future." And that notion, coupled with other programs, helped the company turn the corner on attracting top-flight talent. It is at once focused, forward looking, and energizing to young people.[17]

Talent Acquisition

The talent proposition provides the bait and hook. The talent acquisition question asks if the organization or team uses the right net, casts it in first-rate spots, and catches the right people.

Answering this question requires a candid evaluation of recent hiring decisions as well as missed hiring opportunities. Talent acquisition mistakes and shortfalls can usually be attributed to the following issues. First, are we clear on the type of employees we seek to hire? Second, are we generating the right pool of candidates? Third, are our selection criteria hitting the mark? Experts believe, for example, that only 50% of interviews result in the right hiring decisions.[18] Either we hire the wrong person or we unwittingly screen out a skilled talent. We might as well flip a coin. Fourth, are we losing good people because we can't sell them on the opportunity? Any one of these issues might stand in the way of successful talent acquisition. Progress makers plot a strategy to make sure that does not happen to their organization.

Talent Development and Retention

How should we develop and retain existing talent? This question suggests that leaders should measure the quality of their approaches to employee development. Likewise, they should measure and study retention rates. After all, one of the only common characteristics of the "World's Most Admired Companies" is a "focus on identifying and developing talent globally."[19]

Progress makers capitalize on the strengths of their employees. But they seek to augment their abilities, as well. Any tennis coach can tell you about the difficulty and ultimate reward of teaching a player with a naturally gifted forehand to improve her backhand. The common tendency is to favor her gifted hand and avoid the other. Learning to fight that natural tendency and use the weaker hand with similar ease is exactly what this option entails. It is difficult for gifted explorers to use refining skills (and vice versa), but learning to do so improves the odds that they will win the progress game.

Diversify Your Investments in Employees

The simple translation: "Don't put all your eggs in one basket." Why? Just ask investors who had all their retirement funds invested in Enron stock. Something might happen to that basket. Sure, it's a little more cumbersome to carry extra baskets, but you are more likely to weather financial and organizational storms. What does this notion mean to progress makers?

First, it suggests that progress makers avoid hiring clones

Unfortunately, many managers tend to hire people like themselves—people of similar age, temperament, and academic background.[20] This does not breed the diversity of perspectives needed to sort out complex issues. It does not propagate the kind of dissent needed to take the wisest course of action.[21] Sheep blindly follow the herd. Sheep are cloned; people should not be.

Shifting hiring practices away from clones allows the organization to revitalize itself. A company that only promotes from within risks becoming stagnate, insular, and self-serving. Consequently, some businesses shift the hiring mix, seeking to fill 80% positions with internal talent and 20% from external sources. Likewise, the company may only recruit from a single talent pool, such as a particular university or trade school. It might make sense to draw from diverse talent pools with slightly different perspectives. The King of Madison Avenue, David Ogilvy, did exactly that when he bucked advertising agency trends and hired Jewish executives in his firm.[22]

Second, it suggests that progress makers properly mix the types *of investments they make in individuals*

Leaders make a cardinal mistake in assuming a "one-size-fits-all" approach when investing in talent. You can never know the exact technique that will help someone achieve his or her potential. And even the individual involved might be blinded to what experience or combination of experiences would have the greatest impact. For some it may be personal coaching sessions; for others it might be an overseas assignment or exposure to a new network of associates. The richer the palate of investments, the more likely one will hit the mark (see Table 12.1).

Progress makers strengthen employee skill sets by alternating talent development practices. Broadly speaking, we can sort development practices into two categories: (1) hard technical skills such as Six Sigma, lean manufacturing, and budgeting and (2) soft personal skill such as communication, change management, and group decision making. Progress makers know the importance of both categories. They also recognize the natural tendency of those with well-honed skills in either arena to evangelize from their podium of expertise, often looking down on the "less enlightened." That's not healthy; it's like exercising only one leg. Progress makers need two muscular, toned, and well-coordinated legs to run the race. Therefore, they make sure that employees develop in both areas, never overemphasizing one at the expense of the other. A caveat: Sometimes an organization or team has well-developed skills in one developmental category. It makes sense to pause and focus exclusively on the other category for a time. The proper balance emerges over time.

Table 12.1	Talent Investment Portfolio

- Assessment centers
- Performance appraisals
- Coaching
- Placement services
- Corporate university
- Job/assignment rotation
- Career planning
- Professional development opportunities (e.g., conferences, seminars)
- Sabbaticals
- Networking opportunities

Make Routine Talent Investments

The type of investment is important, but so is the timing. Investing in talent must be routine, significant, and sustainable. Any weightlifter can testify about the importance of rest and recovery between workouts. Three hours of lifting, grunting, and sweating spread out over the week beats a weekly three-hour masochistic muscle marathon. Why? The body needs time to absorb the gains. It can only take so much. Energy wanes. Muscle building halts. It's pain with only marginal gain.

Likewise, developing an individual's talent requires routine investments. A comprehensive yearly marathon performance appraisal will not cut it. Perhaps the supervisor can check it off the "employee development" list. Task completed. Talent enhanced? Not likely. Why? Our neural pathways numb at some point, reducing our comprehension and resisting further input. Like the weightlifter, people need time to recover, reflect, and reenergize. Our intellectual and emotional muscles tire just as our physical ones do.

Similar considerations infuse the thinking of progress makers on a more macro level. They recognize that their organizations or teams need time to absorb new talent. Acquiring a new unit or company might make perfect business sense. Yet, the new talent needs time to graft onto the existing structure.

Regularly Measure, Analyze, and Discuss
the Performance of Your Talent Investments

Investors want to know how their portfolio performs. The overly conscientious check every day. Not a good idea, as compulsively monitoring performance often cultivates a tendency to overcorrect or to act precipitously. Others are more cavalier, checking only during crises. That's equally unwise. The progress maker acts in a more systematic, deliberate manner. Many leaders operationalize these conceptual parameters by reviewing talent investments every quarter.

What happens in the review? Leaders evaluate their talent investments. Are we investing in the right people? In the right way? With the right frequency? Are we seeing the results we wanted? Slice the data. Dice it. Chop it up and chew on it. Talk to your people. Seek insight about what's working, what might, and what's not. Investing in the people, like the market, cannot be too rigidly governed by formula. This is what analysis is all about.

The progress maker collaborates with others to find the right mix of investments to meet organizational and individual goals. You can't plug numbers into a magic formula to find the right mix. Instead, progress makers use the routine discussion to recalibrate their approach. Consider, for example, one of the world's largest financial service companies, Barclays. It could coast on its reputation to secure high-value talent. It doesn't. In fact, the executive committee commits up to 50% of its quarterly meeting time to discussions about talent governance and management.[23]

Devoting time to this enterprise provides the opportunity—but not the guarantee—of success. It necessitates a certain frame of mind best captured by Warren Buffett's partner, Charlie Munger:

> If Berkshire has made modest progress, a good deal of it is because Warren and I are very good at destroying our own best-loved ideas. Any year that you don't destroy one of your best-loved ideas is probably a wasted year.[24]

He picks a yearly fight with the natural human tendency to confirm preexisting beliefs. John Kenneth Galbraith put it this way: "Faced with a choice between changing one's mind and proving there is no need to do so, almost everyone gets busy on the proof."[25] Progress makers approach the entire discussion of talent management with these thoughts in mind. What worked? What didn't? What should we try next time?

An element of trial and error pervades all effective talent management enterprises. For example, many companies rotate star performers through different assignment in the quest to provide rich leadership development opportunities. Sounds great in theory, but the results often prove disappointing. For example, an overly ambitious rotation schedule may result in leaders only focusing on short-term gains and missing out on the opportunities to learn about the long-term repercussions of their decisions.[26] Without discussion and rigorous evaluation of results, the investment cannot be properly evaluated. And an attractive but inadequate talent development philosophy prevails.

Routinely Rebalance the Talent Portfolio

As time passes, personal financial portfolios tend to get out of balance. Why? Because even if all investments enter the starting gate at the same time, some naturally perform better than others. The people portfolio evolves in the same way. Investments in people that work at one point in time tend to absorb more and more resources. Likewise, the people who add value at a point in time get more rewards. The "more is better" philosophy takes over, and their ranks are often expanded.

For example, during the height of the Internet boom, some universities hired a number of computer scientists at very high salaries. Once demand abated, some universities were stuck with a number of high-priced tenured professors who taught fewer and fewer students. Perhaps it's inevitable, but is it wise?

External conditions such as the competitive climate, struggles over talent, technology shifts, and prevailing cultural attitudes play an important role in the success of any one individual or of any one program. These forces often subtly shift the types of people hired and development programs pursued. After all, years ago few organizations contemplated the role the Internet could play in training a global workforce. Today, of course, online universities and training are touted as a cost-effective way of developing talent.

Warren Buffett's mentor, Benjamin Graham, was fond of saying, "You can get in way more trouble with a good idea than a bad idea."[27] Why? Buffet explained the rationale: "because you forget that the good idea has limits."[28] That insight permeates the thinking of a progress maker. Refining is a wonderful organizational strategy. So is exploring. But both have limits. Current success can undermine future success. And that's why progress makers obsess over maintaining the proper balance in the talent portfolio. There are far more opportunities to do so than many leaders suspect.

Modifying the composition of teams, for example, tends to shake up conventional thinking. Teams, like companies, risk stagnation as members become overly familiar with each other's skills, talents, and perspectives. Roles can emerge that pigeonhole people into muted acquiescence. One commentator provided a compelling example:

> Photocopy company Xerox found this out in the 1970s when engineers and scientists, who saw each other as "toner heads" and arrogant dweebs, stopped talking and upper echelons failed to appreciate scientists' ideas . . . Apple Computer ripened them to bear glorious fruit. Miscommunication lost Xerox the PC.[29]

Those conversations can never take place without the right—if sometimes uncomfortable—people at the table. Although diversity may potentially stir creativity, it typically promotes conflict and miscommunication. It also runs counter to the security most individuals experience in working and sharing ideas with past collaborators.[30] Progress makers embrace the uneasiness, knowing that it spurs personal development and often serendipitous insights that yield fruitful enterprises.

Cut Your Losses

Young leaders often struggle with this. Yet, when you ask seasoned executives about their biggest regrets, they often involve not making the personnel switches fast enough. In their gut, they know the person is not a good fit for the job and see dim prospects for future change.[31] Alas, the human caring part of their being stands in the way of doing what they know is correct. The pressure *not to act* multiples exponentially when the person involved has helped you win battles before. That's precisely the issue we discuss in Ron Reed's Progress Maker Profile at the end of Chapter 8. Regrettably, the people who helped refine a platform might not be the people who can build the next one.

If cutting losses was entirely about emotions, it would be easy. Just put on your Mr. Spock persona (e.g., logical) and make the decision. It's not like that, though. There are often quite logical and defensible reasons to keep pouring energy into a losing investment. Consider the following reasonable arguments:

- "This person has always delivered in the past; maybe she will again in the near future."
- "I can see this person's potential. I've worked so hard to mentor him. Someday he will produce."
- "If this person could just get past this one issue, then he could add something great to the team."

Every one of these statements may well be accurate, compassionate, and totally irrelevant. For at the core each statement pits hope against personal experience.

Sometimes the person or persons in question are secretly relieved by a cut-your-losses decision. After all, they may be cutting their losses, as well. They may know the fit is not good. They may not verbalize it, but they may well sense it.[32] And leaders are not doing the employees any favors by continuing to engage the disengaged. The leaders are depriving them of the opportunity to find another position with a better fit and where their skills are more valued.

All that said, releasing an employee troubles, disturbs, and unsettles every leader. Professor George Reed of the University of San Diego has led both soldiers and students. He provides an insightful perspective on the conflicting emotions:

> When we identify someone who is not acting in accordance with the values of the organization—especially in the way that they treat subordinates—we have an obligation to make an effort to develop them. We begin with an assumption that every person has fundamental dignity and worth, and that people can modify their behavior. There comes a point, however, when the development efforts have to stop and the reassignments or firings should begin. In the end, people are either an asset to the organization or they are a liability. When the scale tips to the liability side then the right thing to do for the organization is to move the person out of the organization.[33]

Cutting your losses on talent rests on an act of judgment and courage. The successful hedge fund manager John Armitage once spoke about the challenge of managing billions of dollars: "You have to be obsessive, you have to have guts, you have to know when to stick to your convictions, and when to walk away."[34] Progress makers say much the same about the proper management of talent.

CONCLUDING THOUGHTS

Anyone who invests in markets or talents enjoys great days and endures bad ones. Yet, in the long run, what distinguishes the successful investor from the unsuccessful? It is the right investment approach—one that takes on calculated risks, despite the uncertainties. Will every investment produce progress-making benefits? Not a chance. But the odds are that, in the long run, the entire portfolio will yield results. That's what it means to embrace the vagaries inherent to every human enterprise. And it is the kind of risk taking that might cause you to invest a little time listening to a street musician. He might, after all, turn out to be a world-class musician serenading you to a once-in-a-lifetime treat.

NOTES

1. C. Kearney, "Joshua Bell: Hailed by Peers, Ignored on Street." April 11, 2007. http://www.reuters.com/article/entertainmentNews/idUSN1124665920070411 (accessed February 11, 2009).

2. Ibid.

3. G. Smart and R. Street, *Who: The A Method for Hiring.* New York: Ballantine, 2008, xvii.

4. Ibid., xvii.

5. Personal communication with Nancy Thompson, February 18, 2009.

6. Some people react to the seemingly impersonal nature of the financial metaphor we use to explain this strategy. Fair enough. But we are balancing this metaphor with a more organic one based on cultivating growth. Professor Angela Brenton of the University of Arkansas–Little Rock brought this issue to our attention.

7. S. Jordan-Evans and B. Kaye, "Retaining Employees." In *Business: The Ultimate Resource,* edited by C. Coffin. Cambridge: MA: Perseus Publishing, 2002, 196–97, p. 196.

8. C. Paparone and G. Reed, "The Reflective Military Practitioner: How Military Professionals Think in Action." *Military Review,* March–April 2008, 66–76, pp. 73–74.

9. Quoted in an interview by C. Tkacyk, "Follow These Leaders." *Fortune,* December 12, 2005, p. 1 of special insert.

10. L. Bernstein, *Findings.* New York: Simon & Schuster, 1982, 137–38.

11. www.rci.rutgers.edu/~mwatts/glenn/lennie.html (accessed April 20, 2009).

12. J. W. Dean, P. Brandes, and R. Dharwadkar, "Organizational Cynicism." *Academy of Management Review* 23 (1998): 341–52.

13. K. Hollandsworth, "Hostile Makeover." *Texas Monthly,* November 1995, 128–33+; http://www.marykay.com/company/milestones/default.aspx (accessed March 3, 2009).

14. S. Adams, *The Dilbert Future: Thriving on Stupidity in the 21st Century.* New York: HarperCollins, 1997, 26.

15. R. Baumeister, J. Campbell, J. Krueger, and K. Vohs, "Exploding the Self-Esteem Myth." *Scientific American,* January 2005, 84–91, p. 91.

16. S. McFayden, interviewed by J. Akin, *Wachovia Corporation: Engaging Heads and Hearts in Capturing the People Advantage: Thought Leaders on Human Capital,* edited by T. Kinni, I. Steffen, and B. Worthen. New York: Strategy+business Books, 2008, 207–17, pp. 209–10.

17. K. Mattern and S. U. Vallerien, "E.ON AG: Ensuring Tomorrow's Workforce Today," in *Capturing the People Advantage: Thought Leaders on Human Capital,* edited by T. Kinni, I. Steffen, and B. Worthen. New York: Strategy+business Books, 2008, 55–65.

18. G. Smart and R. Street, *Who: The A Method for Hiring.* New York: Ballantine, 2008, xvii.

19. G. Colvin, "The World's Most Admired Companies." *Fortune,* March 16, 2009, 76–78, p. 78.

20. S. Gebelein, L. Stevens, C. Skube, D. Lee, B. Davis, and L. Hellervik, *Successful Manager's Handbook.* Minneapolis: Personnel Decisions International Corporation, 2001.

21. S. Sidle, "Do Teams Who Agree to Disagree Make Better Decisions?" *Academy of Management Perspectives* 21, no. 2 (2007): 74–75.

22. K. Roman, *The King of Madison Avenue.* New York: Palgrave MacMillan, 2009.

23. C. Korwin-Szymanowska, "Barclays PLC: Less Fluff, More Execution," in *Capturing the People Advantage: Thought Leaders on Human Capital,* edited by T. Kinni, I. Steffen, and B. Worthen. New York: Strategy+business Books, 2008, 20–28, p. 25.

24. C. Munger, *Poor Charlie's Almanack.* 3rd ed. Virginia Beach, VA: PCA Publications, 2008, 56.

25. John Kenneth Galbraith, quoted in W. Bridges, *Managing Transitions: Making the Most of Change.* Reading, MA: Addison-Wesley, 1991, ix.

26. H. Nalbantain and R. Guzzo, "Making Mobility Matter." *Harvard Business Review* 87, no. 3 (2009): 76–85.

27. B. Graham, cited in A. Schroeder, *The Snowball.* New York: Bantam Dell, 2008, 21.

28. W. Buffett, cited in A. Schroeder, *The Snowball.* New York: Bantam Dell, 2008, 21.

29. C. Blyth, *The Art of Conversation: A Guided Tour of a Neglected Pleasure.* New York: Gotham Books, 2009, 214.

30. R. Guimera, B. Uzzi, J. Spiro, and L. Amaral, "Team Assembly Mechanisms Determine Collaboration Network Structure and Team Performance." *Science,* April 29, 2005, 697–702.

31. J. Welch, *Jack: Straight From the Gut.* New York: Grand Central Publishing, 2001.

32. Terri Lowell of PepsiCo, personal communication, April 20, 2001.

33. G. Reed, personal communication, February 25, 2009.

34. J. Armitage, quoted in K. Burton, *Hedge Hunters: Hedge Fund Masters on the Rewards, the Risk and the Reckoning.* New York: Bloomberg Press, 2007, xiii.

❧ 13 ❧

SEEK, NURTURE, AND
EVALUATE ACTIONABLE IDEAS

———◆◆◆———

*By not daring to take the risk of making the new happen,
management takes, by default, the greater risk of being surprised
by what will happen. This is a risk that even the largest and richest
company cannot afford to take. And it is a risk that not even the
smallest company need take.*

—Peter Drucker

Progress makers do many things well, but they obsess over actionable ideas.
Why? Actionable ideas furnish those in the refining mode with incremental
improvements and those in the exploring mode with fresh insights to pursue. No
one better personifies this obsession than the CEO of Apple, Steve Jobs, who has
probably crafted and disassembled more platforms than most Broadway set
designers. This special talent may well explain one major reason why *Fortune*
selected him as its "CEO of the Decade."[1] One colleague captured his mind-set in
this way: "He has the ability to change his mind and completely forget his old opinion about something . . . it's weird."[2] Jobs would explain it this way: "We're doing
what's right today."[3] This ability to quickly shift direction is fueled by intellectual
restlessness bent on the never-ending quest for the next actionable idea.

You do not have to be a genius (as some say of Jobs) to become obsessed
with actionable ideas.[4] But you do need a deep understanding of the notion and

the know-how to build an organization that properly seeks, nurtures, and eval-
uates actionable ideas. We now turn to those issues.

DEFINING THE CONCEPT

Ideas alone cannot drive progress. The ideas must be actionable. In other words,
you must be able to implement the ideas. The distinction is similar to the one
between invention and innovation. Professor Fagerberg from the Centre for
Technology, Innovation and Culture at the University of Oslo put it this way:
"Invention is the first occurrence of an idea for a new product or process, while
innovation is the first attempt to carry it out into practice."[5] In short, invention
equates with an idea, while an actionable idea resembles an innovation.

Actionable ideas may not always result in a tangible innovation in the form of
a new product or process. An actionable idea may consist of an incremental
improvement or tweak to an existing process or product. Logicians would diagram
the relationship as pictured in Figure 13.1: All innovations are considered actionable
ideas, but not all actionable ideas would be considered innovations.

| Figure 13.1 | Actionable Ideas Formula |

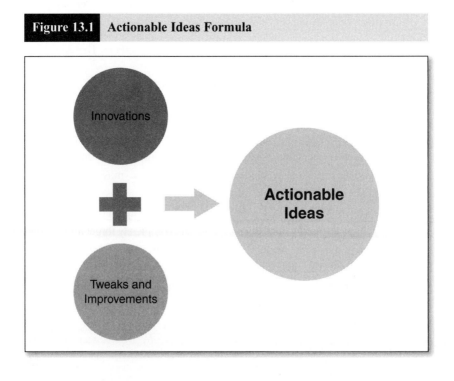

Progress makers recognize their central role in defining what counts as an *actionable idea*. By drawing attention to action, they necessarily divert attention from those deemed not actionable. What counts as *actionable*? Think of the possible questions that a leader must answer:

- *What types of ideas are deemed fair game?* Xerox pioneered the ubiquitous computer mouse and icon-based computer but never deployed it. Apple did.[6] At the time, Xerox believed that the idea did not fit with the existing photocopier business.

- *Who decides whether an idea is actionable?* Jean Lipman-Blumen devoted much of her scholarly career to the study of toxic leaders. She notes that one behavior that toxic leaders employ is "stifling constructive criticism and teaching supporters (sometimes by threats and authoritarianism) *to comply with* rather than *to question* the leader's judgment and actions."[7] Such noxious displays may send the most powerful signal of all about what counts as an actionable idea.

- *What timeframe constitutes "actionable"?* In the 1960s, P & G invented a material that absorbed a lot of water. Many years later, it moved from invention to innovation with the introduction of disposable baby diapers.[8] Clearly, the timeframe for "actionability" differs greatly in a startup firm versus a more established one. Somehow those constraints need to be addressed.

Progress makers ponder answers to these questions. For now, let's assume that you have some responses in mind. In all likelihood, your answer resembles Supreme Court Justice Potter Stewart's famous definition of obscenity: "I know it when I see it."[9] Progress makers face a similar—if less sensational—dilemma as Justice Stewart; they often need to see an idea before determining if it is actionable or not. How leaders respond to this quandary determines the degree and type of progress their organizations actually make.

PHASES TO GENERATE ACTIONABLE IDEAS

Progress makers respond with an elegantly simple process; they (1) seek ideas, (2) nurture the right ideas, and (3) evaluate those ideas. At the end of the process, they generate actionable ideas (see Figure 13.2).

Figure 13.2   **Actionable Ideas Phases**

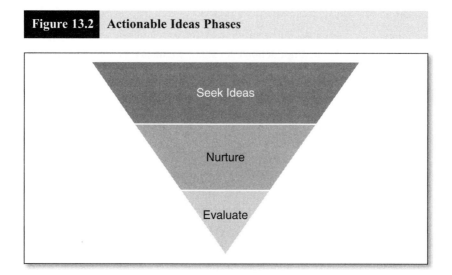

Seek

In this phase, you search for new information, connections, and insights. Stir up these elements in the right proportions and often actionable ideas emerge. The search, though, never ends. The hunter never rests, for tomorrow's sustenance lurks out there in an ever-changing environment. Hunting for different types of cognitive prey requires special methods and skill sets. Tracking down fresh information may appear easy in the Internet age, but it also involves exposing yourself to new experiences, arguments, and people. Sniffing out new connections or patterns requires a hunter's instincts to pick up on weak and subtle clues in the environment.[10]

It also means ignoring some things that others might find pivotal. It's a mind-set captured by the great French scientist Henri Poincaré, who said, "Certain facts are more interesting than others."[11] Why? Because certain facts provide more relevant hints at the underlying pattern. Pursing insights requires the ability to see connections across a wide range of disciplines. It can happen at odd times, such as after a country walk with your dog. When you pull out the burrs sticking to your best friend's fur, you might become fascinated with how the cockleburs adhere to your canine companion. You might even put the burrs under the microscope and discover the exquisite details of the tiny hooks. If years ago you had done that, you might have crafted the insight that led to the development of the hook-and-loop fastener. And that is exactly what the

Swiss engineer, George de Mestral, did. His discovery eventually led to the development of the ubiquitous product we call Velcro.[12]

Seekers cast a very wide net to catch their prey. Yet, seeking is not necessarily a solitary activity. It often requires a willingness to suspend our natural evaluative bent and collaborate with others in a brainstorming activity. Groups that effectively brainstorm operate under some simple rules:

- Generate as many ideas as possible
- Avoid focusing on the quality of an idea
- Write down all ideas (no matter how silly) on a whiteboard or flipchart for all to see
- Resist any evaluation of the ideas until the brainstorming session ends
- Encourage "hitchhiking" or building on the back of other ideas[13]

The rules help people resist their inclination to immediately accept or reject an idea. Evaluating ideas takes place later in the process.

Consider, for example, how Vicki Wilson of Door County Coffee & Tea selects the names for the new coffees she creates. As we discuss in her Progress Maker Profile in Chapter 11, her company regularly rotates in and out new coffees. The company roasts over 30 new coffee blends a year (and drops an equal number). Some companies would do extensive marketing research to pick the proper moniker. Not Vicki. Instead, all the front office, back office, and restaurant staff taste the new brew. Then each employee thinks about a name that best captures the java's essence. In short order, everyone jots down their choice on a slip of paper. After that, all the names are put in a hat and everyone votes on the best name. Simple. Engaging. And fun. Even grandchildren get in on the naming (not tasting) action. The retail manager, Sally, told her grandson, Luke, about her struggle to come up with a name for a blend that tasted like cinnamon and liquor. In flash of childhood brilliance, he blurted out "Cinnarum." The name won the day and the devotion of many customers.[14]

Perceptive readers will note that our approach to the seeking phase integrates both right-brained (intuitive) and left-brained (logical) activities: creativity and logic, instincts and facts, and chaos and order. Those who excel at seeking actionable ideas develop a deeply informed intuition into what might be the next step forward. But they do not stop there. Even keenly perceptive intuitions need to be nurtured.

Nurture

Any parent knows that different children require different degrees of nurturing. The same is true with ideas. Some incremental improvements need very little developmental time and can be launched in short notice. Others require enormous investments of time and energy to reach their potential. James Dyson went through over 5,000 prototypes before perfecting his elegant bagless vacuum cleaner. Before his vacuum cleaner became a consumer hit, he lugged it around for years trying to find the right manufacturer.[15]

During the seeking phase, ideas tend to be rough around the edges and not fully developed. That's fine. These imperfections are addressed in the nurture phase as the ideas are honed, improved, and morphed. Doing so requires three interrelated sensibilities:

- *Willingness to be candid.* Recognizing the strengths and weaknesses of your ideas allows them to be improved, tweaked, and honed. Setting aside time for formal and informal feedback at regular intervals generates the kind of insight, energy, and momentum needed to extract all the potential from an idea. One innovation scholar put it this way: "Innovation is a continuous process. . . . In fact, the first versions of virtually all significant innovations, from the steam engine to the airplane, were crude, unreliable versions of the devices that eventually diffused widely. . . . What we think of as a single innovation is often the result of a lengthy process involving many interrelated innovations."[16] As the iterative loops build up, the tweaks morph the idea into something even more valuable than originally conceived.

- *Tolerance for setbacks.* It would be a capital mistake to assume that innovative ideas move up a smooth linear development track. In fact, the path more often looks like the jagged line of the Dow Jones Industrial average over the past 100 years. Sometimes it's a smooth, steady upward movement, punctuated by some mild downturns. At other times, it moves up and down in dramatic spurts. Either way, progress makers, like long-term investors, learn to build setbacks into their expectations. As parents know, nurturing requires trial and error. The errors, though, if used correctly, provide the means to improve or reshape the idea into something more workable.

- *Patience.* Ideas may mysteriously materialize from the unconscious. Action does not. Action requires concerted energy and effort to implement a process improvement or move a new idea to the marketplace. Even brilliant actionable ideas take time to incubate. Just ask Kim Matheson Shedrick, who spent "16 years growing [her] New York–based Natural Resources into a 15-person, $1 million company that advises developers of high-end spas."[17] For almost half that time she was also contemplating offering her services and products to other, less affluent clients. The economic slowdown in 2008 was the impetus she needed: In that year, she took the plunge and launched a Web site (mySpaShop.com) targeting this market. Was it an instant success? No. Were there bumps in the road? Absolutely. But with diligent tweaking, the new service platform started to yield results. Currently, it generates a nice, growing revenue stream.[18] Her experiences remind us that effective leaders must exercise two different kinds of patience.

First, they must *tolerate* the necessary *developmental cycles.* It works like this: Prototype an idea. Test it. Reconceptualize it. Repeat as often as needed. Even then it may have to jump through a number of organizational hurdles. But the results might be worth it. After all, the first year of the *Seinfeld* sitcom did not garner many fans or executive support. Yet, a few wise executives stuck with the show as the characters, storylines, and comedic style evolved into one of the most successful and widely acclaimed sitcoms in American television history.

Second, they must patiently *tolerate failures.* Most innovative ideas fail to yield expected results. New product ideas have a particularly rocky road to travel. One study found it takes 3,000 raw ideas to generate one commercial success.[19] Clearly, not every idea will be nurtured all the way to the launch cycle. The odds favor the status quo, not the unconventional.

In short, nurturing requires a special temperament. There are few instant successes.

Evaluate

In the final phase, you make the tough calls. Not all ideas—even actionable ones—are worthy of pursuit. Or they may not be worthy of pursuit at that particular time. If you try to pursue every idea, you end up doing nothing well. This is where evaluation comes into play. To evaluate literally means to "place a value on something." That proves particularly difficult because our emotions become so tangled up with our ideas. Or as the founder of the Eureka! Ranch, a corporate innovation and research facility, put it, "The moment anyone becomes emotionally involved in the creation of an idea, discipline leaves as the heart overrules the brain."[20]

Despite the difficulty of the decision, the choice comes down to three options regarding the idea: launch it, morph it, or block it. Launching the idea means giving it the go-ahead for deployment with the expectation it will deliver the intended benefit. At that point it becomes an actionable idea within the organization. Morphing the idea means sending it back for further study, tweaks, and refinement. Blocking the idea means pulling formal sponsorship of the idea.[21]

How do progress makers make this difficult judgment? That depends on the type of idea under scrutiny. Ideas that require large expenditures would undergo greater scrutiny than those that do not. Ideas that cannot be easily abandoned also require greater scrutiny. Consider, for example, a grocery store that is mulling over two different actionable ideas: (1) shifting the positioning of an in-store display and (2) launching a new home delivery service. Shifting the display requires little effort and resources. Just try it out. See if it delivers results. If not, move it back. But the new delivery service would be a much more costly adventure; best to carefully study the idea before launch. For example, what would happen to the store's reputation if the elderly population became dependent on the service but it had to be pulled for financial reasons? In short, the level of scrutiny shifts depending on the type of idea under consideration.

BARRIERS

The seek-nurture-evaluate process appears logical, straightforward, and relatively simple to enact. In theory, yes. In practice, not always. In fact, many barriers often crop up in organizations. We discuss the three most common ones below.

"Sharpshooting"

There are people who make sport of shooting down others' ideas as if they were some clay pigeons at the skeet shoot. Someone proposes an idea, and then the entire group takes shots at it. They aim to criticize it into oblivion or, at least, to wound it. Then someone else proposes another idea. Lock and load. The entire group takes aim at that idea. And the first person who offered up the now dying idea takes particular relish in shelling the next person's idea. Why do they do it? For some, it is a way to assert their intellectual superiority:

"MY ideas are better than yours." For others, it protects their power base: "Letting someone else's idea prevail undermines MY authority." For a few, it is merely a reflex: "I'm just giving my opinion."

Regardless of the reason, such sporting adventures tend to shut down the search for new ideas. This particular "sporting" event forever changes the cost/benefit equation for members of the group. The cost of proposing a new idea rises with each barrage of criticism. Instead of collectively enhancing each other's ideas, the group unwittingly but jointly creates a norm of destroying ideas. No wonder everyone fears suggesting an idea unless it is fully formed and can withstand careful scrutiny. Few initial ideas meet these tests. In fact, the vast majority of ideas—even really good ones—need to be nurtured and improved before they are fully formed. The sharpshooters don't practice this and end up shooting themselves in the foot.

Insular Mind-Set

Psychologists have pinpointed a perceptual bias that almost literally inhibits us from thinking "outside the box." Some call it "perceptual sets" that cause us to fixate on assumed, but not necessarily real, parameters to problems.[22]

Many people, for example, stumble over the famous nine-dot problem. They are instructed to connect all the dots with four connected lines and without retracing any lines (see Figure 13.3). Most people try to solve the problem by sticking within the box or perceptual set. It can't be done that way. Instead, you have to draw lines outside the perceived box.[23]

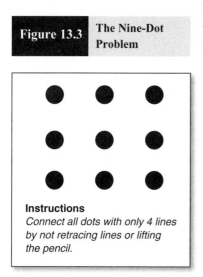

Figure 13.3   The Nine-Dot Problem

Instructions
Connect all dots with only 4 lines by not retracing lines or lifting the pencil.

The nine-dot challenge provides a vivid illustration of how we often put mental blinders on problems and situations that inhibit us from seeing the unusual. That's how experience works against us; it boxes up our thinking into nice, tidy packages that we can neatly file away in our mental warehouse. While that usually expedites our thinking process, it simultaneously hinders us from seeing the novel, unusual, and subtle.

An insular mind-set can pervade an organization as well. No one, of course, openly advocates this inward focus. Rather, it subtly seeps into the culture through everyday conversational declarations like "we've always done it that way before" or "if it's not invented here, it's not good enough." Such sensibilities calcify in the organization's decision-making system, gradually but inevitably clogging out new perceptions, ideas, and approaches. And predictably, the firm suffers a sometimes fatal attack on its long-term viability. Two business strategy thought leaders explain,

> Competitiveness favors those who spot new trends and act on them expeditiously. Therefore, managers must develop insights about new opportunities by amplifying weak signals. These weak signals emerge from insights derived through a deep understanding and interpretations of a wide-variety of information.[24]

This insight became A. G. Lafley's focal point when he became CEO of P & G. When he assumed the position, only 15% of innovations emerged from external sources. He sought to raise that to 50% through his "Connect & Develop" initiative.[25] As shareholders now know, the strategy worked quite well. In sum, the inwardly focused company lacks the competitive instincts to survive because it fails to pick up on the weak signals in the environment.

Phase Imbalance

Similar concerns emerge when any one phase in the process dominates. This can occur for any number of reasons. For example, if your most talented employees relish the evaluation process, it can crowd out those who naturally seek out new ideas. Likewise, if employees get caught up seeking new ideas, they may avoid making hard choices about which ideas to pursue. The perpetual graduate student suffers from this affliction; he or she simply cannot make a choice about a direction because every idea seems so alluring.

Sometimes the proportions are wrong because leaders simply skip a stage. For example, some people bounce between seeking and evaluating as if it were a ping-pong match. They never allow time for an idea to incubate (e.g., lack of nurturing). Sometimes the incubation occurs as we slumber, which allows our unconscious mind to make the subtle connections we could not make in the bright of day. Sleep researchers have concluded that "because new learning processes are inactivated, during sleep we can reorganize and more efficiently store the information already in the brain."[26] Bottom line: If you skip the stage, you will probably jump over actionable ideas necessary for progress.

WHAT TO DO?

Progress makers use a number of tactics to ensure that they generate the right actionable ideas. We highlight below the most important ones.

Build "Discovery Time" Into the Schedule, Surroundings, and Job Duties

Fresh perspectives, new information, and novel experiences provide the raw material of the actionable idea engine. Progress grinds to a halt when deprived of this fuel. Unfortunately, the demands of day-to-day activities crowd out discovery time, leaving the actionable idea engine to run on fumes.

Progress makers respond to this natural tendency of the typical organization by building discovery time into the schedule, surroundings, and job duties. Google, for instance, designated by *Fast Company* magazine as one of the most innovative companies in the world, provides employees the opportunity to hear speakers ranging from religious ministers to rock musicians to Nobel Prize–winning scientists.[27] If employees cannot attend the session, they, of course, can watch proceedings on the Internet.[28] Surrounding employees with such diverse and brilliant minds keeps the ingenuity synapses buzzing as employees discover all kinds of unanticipated connections. They learn to discover subtle patterns, ascertain relationships between diverse fields, and detect weak signals that hint at important discoveries.[29] Companies without those resources can sponsor any number of activities to encourage discoveries:

- Take a tour of the zoo or battlefield or a business in a totally unrelated field
- Set up a resource center with diverse publications and strange gizmos
- Go to conventions about subjects not directly related to the business expertise

In short, effective leaders nudge their employees into serendipitous experiences that might prove valuable. This is what Alexander Graham Bell must have visualized when he said, "Leave the beaten track occasionally and dive into the woods. Every time you do so, you will be certain to find something that you have never seen before."[30]

A note of caution: This is serious play. It's *play* because we need to open our child-like mind to the novel, unusual, and intriguing, much like the anthropologist's mind-set. Tom Kelley, the general manager of IDEO, observed that those who assume the "anthropologist role seem unusually willing to set aside what they 'know,' looking past tradition and even their own preconceived notions. They have the wisdom to observe with a truly open mind."[31] It's *serious* because you expect original observations, connections, and insights to emerge at some point that might prove valuable.

Cultivate Employee Imagination

Albert Einstein once remarked, "Imagination is more important than knowledge. Knowledge is limited. Imagination encircles the world."[32] Since imagination often trumps knowledge, progress makers find ways to cultivate it. That proves difficult because employees frequently develop idiosyncratic ways of stoking their creative fires.

Consider, for example, the company IDEO. This global design consultancy has patented over 1,000 ideas since 1978 and designed an almost dizzying array of products, including the Microsoft mouse, Salad Spinner, Samuel Adams Tap Handle, Swiffer Sweeper, and even Dilbert's ultimate cubicle.[33] If you go into their design studios, you would find an equally zany smorgasbord of unusual items ranging from airplane wings to toys of every shape and size adorning walls, cabinets, and ceilings. This rich over-the-top environment stimulates the designers' imaginations in ways even the strongest cup of espresso couldn't emulate. This kind of visual wackiness works for them. The company is considered America's leading design firm.[34]

Yet, we should be careful about using this wildly successful company as a template. After all, some extraordinarily imaginative people seek out just the opposite environment. Consider the preferred working space of the artist Georgia O'Keefe, whose paintings of flowers, rocks, and landscapes are world renowned. The art world recognizes her as a seminal figure for her ability to blend the abstract and representational artistic tradition. Yet she would shun the crazy IDEO environment. Instead, her biographer explains,

> Georgia needed a neutral space in which to conceptualize her dazzling colors. When the *Eagle* reporter asked in bewilderment, "Don't you like color?" Georgia's face broke into a grin. "Color does something to me," she replied, and she tried to explain why she needed to paint in a colorless room. "I like an empty wall because I can imagine what I like on it."[35]

What can we glean about imagination from these two extreme examples? Cultivating the right environment for the individual employee becomes the pivotal intervention point. The orchid and cactus blossom under very different conditions. The orchid flourishes in the rainforest surrounded by every imaginable type of plant. The cactus flowers in the rugged isolation of the desert. Likewise, progress makers nurture some employees' imaginations with lots of stimulation and others' by minimizing distractions.

Pay Attention to "Lead Users"

The traditional model of innovation is that companies first develop products and services, and then consumers evaluate. Thumbs up: Consumers approve, and the company generates a return on investment. Thumbs down: Consumers disapprove, and the firm loses the innovation lottery. That model still has merit, but it can be greatly augmented by a more co-creative collaboration between users and the company. In particular, companies can develop a lot of actionable ideas by paying attention to lead users of their products and services.

We owe this insight to Professor Eric von Hippel of MIT Sloan School of Management and his colleagues. He summarized his findings:

> Empirical studies show that many users—from 10 percent to nearly 40 percent—engage in developing or modifying products. . . . The findings make it very clear that users are doing a lot of product modification and product development in many fields.[36]

Lead users make modifications without compensation or much acclaim. They also tend to share their ideas willingly with others.

Windsurfers, for example, were frustrated by the tendency to fly off their boards when making aerial jumps. Some enterprising enthusiasts crafted make-shift footstraps for the boards. Presto. Now they could soar and flip and do all sorts of insanely terrifying stunts. These windsurfers were the lead users. Soon manufacturers picked up on the trend and starting crafting boards with their own straps.[37] That's what happens when you notice lead users: They can provide a lot of actionable ideas. We just need to pay attention. And the organizational payoff is not bad either. As Professor von Hippel notes, "The average lead user projects at 3M were conservatively forecast by management to be more than 8 times the sales forecast for new products developed in the traditional manner. . . . In addition, lead user projects were found to generate ideas for new product lines."[38]

Note that paying attention to lead users differs from the proverbial call to "listen to the customer."[39] After all, Henry Ford once said, "If I had asked my customers what they wanted, they'd have said a faster horse." Professor von Hippel advocates something more subtle; pay attention to what the lead users *do,* not necessarily what they *say.* Moreover, it's not a "majority rules" decision. Rather, some users/customers set trends and others do not. Observe the trend setters at the right time and you will increase the likelihood of discovering actionable ideas.

Use the Right Skills at the Right Time

Creativity experts agree that "a big mistake people make is to start visualizing the criticism or the feedback while they're still generating (ideas). That can shut you right down."[40] Criticism, evaluation, and analysis are NOT the culprits. Rather, what robs us of creativity is using these skills at the wrong time. Evaluating an idea immediately after conception steals away time from further exploration, contemplation, and proper nurturing (e.g., sharpshooting). Think of a new idea like an infant: It needs oodles of tender care and praise, not evaluation and criticism. The time for that will come soon enough.

Progress makers paint a sharp bold line between the idea generation phase and the other phases. What's appropriate in one phase is not appropriate in another. In particular, enact this rule: Ban evaluation and critique during brainstorming. No exceptions. But relax the rule when you move to the nurturing phase. Tear up the rule and create new ones in the evaluation phase. That's when assessment skills assume a prominent role. You want to have a sober analysis of the relative strengths and weaknesses of the notion before taking action. That's the right skill at the right time, too.

Insisting on using the "right skill at the right time" sounds effortless. It's not. Why? Because people often do not have equally developed skill sets. It's like being born left- or right-handed. And the less practice we have using our opposite skill or hand, the less likely we are to use it. High school basketball coaches teach their players to shoot both left- and right-hand layups. Progress makers do the same with the naturally right-brained creative types and left-brained analytical types. The good news, for high school coaches and progress makers, is that most people can develop both skill sets. Of course, there are always some people who choose not to do so. And everyone has a natural predominance of handedness and "mindedness." Progress makers take this into account. They marvel at creativity but not the creative speller. They appreciate regimentation but not the regimented creative director. Such are the tensions progress makers manage with aplomb.

Articulate Criteria Used to Evaluate
Ideas at Different Phases in the Process

The business stories that get the press often highlight zany ideas that end up generating stellar results. Fair enough. Progress makers value novelty, as well. But such stories often edit out the hard work done during the nurturing and evaluation phases. The news stories barely mention the countless other ideas rejected by that process. Consequently, people often draw the wrong conclusion from the press reports and focus all their attention on phase one, seeking new ideas. Or worse, they focus on seeking the one "killer idea" instead of bringing numerous possibilities into the process.

Progress makers recognize that the wacky idea that garners all the press attention usually emerges from a thoughtfully developed nurturing and evaluating process. Consequently, progress makers expend a great deal of intellectual capital conceptualizing the success measures in each phase. And then they expend considerable energy communicating the criteria to their people.

The criteria will vary by type of idea and organization. But we can offer some broad brush strokes as a starting point: In the idea-seeking phase, look for a lot of novel ideas from a wide range of perspectives. In the nurturing phase, measure success by asking the following:

- Are we giving useful feedback?
- Are we providing proper resources for development?

- Are we being appropriately patient?
- Are we pursuing the idea in a timely manner?

In the evaluation phase, we would do well to heed the advice of "America's Top New Product Idea Man," Doug Hall. He claims that *Merwyn,* his research-based business idea tester, can dramatically boost the success rate for new initiatives. He boils down the decision during the evaluation phase to three questions:

- What's in it for the customer (specifically, obviously, directly)?
- Why should the customers believe you will deliver on the promise?
- How revolutionary are your benefits and reasons to believe you can deliver on the promise (dramatic difference)?[41]

Progress makers also ask about the benefits their business will derive from pursing the idea. This moves the return-on-investment issue to center stage.

Successful leaders hone these general criteria or craft their own (see Figure 13.4). Regardless, the criteria are widely discussed, illustrated, and championed. Without this concerted educational effort, employees often become confused. They may rely on their natural inclinations or even glean the

Figure 13.4 **Assessment Criteria**

Seeking Phase	Nurturing Phase	Evaluation Phase
• Do we have a *wide range of ideas* from various domains to choose from? • Do we have a *lot of ideas* in each domain to choose from? • Are we involving enough people with *different perspectives*?	• Are we giving useful *feedback*? • Are we providing proper developmental *resources*? • Are we being *appropriately patient*? • Are we pursing the idea in a *timely manner*?	• Are we providing *significantly new benefits* to customers/users? • Are we clearly *articulating* customer/user *benefits*? • Are we providing adequate reasons for the customer/user to *believe we can deliver* the benefits? • Will we see the proper *return on our investment*?

wrong lesson from sexy business press stories. Consequently, progress makers commit to explaining the varying criteria and the related rationale.

Evaluate Ideas by Examining Attributes Rather Than Relying on Initial Impressions

Consider a situation where a team presents a new marketing brochure to the manager. Poor evaluations simply reject or accept an idea out of hand as in, "That's no good" or "Let's go with it." Even the most astute learner would glean little from these comments. A more frequently made—and slightly better—evaluation directs attention to the upside and downside of an idea as in, "I like the texture of the paper but don't like the colors." In this case, the developer can target some improvements. But a great evaluation would focus on key attributes of the packaging and peel off benefits and concerns from each attribute: "The 100-pound paper used for the brochure (attribute) feels sturdy but I'm worried about mailing costs." Note how this last comment (1) invites further discussion about the trade-offs, (2) offers valuable lessons about business constraints, and (3) encourages further development.

We call this the ABC method: Attributes, Benefits, and Concerns. It starts by ascertaining the key attributes or features of the idea. Next you specify the important benefits and concerns of each attribute on a line-by-line basis (see Figure 13.5). Such an approach directs attention first to description and then to evaluation. So what? Those who use this technique soon discover that it promotes more thoughtful discussions centered on objective facts rather than impressionistic judgments. It dampens the "wow" or "ugh" initial reactions in favor of a more sober analysis. ABC veterans soon learn that it is often easier to alter an attribute than an initial emotional impression. And that's exactly the way effective leaders manage the thoughts and emotions of their actionable idea pioneers.

The conundrum is that progress makers cannot pursue ALL ideas. In fact, they need to set aside many ideas in order to devote resources to those that have the greatest probability of yielding fruit. If you use the ABC method, you stop the ideas with the least likelihood of success while not undermining the creative spirit of the idea generators. Sapping inventive energy is startlingly easy to do. It can happen with a mere dismissive roll of the supervisor's eyes. It can occur with a manager's off-the-cuff query, "Are you serious?" It will surely happen when an executive sneers, "That's the stupidest idea I've ever

Figure 13.5 The ABC Method of Evaluation

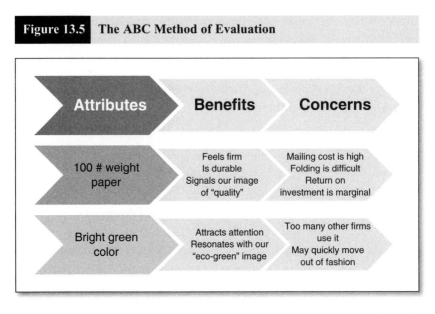

heard." However it materializes, once the creative oomph seeps away, it rarely bubbles back up. That's something progress makers resist with all their ingenuity, vigor, and skill. Instead, they properly frame the negative decision by

- *Praising the investment of personal energy.* Merely recognizing the developer's investment of time and energy sends powerful signals. It indicates that someone noticed and appreciated the effort. It provides some measure of satisfaction: "At least someone seemed to notice." Long after the sting of defeat fades, the *American Idol* losers smile as they remember the applause.

- *Providing perspective.* Suzy Welch, former editor-in-chief of *Harvard Business Review,* wrote a delightful book about the 10–10–10 rule. In a nutshell, she advocates looking at the impact of a decision from the perspective of 10 minutes, 10 months, and 10 years.[42] Such an approach can provide the proper perspective on a rejected idea. Ten minutes after rebuffing an idea, the employee will probably be disappointed, upset, and perhaps hostile. Effective leaders legitimize those emotions and allow employees time to work through them. Even then, though, progress makers offer perspective about (a) why the decision was made, (b) how it was made, (c) what alternatives were considered, and (d) how the decision fits with corporate values/initiatives.[43]

Hopefully, in 10 months, the employee will reflect on how the temporary setback spurred even further innovation. And in 10 years, perhaps the experience will be assimilated into a life lesson about managing setbacks and innovation.

- *Allowing for reflective stubbornness.* Highly innovative companies recognize that their actionable idea filter, like all other filters, occasionally will make mistakes. So some allow their employees to "secretly" work on innovative projects that were formally rejected.[44] Such programs educate employees in powerful ways about the innovation process. Think about the potent signals sent by pairing such programs with a formal actionable idea screening process: (1) The company may have made a mistake rejecting your idea, (2) the company wants you to carefully consider your continued pursuit of the idea, and (3) the company wants you to stubbornly pursue those ideas you believe have merit.

This all boils down to teaching employees the right lessons about actionable ideas. And if leaders don't teach those lessons, then employees will learn the wrong ones. Learning in organizations is inevitable, but learning the *right lesson* is not.[45] That's the job of progress makers because they want to keep the ideas flowing.

CONCLUDING THOUGHTS

Those who dwell in the world of ideas rarely commune with those who move in the world of action. Not many stereotypical professors emerge from their ivory towers to engage in thoughtful conversations with the ruff-hewn members of a professional hockey team. When those worlds *do collide,* the fallout can be an ugly mess. Few fans would pay to see the tweed-coated professor play hockey. Likewise, students would quickly tire of the hockey player attempting to explain the symbolism of Keats's *Ode on a Grecian Urn.* Yet those who *can synthesize* ideas and action create something magical. That's why we marvel at the accomplishments of Leonardo da Vinci, Benjamin Franklin, Thomas Edison, George Washington Carver, Georgia O'Keefe, Twyla Tharp, Richard Feynman, and others. It's what every progress maker knows deep in his or her soul; actionable ideas spark wonder even as they fuel progress. And that's why progress makers obsess over them.

PROGRESS MAKER PROFILE

LAURA HOLLINGSWORTH AND THE *DES MOINES REGISTER* AND GANNETT

Conventional wisdom suggests that newspapers are being strangled to death by bloggers, tweeters, and other assorted digital content movers.[46] Fortunately for the *Des Moines Register* and Gannett, Laura Hollingsworth has made a career out of challenging the conventional wisdom.

Shaking up traditions started early in her career when she was thrust into a supervisory role at the tender age of 22. Her task? Manage and refocus a group of seasoned newspaper ad personnel. Her challenge? Amid her team of six, several had decades more experience in traditional newspaper advertising sales than she did. Some did not readily embrace Laura's vision. She got push-back on many ideas she advocated, with retorts such as, "We've tried it before" or "That's just a new twist on an old idea." Her goal at the time was to shift the mind-set of her ad employees from "selling space" in the newspaper to "selling advertising ideas." This meant moving from a more passive to active role by seeking out new clients with products or services that could be advertised in the paper. It worked: With a focus on building customer relationships and offering creative new ideas and packaging, advertising sales in her territories of responsibility soared in the double digits. Laura's career took the same trajectory as she was promoted twice in the following 3 years.

This was a galvanizing experience. Laura realized early in her career that "either I'm going to be a catalyst for change or I'm going to go crazy and have to get out of it." So she became a change agent. Some changes were refinements of existing processes or products. For example, in 2000, Laura led the redesign of traditional classified sections to colorful, interactive content that were tied to Web components. That redesign was then duplicated in all of Gannett's community newspapers. Other changes came from exploring new opportunities. For example, in 2001, Laura was part of a team of Gen-X employees that designed highly successful new print and Web products designed for the 25–34 age group. Progress was always her central priority, which she measures by looking for "the growing viability and value of your products/services" in a fast-moving marketplace.

Laura readily acknowledges that making timely progress in large, complex, and decentralized organizations proves exceedingly challenging.

She looked back on her career in the newspaper industry and asked some fascinating questions:

> Why didn't newspaper executives create eBay? After all, we sold all kinds of second-hand products in the classified ads. Why didn't we create Craigslist? After all, newspapers pioneered personal ads, help-wanted ads, and the like. We owned the connecting point and that marketplace. Why didn't we lead the charge toward blogging? After all, for decades newspapers have published "Letters to the Editor."

These are troubling questions because eBay, Craigslist, blogs, and others represent forgone opportunities. Laura candidly admits that the newspaper industry "missed numerous potential launch points." It is what the former CEO of Intel, Andy Grove, described as strategic inflection points, which he defined as occurring "when the balance of forces shifts from the old structure, from the old ways of doing business and the old way of competing, to the new."[47] If you miss those points, you miss major opportunities. And that's exactly what happened in the newspaper business: The Internet separated the "news" from the "paper" by providing alternative delivery mechanisms for the news.

So why did the industry miss the opportunities? That's the question that Laura pondered. It was not for lack of imagination or ideas. Nor was it due to a shortage of intelligence or insight. Years before the Internet blossomed, Laura was involved in numerous discussions with very smart, well-informed employees about the possibilities of the World Wide Web. Early on they saw the potential of the Internet for classified ads, marketplaces, community "bulletin boards," and dating sites.

Why did the digital entrepreneurs win out? Laura believes it boils down to three issues. First, the traditional newspaper was a very profitable business at the time of these imaginative discussions, and there was a huge amount of revenue to be lost or given up with "free" models. It was extremely difficult to shift resources away from a large, steady revenue stream—particularly to a new, less certain platform—even when executives saw threats out in the future. Second, there was a lack of urgency. There were no signal flares announcing the perfect time to launch a new enterprise. Third, since individual newspaper sites operated autonomously, there was "no mechanism to channel these discussions and easily pilot new ideas."

(Continued)

(Continued)

These insights influence her thinking to this very day, particularly in her role as president and publisher of the *Des Moines Register* and West Group President of Gannett's U.S. Community Publishing division. Laura vigorously seeks way to break this pattern of brilliant discussions followed by anemic reactions that lead to missed opportunities.

Her approach congealed into three firm convictions: First, organizations must dedicate resources to unproven ventures, particularly during the "good times." Second, no one can tell you the precise moment to launch a new platform. When she first saw the Progress Model, she immediately focused on the final node of Platform 1. She asked, "How do you know when you are at the bottom node and it's time to jump to a new platform?" She answered her own question moments later: "No one can tell you. You just have to sense it. You can only determine that by using your 'gut instinct' based on a deep understanding of the business and of people." Third, organizations need a formal mechanism or structure to surface and act on the ideas generated in exploratory discussions. So how did Laura put this idea into action? "We've built innovation centers, held creative workout sessions, and encouraged local exploration time. Ideas can start at the front line and make their way to fruition. Those channels didn't exist even 10 years ago. And the people in the industry are finally working well together toward our future."

While these convictions ground her leadership philosophy, she also recognizes that others might not understand them in the same instinctive way. Many journalists see the blogs and other uncensored electronic outlets as a threat to their professional careers. She does not. She intensely believes that in-depth, high-quality, and engaging news and information will always be a top priority for consumers. How it gets received, whether it be via print or electronically, matters less. She reassures the professionals by noting, "If we shut down the newspaper today, someone would open up an operation across the street doing what we do. Maybe they would do a better job because they wouldn't put hindrances we put on ourselves. They'd seize a huge opportunity and make a lot of money. Why don't we just do it instead of them?" She often repeats statements like this, which blends reassurance and a challenge into an elixir to move people forward. She believes that "the customer should be able to have access to their information in any form, at any time, with any frequency and at any level of depth that they choose." That's why she readily embraces the new technology some journalists fear or shun.[48] It also explains her relentless pursuit of progress; the forms change rapidly, and consumer demands shift constantly.

Such sentiments led her to form a "client solutions group" under the business umbrella of the *Des Moines Register*. The group's mission is to extend on the strategic shift she advocated as a young supervisor. In particular, she set up a division designed to help clients coordinate their advertising campaigns, improve brand positioning, and better utilize emerging technology. The staff uses their extensive knowledge of traditional newspaper readers and users of other media. The division advises clients on key marketing and advertising decisions and takes an active role in measuring the results of the advertising. As a result, the division produces "killer creative" for the client.

All these activities may sound like nothing more than a traditional marketing or advertising firm. That perspective understates the uniqueness of this particular division by failing to take into account several salient facts. First, Laura had to persuade others of the wisdom for this move. After all, this dramatic step represented a major departure from the traditional role of the newspaper. It was a move into more of a consultancy role rather than simply being a provider of services. It would be like a grocery store offering nutritional counseling as well as merchandise. Second, the expertise for this kind of operation did not exist in the organization at the time of the proposal. She recruited the former vice president of a respected advertising agency with unique marketing experience to head up the division. The now successful leader originally rebuffed Laura's offer because it was a "crazy idea for a newspaper to have a marketing arm like we envisioned." Third, other newspapers under the Gannett umbrella have started similar divisions as a result of Laura's original idea. Importantly, the division has become a major profit center for the company. In short, the client solutions group represents a successful new platform that stands in contrast to previous missed opportunities.

Laura says that rapid technology innovations, competition, and the global economic crisis have driven and opened the industry to change faster than at any other point in the past. She continues in her progress-making role for the Gannett Company and says with a laugh, "I don't foresee a shortage of opportunities to lead change and make things happen."

(Continued)

(Continued)

LESSONS LEARNED

- **Trust your gut instinct when deciding to leap to a new platform.** No one can give you a formula for when you should launch a new endeavor. You have to rely on your thorough knowledge of the business, stakeholders, and opportunities. Leaders have to define the entry point and get others on board.

- **Resist the lure of predictable, solid profits.** Why? It can only last so long. How long? If you can think of the possibilities, someone else will, as well. And they will act on it. Therefore, wise executives use the predictable profits to fund new initiatives that may yield significant returns.

- **Create organizational structures that institutionalize listening, exploring, and innovation.** It is not enough to just have discussions about new trends. You need mechanisms that allow you to fund and implement new ideas.

NOTES

1. A. Lashinsky, "The Decade of Steve." *Fortune,* November 23, 2009, 93–100.

2. P. Elkind, "The Trouble With Steve." *Fortune,* March 17, 2008, 88–98, 156, p. 94.

3. Ibid., 94.

4. L. Kahney, *Inside Steve's Brain.* New York: Portfolio, 2008.

5. J. Fagerberg, "Innovation: A Guide to the Literature," in *The Oxford Handbook of Innovation,* edited by J. Fagerberg, D. Mowery, and R. Nelson. Oxford, UK: Oxford University Press, 2006, 1–26, p. 4.

6. G. Colvin, "Xerox Inventor-in-Chief." *Fortune,* July 9, 2007, 65–72.

7. J. Lipman-Blumen, *The Allure of Toxic Leaders.* New York: Oxford University Press, 2005, 20.

8. "How P&G Plans to Clean Up." *BusinessWeek,* April 13, 2009, 44–45.

9. See Supreme Court case *Jacobellis v. Ohio,* 378 U.S. 184 (1964).

10. C. Prahalad and M. Krishnan, *The New Age of Innovation: Driving Co-Created Value Through Global Networks.* New York: McGraw-Hill, 2008.

11. H. Poincaré, *The Foundations of Science,* translated by George Bruce Halsted. New York: The Science Press, 1921, 355.

12. K. Rockwood, "Truly Intelligent Design." *Fast Company,* October 2008, 129–38.

13. J. Keyton, *Group Communication: Process and Analysis.* Mountain View, CA: Mayfield, 1999.

14. Personal interview, May 2, 2009.

15. "Suck It and See." *The Economist,* February 3, 2007, 8.

16. Fagerberg, "Innovation: A Guide to the Literature," 5.

17. A. Field, "Chart a New Course." *BusinessWeek SmallBiz,* August/September, 2009, 46–49, p. 46.

18. Ibid., 49.

19. D. Hall, *Jump Start Your Business Brain.* Cincinnati, OH: Eureka! Institute, 2001.

20. Ibid., 39.

21. However, some highly innovative companies allow their employees to use 15% of their work time to pursue their own original ideas. See the chapter on innovation in P. Clampitt, *Communicating for Managerial Effectiveness.* 4th ed. Thousand Oaks, CA: Sage, 2010.

22. R. Weisberg, *Creativity: Understanding Innovation in Problem Solving, Science, Invention and the Arts.* Hoboken, NJ: John Wiley, 2006.

23. Ibid.

24. Prahalad and Krishnan, *The New Age of Innovation,* 81.

25. J. Howe, *Crowdsourcing: Why the Power of the Crowd Is Driving the Future of Business.* New York: Crown Books, 2008, 9.

26. J. A. Hobson, *Sleep.* New York: Freeman, 1989, 189.

27. "The World's Most Innovative Companies." *Fast Company,* March 2009, 52–97.

28. http://www.youtube.com/user/AtGoogleTalks (accessed June 15, 2009).

29. R. Baron, "Opportunity Recognition as Pattern Recognition: How Entrepreneurs 'Connect the Dots' to Identify New Business Opportunities." *Academy of Management Perspectives,* February 2006, 104–19.

30. G. Linder, *Alexander Graham Bell.* Mankato, MN: Capstone, 1999, 20.

31. T. Kelley, *The Ten Faces of Innovation.* New York: Doubleday, 2005, 17.

32. A. Einstein, as quoted in A. Calaprice (editor), *The New Quotable Einstein.* Princeton, NJ: Princeton University Press, 2005.

33. www.ideo.com (accessed June 30, 2009).

34. T. Kelley, *The Art of Innovation: Lessons in Creativity From IDEO, America's Leading Design Firm.* London: Profile Books, 2004.

35. L. Lisle, *Portrait of an Artist: Georgia O'Keefe.* New York: Pocket Books, 1986, 184.

36. E. von Hippel, *Democratizing Innovation.* Cambridge, MA: MIT Press, 2005, 4.

37. Howe, *Crowdsourcing.*

38. Ibid., 15.

39. M. Treacy, "Ignore the Consumer." *Point,* September 2005, 15–19.

40. R. Epstein, in an interview conducted by M. DiChristina, "Let Your Creativity Soar." *Scientific American Mind,* June/July 2008, 24–31, p. 29.

41. Hall, *Jump Start Your Business Brain,* 63.

42. S. Welch, *10–10–10: A Life-Transforming Idea.* New York: Scribner, 2009.

43. P. Clampitt and M. L. Williams, "Decision Downloading." *MIT Sloan Management Review* 48 (2007): 77–82.

44. Clampitt, *Communicating for Managerial Effectiveness.* 4th ed.

45. G. Hirst, D. van Knippenberg, and J. Zhou, "A Cross-Level Perspective on Employee Creativity: Goal Orientation, Team Learning Behavior, and Individual Creativity." *Academy of Management Journal* 52, no. 2 (2009): 280–93.

46. N. Baker, "A New Page." *The New Yorker,* August 3, 2009, 24–30.

47. A. Grove, *Only the Paranoid Survive: How to Exploit the Crisis Points That Challenge Every Company.* New York: Doubleday, 1996, 32–33.

48. E. Schmidt, "How Google Can Help Newspapers." *Wall Street Journal,* December 3, 2009, A23.

☆ 14 ☆

SELECT, DETECT, AND
CORRECT THE PROPER ERRORS

———•◦•———

Every company needs people who have made mistakes and then made the most of them.

—Bill Gates

Comedians revel in our shortcomings, foibles, and day-to-day mishaps. They satirize celebrities' idiosyncrasies, ridicule politicians' verbal miscues, and laugh at our mistakes. But one comedian was not the least bit amused by a mistake that befell him. It was a simple error that almost had fatal consequences.[1] His heart surgeon performed bypass on the wrong artery—one of his good ones. He had to endure two bypass surgeries: one life saving, another unnecessary. He was in no mood for joking when he slapped a lawsuit on the surgeon. Who would be?

Errors, mistakes, and mishaps are inevitable, but they have different consequences. After all, Dana Carvey made a pretty good living skewering politicians, celebrities, and religious leaders. That's relatively harmless stuff. But operating on the wrong artery, well, that's on the complete other end of the spectrum. In fact, data from studies during the 1990s indicated that tens of thousands of people died each year due to medical errors in U.S. hospitals.[2] Of course, it's not just medical institutions that are susceptible to errors; this problem occurs in every organization. Unfortunately, "most organizations do a poor job of learning from failures, large and small."[3]

BACKGROUND

The English word *error* originated from the Latin word *errare,* which meant "to stray." Today the word retains shades of that meaning because we use the word *error* to designate when something strays from the proper path. That does not mean, though, that all disappointing results are caused by errors. For example, a successful operation on the proper artery does not guarantee the patient will survive. In short, we want to distinguish errors from "decisions or acts that lead to suboptimal results."[4] Results may disappoint, but in some situations, this may not have occurred because of an error in the procedure or decision-making process.

Long before the concept of the "learning organization" became a buzz phrase, Chris Argyris and Donald Schön published a book titled *Organizational Learning.*[5] In fact, Professor Argyris noted that his publisher asked him at the time, "Do you think this topic will ever be of interest to the business community?"[6] He explained that learning was fundamental to organizational performance because it involved the "detection and correction of error."[7] Indeed, it is hard to see how any organization could heed the advice of the latest business gurus without properly learning from error. If a company wants to go from "Good to Great," then it will need to rectify errors. If a company wants to train a cadre of "Six-Sigma Black Belts," then it better start focusing on error management. Indeed, toolkits designed to assess an organization's learning capability place considerable weight on the ability to analyze and share lessons learned.[8]

Moreover, highly effective companies often attempt to front-load errors for prevention and innovation purposes. For example, engineers use programs such as Autodesk to catch mistakes early in the design process for products ranging from escalators to mountain bikes. This often results in significant time and dollars savings.[9]

ERROR MANAGEMENT FRAMEWORK

During World War II, the Allies developed sophisticated radar to help them track enemy planes. This was brilliantly chronicled in an aptly titled book, *The Invention That Changed the World: How a Small Group of Radar Pioneers Won the Second World War and Launched a Technological Revolution.* The author, Robert Buderi, concludes that "the Atomic bomb only ended the war. Radar won it."[10] Buderi's conclusion should cause us to pause and reflect for a moment. He suggests that the historical accounts and headlines often do us a disservice when attempting to discern important success factors. Organizations' error management practices possess the same stealthy characteristics of radar: They're often hidden from view but vital to victory.

Radar provides a useful metaphor for discussing error correction processes. Different types of radar are used to spot aircrafts, cars, ships, and weather formations. The police officer's radar gun would not be very helpful in predicting the next thunderstorm; best to use the NEXRAD high-resolution Doppler weather radar for that task. In short, the radar system you develop determines what you choose to pay attention to.

First, you have to select the type of errors you want to identify and the appropriate radar for the situation (see Figure 14.1)

Effective error management, like radar, starts with proper selection. Many discussions of error management focus attention on detection and correction. That presupposes that everyone agrees on what counts for an error. Sometimes that's an accurate assumption, such as an obvious spelling error. Other times

Figure 14.1 **Error Management Model**

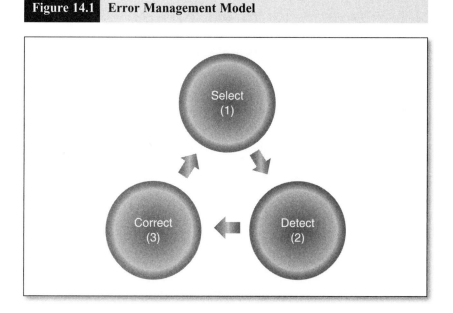

it's not. Why not? Just as the radar pioneers during World War II thought about the types of objects they desired to identify, progress makers ask about the types of errors they wish to discover (see Figure 14.2). Those choices are critical. Should we aim our radar at errors of omission or commission? Random errors or systematic ones? Latent errors or apparent ones? Minor errors or major ones? In an ideal world, the answer would be "all of the above." Unfortunately, few organizations can claim to have such a robust error management system.

Figure 14.2	Basic Types of Errors

Error Types			
Omission	Random	Latent	Major
Commission	Systematic	Apparent	Minor

Second, you use the selected radar to detect errors

Click on your computer's automatic spell checker and it highlights potential spelling errors. It cannot detect all the errors, but it does a pretty good job. Sometimes you get "false positives" or spellings that the radar detects as an error but are not. For example, many spell checkers will flag the word *organisation* as a misspelling, but it's not considered an error in the United Kingdom. At other times, you get "false negatives" when the spell checker fails to pick up an error that would be obvious to an English teacher. Consider the sentence, "Jack Welch is defiantly the best CEO General Electric ever had." Jack Welch was *definitely* the CEO of GE. Was he *defiant*? We'll leave that debate to others. All radar, no matter how sophisticated, suffers from these potential problems.

Third, you correct certain errors exposed by the radar detector

Detection often leads to correction—but not always. The skilled writer, for example, does not accept every spell checker recommendation (false positives). Nor does the writer trust the spell checker as the final authority (false negatives). Experts use their judgment to decide which errors to confront and when to correct them. This act of judgment can only be made in the context of the priorities at hand. Parents, for example, avoid correcting every syntax error of their 2-year-old.

In Figure 14.1, we show an arrow between correction and selection. We do this because sometimes unseen objects slip through the radar, fouling up the most thoughtful plans. In fact, the radar itself often needs to be fine tuned. For example, despite the most sophisticated radar in the world, Canadian geese brought down US Airways Flight 1549 in New York City. After Captain Sullenberger's heroic landing on the Hudson River, engineers started looking at how to develop radar specially designed to detect large flocks of geese in the path of airplanes.[11] Likewise, unidentified organizational errors often prompt executives to look for more refined tools to prevent similar incidents in the future.

THE COUNTERFORCES

Given the potential benefits of learning from error, it would seem reasonable that organizations would readily embrace error detection and correction. Most do not. Why not? There are very strong personal and organizational forces pushing against proper error management.

First, the natural human tendency to "save face" often inhibits employees, managers, and executives from acknowledging mistakes

A host of well-documented "defensive behaviors," such as making overly evaluative comments, showing expressions of superiority, and creating appearances of certainty, serve to protect fragile egos.[12] As two scholars wrote, "Honest acknowledgment of one's failures is not only unpleasant, it also can strike a blow to one's self-esteem, self-image, and identity."[13] When most people are given a choice between preserving their self-esteem and admitting they made an error, most will opt for self-esteem. Many people equate admitting error with admitting failure. As a result, they end up deceiving themselves and placing blame elsewhere. This keeps their self-confidence intact at the expense of a more realistic analysis of the situation.

For some people, this may be a passive reflexive response, but for others, error avoidance takes on a more active verbal character. In fact, this is not a silent majority; it is often a quite vocal one. Consider a situation in which someone forgets to place contact information on a brochure sent to potential clients. A week later, after thousands were mailed to consumers, one astute executive, not involved in the decision, notices the omission. Now what? Think of the face-saving possibilities:

- "I was involved in another aspect of the brochure. Someone else was supposed to check the final edition." (*Shifting blame*)
- "Our energies were devoted to developing an innovative design that would really impress our customers. While we were trying so hard to be innovative, creative, and ground-breaking, I guess we just forgot that detail." (*Maximizing motives*)
- "The decision was made by a committee." (*Obscuring ownership*)
- "This was just an image campaign, and besides, they can get the contact information on our Web site." (*Minimizing impact*)
- "You've made your share of minor gaffes, as well." (*Attacking the accuser*)

These statements have one common attribute: No one takes responsibility for the error or acknowledges their own fallibility. They all envelop the employee in a cloak of what we might call "ego-protective foolhardiness."[14] The authors of the wonderfully titled book, *Mistakes Were Made (But Not by Me),* sum up these tendencies best: "When we make mistakes, we must calm the cognitive dissonance that jars our feelings of self-worth. And so we create fictions that absolve us of responsibility, restoring our belief that we are smart, moral, and right—a belief that often keeps us on a course that is dumb, immoral, and wrong."[15]

Second, the "confirmation bias" amplifies all of our error-deflecting tendencies[16]

That is, humans actively seek out information that confirms preexisting opinions. Rather than acting like a respectable scientist, most people fail to seek out counterevidence. So, those employees who view themselves as competent will actively avoid any evidence that hints at a counterview.

Consider, for example, the candid revelations of the world-class physicist Freeman Dyson. As a young man, his collegiate career at the University of Cambridge was interrupted by World War II. He served in the Operational

Research Section of the British Royal Air Force's Bomber Command. His group's job was to provide scientific advice about the effectiveness of bombing campaigns and force protection measures. At the time, the prevailing wisdom was that as bomber crews gained more experience, their chances of survival significantly increased. That was a myth. Dyson acknowledged years later that "experience did not reduce loss rates."[17] He continues,

> The evidence showed that the main cause of losses was an attack that gave experienced crews no chance either to escape or to defend themselves. If we had taken the evidence more seriously, we might have discovered the Schräge Musik in time to respond with effective countermeasures.[18]

The mysterious weapon, the Shräge Musik, allowed German fighters to fly underneath the bombers and fire up at a 60-degree angle. As a result, the British bombers incurred substantial losses—they never knew what hit them. Unfortunately, that's how the confirmation bias works. We see what we want to see. We don't see the errors of our ways and are doomed to repeat them (ego-protective foolhardiness at work). The experience myth held powerful psychological sway, inhibiting careful assessment that could have revealed a thinking error and saved countless airmen's lives.

Third, organizational cultures can inhibit proper error management

Some federal regulators, for example, who tried to warn members of Congress about the potential financial troubles of Fannie Mae and Freddie Mac were ridiculed and denounced. Years later, many believe the defaults by these two quasi-governmental entities helped ignite a worldwide recession.[19] These types of organizational practices and reactions can lead to widespread suppression of error reporting. Employees will naturally engage in a cost-benefit analysis before discussing an error: They will weigh the benefits of reporting against the material costs, effort costs, and damage to personal reputation.[20] Often, they will choose silence and pass on those high costs to the organization or others—including taxpayers.[21]

Error reporting and analysis tends to diminish when an organization fails to create a shared problem-solving climate and the proper psychological safety for employees.[22] Conducting candid discussions about mistakes poses a special challenge for supervisors because they might be tempted to punish those who admit errors. Unfortunately, many supervisors relish playing the "train 'em & blame 'em" game. On the flipside, a cooperative problem-solving climate helps change employees' cost-benefit analysis. For example, the U.S Air Force will not penalize pilots for reporting errors within 24 hours of an incident.[23]

WHAT TO DO?

Few people would argue against the *idea* of proper error management. Yet, as we have discussed, many powerful personal and organizational forces are aligned against the *practice* of it. Progress makers mount an equally potent counterattack against these forces. They know how to put the idea of effectively managing errors into practice. That's our focus in this section.

Conceptualize the Errors You Wish to Monitor

All errors are not created equal, nor should they be treated that way. The military uses different types of radar for different threats. Likewise, progress makers envision the types of errors they want others to pay attention to. That depends greatly on whether you are in the exploring or refining modes.

Exploring Errors

The exploring mode requires a different type of radar than the refining mode. When exploring or seeking innovations, there needs to be a high tolerance for what many might call errors or mistakes. Bell Labs, for instance, made a "deliberate mistake" by offering "no deposit" services to 100,000 high-risk consumers. Why? They wanted to test the assumptions of their financial models, which stipulated that those customers should pay a substantial deposit. The high deposits protected the company and discouraged some customers from purchasing the service. It turned out the models were flawed and the company learned something significant. Indeed, these "high-risk" customers ended up adding "on average, $137 million to the Bell System's bottom line every year for the next decade."[24] In short, they intentionally committed an "error" to test the assumptions of their business model.

Innovators embrace "mistakes." We should be disappointed when a promising AIDS vaccine fails a clinical trial but not surprised.[25] Innovation is about adroitly playing the odds. Even with the most brilliant insights, overflowing energy, and the right resources, some new ideas or platforms just don't work out. How, then, should a leader define "error" when exploring, innovating, and establishing a new platform? Answer "no" to any of the questions below and you may be committing an exploring error.

- *Did we exercise due diligence before launching the innovative venture?* Researchers suggest that 80% to 90% of new products or services will fail within a year or two. Why? Two scholars conclude "they fail primarily because customers didn't want them."[26] Clearly, not every new platform will be successful. But the research suggests that the failure rate could be significantly reduced with more emphasis on better market research.

- *Did we fail early enough in the process?* Before the official launch of Amazon.com, Jeff Bezos asked his employees to engage friends in testing the site by making mock purchases. The test run lasted 3 months and eventually involved 300 people from various walks of life. By discovering and fixing these errors early in the process, the company was able to launch a virtually bug-free site.[27] The former CEO of Proctor & Gamble, A. G. Lafley, echoed Bezos's sentiments: "You learn more from failure . . . but the key is to fail early, fail cheaply, and don't make the same mistake twice."[28]

- *Did we identify lessons learned?* Zappos.com has sold more shoes online than anyone in the world. CEO Tony Hsieh walks with a calm confidence because he learned early in his career about the power of a company's culture. And if employees don't buy into the values quickly enough, best to quickly cut your losses and ask them to leave. Perhaps that explains the company's policy of offering "$2,000 to anyone who completes the week-long training program and doesn't want to stay."[29] Few choose to walk away with the cash.

Refining Errors

When refining or executing a routine task, the error detection radar shifts to other matters. Professor Lee Williams helped to design a special research project for this book about this particular issue.[30] He identified 17 typical errors that organizations often seek to manage such as customer service, information management, and scheduling. The research revealed that for most organizations, customer service and quality errors were the most likely to be selected and detected (see Table 14.1). These results were not particularly surprising.

Table 14.1 **Types of Errors Most Organizations Recognize**

Type of Recognized Error	Rank	Mean[a]	Likely to Recognize Errors (%)[b]
Customer service	1	5.5	62
Quality of product or service	2	5.3	57
Hiring decisions	3	5.0	46
Production	4	5.0	43
Management of crises	5	4.9	46
Public relations	5	4.9	43
Training	7	4.9	45
Scheduling	8	4.9	40
Use of technology	9	4.8	44
Marketing	10	4.6	34
Strategic direction	11	4.6	36
Purchasing decisions	11	4.6	31
Management of employee performance	13	4.6	32
Employee communications	14	4.5	32
Personnel promotions	15	4.5	30
Management of change	16	4.4	30
Management of information	17	4.3	31

a. Mean for a scale ranging from 1 = *highly unlikely to learn from errors* to 7 = *highly likely to learn from errors*, with 4 being *neutral*.

b. Collapsed *highly likely* (7) and *moderately likely* (6) to create *likely to recognize errors*.

However, the research about the different error detection practices used by well-led versus less well-led organizations raised a few eyebrows (see Table 14.2).

The research clearly demonstrated that well-led organizations chose significantly more issues to monitor than their less well-led counterparts.[31] In particular, Figure 14.3 compares the radar screens of well-led organizations to their counterparts. Note that the well-led organization paid attention to 12 issues; their counterparts only matched their concerns on two issues. Well-led organizations

Table 14.2	Learning From Errors: The Difference Between Well-Led and Not Well-Led Organizations

Type of Error	*Well-Led Organizations (%)*	*Not Well-Led Organizations (%)*	*Significant Difference*
Customer service	73	43	*
Quality of product or service	71	31	*
Management of crises	64	23	*
Use of technology	55	30	*
Production	63	25	*
Public relations	49	23	*
Strategic direction	51	16	*
Hiring decisions	56	24	*
Training	54	23	*
Scheduling	47	28	*
Purchasing decisions	40	28	*
Management of information	50	9	*
Marketing	38	19	*
Management of change	36	11	*
Employee communications	35	9	*
Management of employee performance	36	16	*
Personnel promotions	40	15	*

NOTE: The scale ranged from 1 = *highly unlikely to learn from errors* to 7 = *highly likely to learn from errors,* with 4 being *neutral.* The results were tabulated by adding the *highly likely* (7) and *moderately likely* (6) to create percentage of *likely to learn from errors.*

*A significant difference was noted when the *T* tests performed met the $p < .001$ criteria.

do something further; they tend to pay attention to more and "smaller" errors. They recognize that proactively and doggedly addressing "small errors" helps prevent larger ones.[32] For example, the quick detection and correction of scheduling errors can clearly decrease the likelihood of major customer service errors.

| **Figure 14.3** | **Radar Screens of Well-Led and Less Well-Led Organizations** |

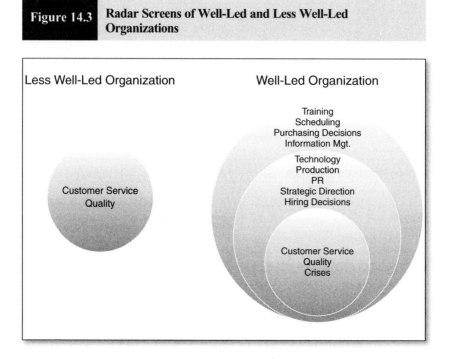

A note of caution: We've implied that the radar might vary from department to department or from time to time. This is the crucial "selection" part of the process. But these shifts may lead to employee confusion. In particular, they might ask, "Why are the rules so different for that division?" "Why are the rules so different now?" Progress makers clearly, confidently, and directly answer the inquiry, even when the query has not been verbalized. They do not apologize for the variation. Instead, they use this as an educational opportunity to explain how the rules of the game have changed because they're now playing a different game. No one would expect the rules of ballroom dancing to be the same as those in football. Likewise, when you move from exploring to refining (and vice versa), you have to shift the error radar screen.

Systematically Document and Analyze Errors to Discern Underlying Error Patterns

"Error documentation" sounds about as appealing as cleaning dishes. Everybody wants the results, but few get very excited about putting in the work to make it happen. Anyone who has used a Microsoft product has, at one time or another, been confronted with an annoying pop-up box that says, "The program is not responding . . . Please tell Microsoft about this problem." Every user benefits if the next version of the software eliminates the bug. Fortunately, many people do report their errors, resulting in upwards of 50 gigabytes of e-mails on an error-prone day.[33] Microsoft uses the reports to detect underlying software error patterns and make corrections in subsequent updates. Yet, many people blithely punch the "Don't send" button when they encounter this minor error reporting hassle. Even though most people know it helps build better software, they brush aside their mild obligation to the user community. After all, pushing the "Send" button may disrupt your thought process or interrupt a task; best just to ignore the report process and move on.

Unfortunately, such sentiments inhibit learning. Surgeon and MacArthur fellow Atul Gawande provides a more conscientious perspective. He offered some unusually simple advice to medical students: "count something."[34] In his quest to be a "positive deviant" (aka "a progress maker"), he notes that "if you count something you find interesting, you will learn something interesting."[35] He counted the number of times and situations in which surgical patients were sewed up with instruments or sponges inadvertently left in them. The patients with 13-inch retractors left in them weren't too happy with their surgical souvenirs. But it happens. More important, Dr. Gawande discovered a pattern to these incidents that could be corrected. In particular, the errors were far more likely to occur during emergency operations or when something unexpected happened during the procedure.

It was not an eclectic bunch of random errors but a systematic one. That's what positive deviants seek out and destroy. A random spelling *errror,* such as the one in this sentence, can be easily corrected and does not require any deep analytical investigation into underlying causes. Anyone—even the Scripps National Spelling Bee champion—who writes enough sentences will commit a random error. However, distinguishing between random and systematic errors is not always easy. In fact, the only way to do so is by (1) documenting all errors and (2) methodically analyzing them with an eye toward underlying patterns. The instructor, for instance, who notices a particular student's penchant for run-on sentences might encourage the student to head down to the writing center for some specialized instruction. In the ideal world, it would work just like that.

Rigorous documentation and analysis have allowed researchers to discover a number of intriguing patterns that have practical implications:

- DNA evidence has overturned a number of convictions. Eyewitness testimony errors accounted for the majority (71%) of the evidence used in these wrongful convictions. *So what?* Investigators should be wary of eyewitness accounts and focus on other types of evidence.[36]

- Researchers determined that professional tennis referees "called many more balls 'out' that were actually in play rather than vice versa."[37] *So what?* In tournaments where the players can challenge calls, they should "concentrate their challenges on balls that are called 'out.'" Or maybe the French have it right: Everyone should use clay courts. Then you can see the ball's skid mark.[38]

- Studies have shown that when gastroenterologists make errors conducting and reading colonoscopies, they usually miss the polyps on the right side of the colon. *So what?* Specialists speculate on several possible sources of this systematic error. But clearly one actionable idea is for gastroenterologists to be more vigilant during the procedure when examining the right side of the colon.[39]

In each of these cases, there are some powerful, natural human perceptual biases at the root of the error. For example, the tennis ball judgment error springs from a common and well-known perceptual mistake. These underlying causes may be important in crafting responses. Progress makers seize on the next steps or the "so what's." Doing so increases the likelihood of progress.

Evaluate, Recalibrate, and Adjust the Radar Detectors

Statisticians warn of two distinctly different types of errors that are inherent to any kind of testing: false-positive and false-negative errors.[40] As we discussed above, false-positive errors (Type I) occur when an error has been detected but did not actually occur. For example, when the spam filter on your computer incorrectly flags a message from your boss as spam, it commits a Type I error. False-negative errors (Type II) occur when a test fails to pick up an error that actually occurred. In this case, the spam filter fails to detect that the e-mail from a Tanzanian bank official promising riches is nothing more than a spam scam.

Statisticians tweak their methods and procedures to avoid both types. Their preoccupation with these concerns arises from the inherent nature of the process of error detection. Ironically, the more often you look for errors, the more likely you are bound to make errors. That does not mean you stop trying to detect the errors; rather, you seek to minimize the possibilities of either type of error. You don't throw away the spam filter because it makes mistakes; instead, you recalibrate and hone the decision-making rules.[41]

Progress makers confront similar issues. Unfortunately, grappling with flaws in the error detection radar screen often proves trickier than adjusting the spam filter decision rules. Consider, for example, the difficulty of accurately ascertaining who genuinely suffers a posttraumatic stress disorder (PTSD). How do you distinguish between war veterans experiencing the normal readjustment period to civilian life and those with PTSD? We would expect veterans to have some hellish nightmares. When does that cross over into PTSD? Richard McNally, a Harvard psychologist, argues, "PTSD is a real thing, without a doubt, but as a diagnosis PTSD has become so flabby and overstretched, so much a part of the culture, that we are almost certainly mistaking other problems for PTSD and thus mistreating them."[42]

Debating a complex issue like this reveals the difficulty and importance of confronting false-positive (Type I) errors. Those who raise such issues often encounter resistance to those with a vested interest in addressing the errors. In this case, some members of the psychiatric community deride Professor McNally's notions. Yet, the debate challenges should not obscure the importance of getting this right. If this particular error becomes institutionalized, then the misdiagnosis will result in soldiers receiving the wrong treatments and, in some cases, will actually promote chronic disability. Such are the stakes when someone selects a defective radar screen.

Similar dire consequences emerge from false-negative results. Progress makers also ask why they failed to pick up on a particular type of error earlier in the process. In other words, how do we adjust our radar screen to avoid false-negative (Type II) errors? Why, for example, would institutional investors such as Fairfield Greenwich Advisors and Bank Medici fail to recognize Bernie Madoff's massive Ponzi scheme?[43] Why would the editors of the *New York Times* fail to pick up on the almost propagandistic reports from their correspondent, Walter Duranty, about Stalinist Russia?[44] How could the reporter have missed the Stalin-induced Ukrainian famine-genocide that starved to death millions in the Ukraine? In both cases, the existing radar detectors failed to detect a blip as massive as a formation of military cargo planes. The consequences of false negatives are worse than false positives. In these cases, we have executives, investors, and policymakers infused with false confidence.

Confronting both types of errors may seem complex, difficult, and potentially contentious. Correct on all counts. Nevertheless, the importance far outweighs the costs of getting the radar screens in place and making them function in the way intended.

Adjust Error Detection and Correction
Responsibilities of Stakeholders

Can a quality control department or quality inspectors effectively reduce errors? Perhaps. But as one founder of the quality movement, W. Edwards Deming, wrote long ago in his ground-breaking book, "Unfortunately, quality control departments have taken the job of quality away from the people that can contribute most to quality—management, supervisors, managers of purchasing, and production workers."[45] Thoughtful leaders carefully think about who should have the primary error detection and correction responsibilities. Consider the following examples:

The U.S. Army—The U.S. Army prides itself on getting the mission accomplished whatever the odds. How do they do it? One widely emulated practice is the Army's After Action Review process or AAR (it's not official in the military without an appropriate acronym). What is it? The official definition: "a professional discussion of an event, focused on performance standards, that enables soldiers to discover for themselves what happened, why it happened, and how to sustain strengths and improve on weaknesses."[46] The discussion can be formal or informal. Regardless, the objective is to candidly detect and correct errors as quickly as possible. By doing so, they can weave the improvements into the next mission. That may be why the U.S. Army claims a difference between being "strong" and "Army strong." Indeed, businesses that make extensive use of AARs soon learn that "employees work harder to detect flaws and concoct fixes, because their ideas will live on long after the project has ended."[47]

Wikipedia—The vast majority of college students know that Wikipedia is "a freely licensed encyclopedia written by volunteers in many languages" and available to any Internet user.[48] Ready accessibility entices many, but so does the Wikipedia's breathtaking scope. By containing over "10 million articles across some 200 languages," it is many times larger than two comprehensive competitors: *Encyclopedia Britannica* and another online encyclopedia, *Encarta*.[49] Sounds great, but what about quality? Since Wikipedia literally changes every second, any assessment about quality must be provisional. Therein lurks the hidden hazard and transparent allure. The hazard is that some in the digital community will vandalize the site or push political agendas.[50] To guard against these problems, Wikipedia has tightened its editing rules.[51] The allure of Wikipedia, though, allows users to quickly address its impurities, imbalances, and imperfections. The moment someone notices an error of omission or commission, it can be corrected. No one has to wait for *World Book Encyclopedia* to send out the amendment "stickers" to correct errors or add updates. In fact, Jimmy Wales remembers dutifully applying the stickers to the appropriate pages in this treasure trove of knowledge.[52] Who is Jimmy Wales? He's the one we have to thank for Wikipedia. He founded the enterprise.

In each of these cases, the responsibility for error detection, selection, and correction shifted from those who would have had the customary duty. The U.S. Army shifted away from a strictly hierarchical approach to error management, and Wikipedia moved error detection away from the experts to all the Netizens of the world. The responsibility shift builds three important attributes into the error management process: speed, habit, and collaboration.

First, in each case, the errors are quickly detected and corrected

The moment Wikipedia volunteers spot an error, they address it. Immediately after a mission, the Army unit can identify concerns and move on to the next mission. Speed combats our natural self-deception mechanisms, such as altering our memory of events and shifting blame.

Second, error detection and correction is considered
a regular, routine part of day-to-day activities

Such practices certainly square with the advice of Joseph Hallinan, the author of *Why We Make Mistakes*. His advice about how to make fewer mistakes? "Think small."[53] We think small by making it a habit to routinely root out the everyday mistakes and learning the proper lessons.

Third, each example involves collaboration with others

Wikipedia involves a global alliance of volunteers checking, monitoring, and updating on a routine basis. In the U.S. Army, the team gets down to the nitty-gritty details in these candid discussions that even superiors might not recognize as potential problems. They heed Albert Einstein's maxim that "Not everything that can be counted counts and not everything that counts can be counted." A collaborative team engaged in a candid AAR discusses both the quantifiable results as well as more hazy impressions. This allows the team to develop a convergent view of events in order to better respond to similar situations in the future. And it combats our natural tendency to poorly understand the root causes of error.[54]

Champion Productive—as Opposed to Defensive—Learning

Auditors, copy editors, fact checkers, and aficionados of moviemistakes.com may delight in detecting and correcting errors.[55] But most people don't. That presents a challenge to any organizational leader. How do progress makers lead people out of this motivational ravine? They carry the banner of productive learning while adroitly navigating around various psychological boulders that impede progress.

Productive learners discover how to avoid similar errors in the future. They take into account a wide variety of potential sources of error such as latent design issues. For instance, many of the most deadly surgical mistakes used to occur when the anesthesiologist turned the drug-delivering valve the wrong way. How could this happen to such well-educated specialists? It turns out that many hospitals used two different anesthetizing machine models with two different ways to appropriately twist the valve. Once valve twisting was standardized, these problems abated and so did many of the deadly errors.[56] In fact, a growing body of evidence suggests that when hospital officials "own up to errors" and take active steps to prevent similar mishaps, they actually decrease the likelihood of lawsuits.[57] One study at the University of Illinois Medical Center in Chicago found that their formal apology program resulted in a 40% decline in the number of legal claims, despite a "20% increase in clinical activity."[58]

Defensive learners, on the other hand, concentrate their energy on avoiding responsibility and shunning change. They might, for example, excuse an unnecessary flap with a customer by saying, "I was having a bad day. The customer was pushing me and I let her know she couldn't talk to me that way. She left in a huff. What choice did I have?" Such responses inhibit learning because they transform choices (e.g., words chosen) into inevitabilities (e.g., words spoken). In some organizations, employees discover devilishly creative ways to play "shift the blame," "obscure the owner," and "attack the accuser." And they don't hesitate to entice others to play the game with them. The result: not continuous improvement but continuous accountability avoidance.

Productive learning stands in sharp contrast to defensive learning; they take organizations in two completely different directions (see Figure 14.4). The progress maker accelerates productive learning and pushes the brake pedal on the defensive learning.

Easier said than done. Putting the brakes on defensive learning requires the progress maker to have some back-pocket retorts ready for the typical face-saving attempts. Let's revisit the brochure example in the "Counterforces" section as a case in point. When the employee attempts to shift blame for the omission of the contact information to other people, how would a progress maker respond? A progress maker might convey, "I'm less interested in fixing blame than in fixing the problem and never repeating the mistake again. How can you help us achieve those goals?" Note that the progress maker deflects the face-saving attempt, assigns responsibility, and seeks action. In Table 14.3, we provide additional ideas for dealing with the other tactics defensive learners might use.

While progress makers recognize that new processes and technical fixes can eliminate many errors, they also know that human error is the source of most problems. After all, 90% of car accidents, 70% of airplane crashes, and 90% of workplace mishaps ultimately come down to human mistakes.[59]

Progress makers hold people accountable while encouraging personal growth. The balance between the two is often tenuous. If you come down too

Figure 14.4   Types of Learning Gleaned From Errors

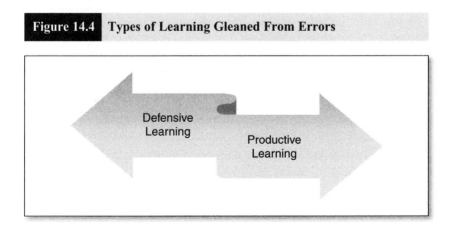

Table 14.3   Responses to Defensive Tactics

Defensive Tactic	Example	Progress Maker Retort
Shifting blame	"I was involved in another aspect of the brochure. Someone else was supposed to check the final edition."	"The chain of responsibility is an important issue that merits further discussion in the future. Today, I want to focus on that fact that the entire team shares a responsibility to meet the customers' needs. That did not happen in this case."
Maximizing motives	"Our energies were devoted to developing an innovative design that would really impress our customers. While we were trying so hard to be innovative, creative, and ground-breaking, I guess we just forgot that detail."	"We are not questioning anyone's motives. Rather we are focusing on how to get the performance up to customer expectations."
Obscuring ownership	"The decision was made by a committee."	"Who made the decision is really less important than making sure we meet our obligations to the customer."
Minimizing impact	"This was just an image campaign, and besides, they can get the contact information on our Web site."	"We want to make it easy for our customers to find out about us. We have to make our brochure as user-friendly as possible."
Attacking the accuser	"You've made your share of minor gaffes, as well."	"Shifting focus away from the present concerns will not solve the problem."

hard on accountability, you risk your team members becoming overly defensive, not talking about their shortcomings, and hiding their errors. Yet, emphasizing learning at the expense of accountability undermines progress. Progress makers would never stop giving tests and issuing grades in order to emphasize "natural" learning. If they did, it would actually undermine learning because employees would not receive the feedback they need to gauge performance and make necessary adjustments.

Acting with patient accountability strikes the right balance. A progress maker's patience allows the team to learn, align, and move forward. Progress makers avoid fretting about fixing the blame for errors and focus on fixing the problems, procedures, and responsibilities. They demand productive learning and then move on. They don't get mired in a finger-pointing kind of accountability. Instead, they tolerate mistakes even as they create accountabilities, expecting progress-making lessons to be learned in the process. Dr. Jerome Groopman of Harvard Medical School may have summed up this ideal best:

> Studies show that expertise is largely acquired not only by sustained practice but by receiving feedback that helps you understand your technical errors and misguided decisions. During my training, I met a cardiologist who had a deserved reputation as one of the best in his field, not only a storehouse of knowledge but also a clinician with excellent judgment. He kept a log of all the mistakes he knew he made over the decades, and at times revisited this compendium when trying to figure out a particularly difficult case. He was characterized by many of his colleagues as eccentric, an obsessive oddball. Only later did I realize his implicit message to us was to admit our mistakes to ourselves, then analyze them, and keep them accessible at all times if we wanted to be stellar clinicians.[60]

CONCLUDING THOUGHTS

Sports broadcasters ushered in something unexpected when they introduced instant replay and slow motion to U.S. football fans. Not only could the highlights be endlessly replayed and analyzed, but so could the obvious errors by officials. Most were inconsequential; others were game changers. What happened after this innovation? At first nothing much. In fact, there was even resistance to using the tool as a hedge against officiating errors. The arguments against using instant replay were plentiful as well as persuasive: (1) it would slow down the game, (2) it would undermine the credibility of officials, and (3) it would destroy fan confidence in the integrity of the game. Today, of course, coaches and officials in the booth rely on instant replay to correct important errors on the spot.[61]

The story of the evolving role of instant replay proves instructive. Managers, like many in the NFL, often resist discussing errors for fear of undermining their credibility or even slowing down production. The research suggests, though, that well-led organizations monitor many potential error sources and learn the relevant lessons. This can only happen by selecting, detecting, and correcting the proper errors. That's the kind of progress every explorer or refiner craves.

NOTES

1. T. Nordenberg, *Make No Mistake: Medical Errors Can Be Deadly Serious.* http://www.fda.gov/fdad/features/2000/500_err.html (accessed October 31, 2008).

2. M. Chiang, "Promoting Patient Safety: Creating a Workable Reporting System." *Yale Journal on Regulation* 18 (2001): 383–407.

3. M. D. Cannon and A. C. Edmondson, "Failing to Learn and Learning to Fail (Intelligently): How Great Organizations Put Failure to Work to Innovate and Improve." *Long Range Planning* 38, no. 3 (2005): 299–319, p. 300.

4. B. Zhao and F. Olivera, "Error Reporting in Organizations." *Academy of Management Review* 31, no. 4 (2006): 1012–30, p. 1013.

5. C. Argyris and D. Schön, *Organizational Learning: A Theory of Action Perspective.* Reading, MA: Addison-Wesley, 1978.

6. M. Crossan, "Altering Theories of Learning and Action: An Interview With Chris Argyris." *Academy of Management Executive* 17, no. 2 (2003): 40–46, p. 40.

7. Ibid., 40.

8. D. Garvin, A. Edmondson, and F. Gino. "Is Yours a Learning Organization? *Harvard Business Review* 86, no. 3 (2008): 109–16.

9. K. Johnson, "Is It Real, or Is It Autodesk?" *Business 2.0,* July 2007, 42–44.

10. R. Buderi, *The Invention That Changed the World: How a Small Group of Radar Pioneers Won the Second World War and Launched a Technological Revolution.* New York: Simon & Schuster, 1996, 246.

11. S. McCartney, "On the Radar, Bird-Proofing U.S. Air Traffic." *Wall Street Journal,* May 26, 2009, D1, 4.

12. D. Rothwell, *In Mixed Company: Communicating in Small Groups and Teams.* Belmont, CA: Thomson Learning, 2007.

13. Cannon and Edmondson, "Failing to Learn and Learning to Fail (Intelligently)," 7.

14. L. Gonzales, "Why Smart People Make Dumb Mistakes." *National Geographic Adventure,* August 2007, 45–51, 85–86; "Margin for Error." *National Geographic Adventure,* November 2004, 53–58, 87–89.

15. C. Tavris and E. Aronson, *Mistakes Were Made (But Not by Me).* New York: Harcourt, Inc., 2007, cover flap.

16. L. Mlodinow, *The Drunkard's Walk: How Randomness Rules Our Lives.* New York: Pantheon, 2008; D. Ariely, *Predictably Irrational: The Hidden Forces That Shape Our Decisions.* New York: HarperCollins, 2008.

17. F. Dyson, "A Failure of Intelligence." *Technology Review,* November/December 2006, 62–71, p. 67.

18. Ibid., 68.

19. L. McDonald and P. Robinson, *A Colossal Failure of Common Sense: The Inside Story of the Collapse of Lehman Brothers.* New York: Crown Business, 2009.

20. Zhao and Olivera, "Error Reporting in Organizations."

21. L. Perlow and S. Williams, "Is Silence Killing Your Company?" *Harvard Business Review* 81, no. 5 (2003): 52–58.

22. D. Tjosvold, Z. Yu, and C. Hui, "Team Learning From Mistakes: The Contribution of Cooperative Goals and Problem-Solving." *Journal of Management Studies* 41, no. 7 (2004): 1223–45.

23. N. Ron, R. Lipshitz, and M. Popper, "How Organizations Learn: Post-Flight Reviews in an F-16 Fighter Squadron." *Organization Studies* 27, no. 8 (2006): 1069–89.

24. P. Schoemaker and R. Gunther, "The Wisdom of Deliberate Mistakes." *Harvard Business Review* 84, no. 6 (2006): 108–15, p. 110.

25. J. Cohen, "Promising AIDS Failure Leaves Field Reeling." *Science* 318 (2007): 28–29.

26. C. Carlson and W. Wilmot, *Innovation: The Five Disciplines for Creating What Customers Want.* New York: Crown Business, 2006, 5.

27. "This Is How It's Done." *Inc.,* April 2009, 90–95.

28. Quoted in an interview by Roger O. Crockett, "How P&G Plans to Clean Up." *BusinessWeek,* April 13, 2009, 44–45, p. 44.

29. J. McGregor, "Zappos' Secret: It's an Open Book." *BusinessWeek,* March 23 & 30, 2009, 62.

30. P. Clampitt and M. L. Williams, "The Selection, Detection and Correction of Organizational Errors: The Role of Communication." Paper presented at the International Communication Association, May 2009, Chicago. Available at www.imetacomm.com under the "Other Publications" tab.

31. For a discussion of how the researchers distinguished between well-led and less well-led organizations, see Clampitt and Williams, "The Selection, Detection and Correction of Organizational Errors."

32. McGregor, "Zappos' Secret."

33. L. Gomes, "Rage, Report, Reboot, and, Finally, Accept Another System Crash." *Wall Street Journal,* October 31, 2007, B1.

34. A. Gawande, *Better: A Surgeon's Notes on Performance.* New York: Metropolitan Books, 254.

35. Ibid., 255.

36. M. Saks and J. Koehler, "The Coming Shift in Forensic Identification Science." *Science* 309 (2005): 892–95.

37. D. Whitney, N. Wurnitsch, B. Hontiveros, and E. Louie, "Perceptual Mislocalization of Bouncing Balls by Professional Tennis Referees." *Current Biology* 18, no. 20 (2008): R947–49.

38. Ibid.

39. N. Baxter, M. Goldwasser, L. Paszat, R. Saskin, D. Urbach, and L. Rabeneck, "Association of Colonoscopy and Death From Colorectal Cancer." *Annals of Internal Medicine* 150, no. 1 (2009): 1–9.

40. L. Meyers and N. Grossen, *Behavioral Research: Theory, Procedure, and Design.* San Francisco: Freeman, 1974, 87.

41. G. Gigerenzer, W. Gaissmaier, E. Kurz-Milcke, L. Schwartz, and S. Woloshin, "Knowing Your Chances." *Scientific American Mind* 20, no. 2 (2009): 44–51.

42. R. McNally, quoted in D. Dobbs, "The Post-Traumatic Stress Trap." *Scientific American,* April 2009, 64–69, p. 67.

43. R. Chernow, "Madoff and His Models." *New Yorker,* March 23, 2009, 28–33.

44. D. McCollam, "Should This Pulitzer Be Pulled?" *Columbia Journalism Review,* November/December 2003, 43–48.

45. W. E. Deming, *Out of the Crisis.* Cambridge: Massachusetts Institute of Technology, 1986, 133–34.

46. http://www.au.af.mil/au/awc/awcgate/army/tc_25–20/chap1.htm.

47. L. Buchanan, "Leadership: Armed With Data." *Inc.,* March 2009, 98–100, p. 100.

48. A. Lih, *The Wikipedia Revolution: How a Bunch of Nobodies Created the World's Greatest Encyclopedia.* New York: Hyperion, 2009, xv.

49. Ibid, xv.

50. Ibid., 213.

51. J. Angwin and G. A. Fowler, "Volunteers Log Off as Wikipedia Ages." *Wall Street Journal,* November 23, 2009, A1, 17.

52. Ibid., 19.

53. J. Hallinan, *Why We Make Mistakes.* New York: Broadway Books, 2009, 210.

54. Ibid., 189.

55. J. McPhee, "Checkpoints: Fact-Checkers Do It a Tick at a Time." *New Yorker,* February 9 and 16, 2009, 56–63; B. Newman, "In Movies, to Err Is Human, to Nitpick Is Even More So." *Wall Street Journal,* March 25, 2010, A1, A6.

56. Hallinan, *Why We Make Mistakes,* 6.

57. L. Landro, "Hospitals Own Up to Errors." *Wall Street Journal,* August 25, 2009, D1–D2.

58. C. Arnst, "10 Ways to Cut Health-Care Costs Right Now." *BusinessWeek,* November 23, 2009, 34–39, p. 39.

59. Ibid., 2.

60. J. Groopman, *How Doctors Think.* Boston: Houghton Mifflin, 2007, 21.

61. Personal interview with Mark Murphy, Green Bay Packers President and CEO, March 10, 2010.

⚹ 15 ⚹

PRACTICE RECEIVER-CENTRIC, STRATEGY-BASED, FEEDBACK-DRIVEN COMMUNICATION

The greatest problem in communication is the illusion that it has been accomplished.

—George Bernard Shaw

Almost any leadership expert will implore you to "communicate, communicate, communicate!" Who could quibble with that maxim? Communication experts could.[1] While they would applaud the spirit of the maxim, they would ask some critical questions before jumping on the bandwagon. For example, is the focus of the communication on the sender or receivers? Everybody knows someone with the "gift of gab" that we might prefer to occasionally give a swift jab to the abs. They "communicate, communicate, communicate," and all we want them to do is clam up, shut down, and go away.[2] Likewise, communication experts would need to know, *what* are you intending to communicate? *How* are you intending to communicate? Who, for example, can claim they haven't heard the message about the dangers of smoking? Millions of dollars have been poured into public service announcements. Clearly, the government abided by the dictum "communicate, communicate, communicate." Yet, still there are millions of people who continue to smoke and chew tobacco.

Any communication expert will advise you about the inevitable gap between the message conceived and the one perceived. The proof? One survey found that only 26% of business executives believe their business strategies are "well communicated and understood."[3] Other researchers found that only half of employees are satisfied with communication in their organization.[4] Lurking behind the communication experts' quibble with the "communicate, communicate, communicate!" crowd is a deep concern over how the maxim gets translated into action. If it means leaders use their megaphone to frequently send "loud and clear" messages, it might actually undermine communication effectiveness. What's "loud and clear" to the leader may not be so to receivers. The solution may not be "get a bigger megaphone." Rather, it may be to develop a better communication system. And that's the focus of this chapter.

DEFINING THE CONCEPT

If you studied accounts of successful leaders, you would develop a deep understanding of the fundamental attributes of world-class communication practices.[5] When we culled through the research literature and discussed communication practices with progress makers, we discovered three fundamental and interrelated attributes of the approach they take (see Figure 15.1). These are discussed in this section.

| Figure 15.1 | Attributes of World-Class Communication Practices |

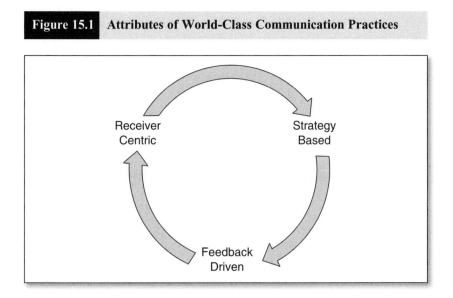

Receiver Centric

The first principle of communication is that *message sent* rarely equals *message received,* and people rarely notice the disconnect between the two. In contrast, progress makers take this principle into account. They are acutely aware of how the same message can be interpreted in different ways by different people with different mind-sets. Progress makers' commitment to receiver-centric communication explains their emphasis on audience analysis. What is it? Simply stated, it is anticipating how different groups of people will respond to a particular message and then planning accordingly.

How do progress makers analyze their audiences? First, they determine which groups of people congeal around a general point of view on the issue. Second, they isolate key facts they *know* about each audience. Third, they speculate on what they can reasonably *infer* about the audience's reactions. Fourth, they ask, "So, what should I *do?*" And fifth, they ask, "So, what should I *avoid doing?*"

Consider the executive who wants to educate her team about the concept of progress making. She conducts a simple audience analysis by breaking her team into extroverts and introverts. The sample KISS chart (<u>K</u>now, <u>I</u>nfer, <u>S</u>o what should I do? <u>S</u>o what should I avoid?) demonstrates how such an audience analysis provides a tool for advancing the progress maker's agenda (see Figure 15.2). Why? Because it improves the probability of crafting resonant messages and avoiding hidden dangers. And it improves the odds of securing the support of various stakeholders when refining a platform or moving to the next one.

Strategy Based

Progress makers develop a communication strategy because they realize that they can communicate *anything* but they cannot communicate *everything.* That means they must make the right trade-offs. Consequently, they must weigh the relative costs and benefits of properly communicating particular messages. We can broadly define communication strategy as the *"macro-level communication choices we make based on organizational goals and judgments about others' reactions, which serves as a basis for action."*[6] Note that the choices are driven by organizational imperatives and likely employee reactions. Discussions about those issues should yield a communication strategy that answers three important questions.

Figure 15.2 **"KISS" Chart for Audience Analysis**

	Know	_Infer_	_So what should I do?_	_So what should I avoid?_
Introverts	Think before they speak. Value time alone.	They will need to read the book before thinking of action steps.	Ask them to read the book. Write down the implications of the book.	Spring a discussion on them about the book. Press them for detailed reactions.
Extroverts	Speak before they think. Value time with others.	They will make sense of the concepts by discussing them with others.	Ask them to scan the book or read synopsis. Discuss the implications in a meeting.	Demand they read the book and submit a written list of implications. Hold them accountable for every reaction to the book.

First, what are the communication goals?

These can range from the simple to the difficult (see Table 15.1). The costs, for example, of informing employees in our technology-laden world are fairly low. The benefits, though, are often illusory. After all, with a few keystrokes, anyone can instantly access the latest news on health and fitness on the Internet. Yet, it may not be enough to persuade most people to change their behavior. In contrast, the costs of educating (creating deep understanding) are often quite high. The benefits, though, are often quite high as well because employees are more likely to build enduring patterns of success. If, for example, employees develop a deep understanding of their business's cost structure, then they might develop innovative solutions to significant challenges.

Second, what are the core messages?

There are limits to what humans can comprehend and process. A core message provides the cognitive scheme to shape interpretations and help us

Table 15.1	Types of Communication Goals	

Goal	Example	Difficulty
Informing	Update others on project status. Relay wage and benefit information.	●
Training	Demonstrate how to do a task. Document a process.	●●
Relating	Build rapport. Provide recognition.	●●
Coordinating	Negotiate common standards across units. Integrate priorities of different units.	●●●
Inspiring and influencing	Provide a sense of direction. Frame information in a meaningful and useful way.	●●●●
Educating	Teach about how executives make major decisions. Clarify links between organizational and employee goals.	●●●●●

NOTE: ● represents the number of balls you have to juggle to be successful; the more balls, the more difficult the task.

make sense of the never-ending, contradictory sensory whirlwind we are immersed in on a daily basis. It's what helped George Orwell's pigs in *Animal Farm* dominate with their slogan, "Four legs good, two legs bad," which was a pithier version of Snowball's (the Alpha pig) Seven Commandments for the Manor Farm animals.[7] Simple, memorable, and useful—at least to the pigs. It provided the prism through which to view events, information, and contradictory sentiments. And that's what a useful core message can do—even one those with two legs might not appreciate.

Third, what is our general plan to move forward?

The word *strategy* was derived from the Greek term *strategos,* signifying a general viewpoint. For instance, the term indicates the perspective military commanders adopt when planning large-scale campaigns. A sound strategy focuses on the "big picture" issues, which are designed to advance the communicative goals. Often, this takes the form of a series of phases in a communication campaign. For example, first establish awareness of a key organizational problem. Second, educate employees on the alternatives. Third, advocate a particular alternative. More specific plans would emerge around the phases.

Feedback Driven

Progress makers know that feedback is something more than a response. It is, in a deeper sense, a mechanism designed to check for transmission errors and then respond accordingly. To scientists, it is "essential to the life of every cell of every organism."[8] To progress makers, it is essential to the life of every message of every communication strategy. Why? Because progress makers want to know how messages were actually interpreted by receivers. If there is a misinterpretation or unintended consequence, they want to know about that today rather than tomorrow in order to correct it.

Feedback can be as simple as the fast-food clerk repeating your order. Or it can be as involved as conducting focus groups after an executive rolls out a major initiative. Either way, the senders check message fidelity by seeking out receivers' reactions. The process of actively seeking feedback distinguishes the communicative style of the progress maker from the merely gifted speaker.

Feedback allows the progress maker to determine if speculations about the audience were on target and if the communication strategy produced the intended results. If not, then shift the strategy or the related tactics. If it works, then progress makers glean lessons learned and use them in their next communicative endeavor.

BARRIERS

Unfortunately, roadblocks crop up when leaders attempt to use communication practices that are audience centric, strategy based, and feedback driven. All too often, communicative efforts drift off the intended path. We review the most pernicious and common reasons below.

Spray-and-Pray Strategy

Many leaders have the right sentiments but wrong approach. In particular, they often approach communication with a spray-and-pray strategy. They spray information of all sorts to every conceivable audience and then pray everyone understands.[9] They spray with the best of intentions such as "keeping everybody informed." Who could argue with that? We don't question the motivation, just the effectiveness. Unfortunately, their prayers often go unanswered.

The spray-and-pray strategy rests on two untenable assumptions. *First, it assumes that the communication will be understood as the sender intended.* Consider, for example, the potter who was having a bad day at a local art fair. An interested buyer enthralled with his pottery asked the potter, "Could you knock a little bit off the coffee mug?" The buyer, of course, was using a time-honored cliché to enter into a price negotiation. The irritated potter responded by grabbing a hammer and whacking off the coffee mug's handle. The customer's message was sent but definitely not received as intended.

Second, it assumes that more information equates with better communication. That's rarely the case. In fact, many times more information becomes toxic. Why? It can overwhelm people as they cope with the overload and they simply tune out. It can also slow decision making to a crawl as people spend an inordinate amount of time sifting through and evaluating the information.[10] There is never enough information to act with complete certainty.[11] Searching for certainty by seeking more information may ease our apprehensions but ends in futility.

In essence, the spray-and-pray mind-set conflicts with a receiver-centric orientation. The sender both sprays and prays. The receiver may not be willing or capable of answering the supplications.[12]

Technology-Driven Communications

When we ask leaders about the effectiveness of their communication systems, many respond by proudly listing all the communication technologies deployed in their organization. They tweet, blog, videoconference, text message, and so on. It's thrilling, impressive, and often irrelevant. In essence, these leaders equate communication technologies with communication effectiveness; more technology equals enhanced communication effectiveness. Maybe. Maybe not. It all depends on how the leaders employ the technology.

A technology-driven communication system is the antithesis of a strategy-based one. Why? Because the technology should provide the *means,* not be the *end,* of a communication strategy. Communication technology, like an automobile, should provide a method to get from Point A to Point B. Communication strategy defines Points A and B. The technologies can help transport you from A to B. And some are better than others for getting you to your particular destination. If your goal is to speed up communication, then perhaps tweeting and e-mailing best serve the purpose. If your goal is education, then tweets or e-mails are about as useful as your automobile on a transcontinental trip. It probably requires face-to-face communication. For example, many higher education administrators buzz about the possibilities of "distance learning" through the Internet, videoconferencing, and the like. To be fair, it may have a place in the curriculum. But would you be comfortable knowing that the surgeon holding the scalpel poised above your torso has a medical degree from the world's greatest online medical school?

Gap Between Desire and Resources

Most leaders sincerely desire to effectively communicate. Their problem is that they simply do not devote enough time and energy to *crafting, executing,* and *evaluating* their communication strategy.

The *crafting* presents a special challenge. First, few people have the necessary expertise. Second, it takes energy to locate this resource. Third, once these experts are located, it takes still more energy to craft the proper strategy. To be sure, there are many experts with the skill to construct a captivating Web site, ghostwrite a compelling speech, or fashion convincing talking points. But their tactical expertise often overshadows their strategic thinking abilities. Bottom line: The abundance of tactical expertise coupled with the scarcity of communication strategists undermines many leaders' desire for an effective communication strategy.

Executing a sound strategy requires resources as well. One great speech or one scintillating article will not do. Progress makers know that it requires multiple communications in different channels to different groups under different circumstances to move an organization forward. Progress makers eagerly invest the resources because they believe if something is poorly communicated, it will take even more resources to correct the problem later. So it is best to invest the resources up front.

Progress makers wince when they hear the statistic that only 50% of organizational decisions are actually implemented and sustained.[13] That's why they invest time in *evaluating* the effectiveness of their approach. They could never live with the fact that half the energy they put into decision making wastes away in some cosmic organizational black hole. And they realize the effective development, execution, and evaluation of their communication strategy greatly increase the odds of successful implementation. In short, they narrow the desire-resource gap.

WHAT TO DO?

Progress makers possess a deeper appreciation than most people of the value of communication. They viscerally understand the benefits of effective communication such as improved alignment, enhanced trust, and reduced destructive conflict. And they willingly pay the costs by devoting time, personnel, and other resources to the quest. When progress makers invest in an audience-centric, strategy-based, and feedback-driven communication system, they are guided by the following best practices.

Select a Rich and Meaningful Signature Message

Great leaders often craft a core or signature message that captures the essence of their vision at a particular time. Even the casual student of World War II instantly recognizes Winston Churchill's raised arm flashing the "V" for victory sign. More serious students will recall Churchill's first speech as prime minister:

> You ask, what is our aim? I can answer you in one word: Victory—victory at all costs, victory in spite of all terror, victory, however long and hard the road may be; for without victory there is no survival.[14]

That singular idea, "victory," became the signature message that framed all other issues. Expenditures, hardships, disappointments, conflicting stories, and unpleasant decisions could be explained through the lens of Churchill's signature message. *In short, the power of a signature message surges in direct proportion to the number of major issues that can be framed around the notion.*[15]

Business leaders may operate on a less dramatic stage, but signature messages retain their powerful influence over their employees. Former CEO of Intel Andy Grove held sway over the company with his famous quip, "Only the paranoid survive" or some variant on the theme.[16] Likewise, early in his career, Jack Welch, the former CEO of General Electric, insisted that every GE business must be "number one or two" in its marketplace or it should be "fixed, closed or sold."[17] And he meant it. All his major decisions were predicated on this core message, and he expected those who reported to him to do the same. In fact, when one manager joked about being number one or two, he was promptly given the hook. Effective leaders take jokes in stride, but they do not tolerate employees masquerading as comedians when they start joshing about their signature messages. Why? Behavior scientists found that "signs of inappropriate behavior like graffiti or broken windows lead to other inappropriate behavior (e.g., litter or stealing)."[18] Likewise, tolerating the inappropriate joke introduces contagion into the organization. Moreover, the tolerance diminishes the power of the message by signaling a leader's disingenuousness or lack of resolve. No one—not even the comedians—joked about victory in front of Churchill.

Use Multiple, Credible Channels for Important Messages

Most people choose their channels based on their own personal convenience. Even if you happened to be an amateur telegraph operator, you probably would not send Morse code signals to your boss. Yet people do the functional equivalent every day. The bride and groom who send out a mass e-mail thanking friends and family for their wedding gifts fall into this category. So does the manager who calls a face-to-face meeting with her staff of 15 employees for the sole purpose of soliciting agenda items for the "real" meeting with the same group a week later. In the first case, the communicators chose an overly impersonal channel to send a message that should be warm and personal. In the second case, the manager selects an overly rich and interactive channel for a relatively simple task that could be handled with text messages or e-mails. Note that there is nothing inherently wrong with e-mail, text messaging, face-to-face meetings, or any other channel. The problem revolves around the mismatch between the channel and the nature of the message and receiver needs.[19]

Effective leaders think about the dynamics of their message and their receivers' needs when selecting communication channels. This includes being attuned to the channels that receivers view as credible. For instance, they recognize that complex, difficult, and potentially conflict-laden issues are best handled face-to-face by highly credible sources. The immediacy of feedback, the rapid give-and-take, and the ability to detect a variety of subtle cues make this channel the richest and best possibility in these situations. Lean channels such as mass e-mails or Web postings should be reserved for unambiguous tasks and routine information sharing.

If leaders use an array of channels from rich to lean, then there's a pretty good bet they are making strategic choices. If, on the other hand, they tend to rely on only one particular rich OR lean channel, then the odds are that they make choices based on personal convenience. That indicates they lack a receiver-centric outlook, which in turn undermines their communicative effectiveness.

Translate Your Agenda for Different Audiences

Douglas Feith served as the Under Secretary of Defense for Policy during George W. Bush's presidency. He was trained as a lawyer, not a strategic communicator. Yet his insights about communication failures during the Gulf War are extraordinarily insightful:

> The Reagan White House encouraged *all* its officials, not just those at the cabinet level, to tailor messages to our various audiences. When addressing lawyers' groups, for example, we offered legal analysis. In academic settings, we would explain our thinking in greater depth than in television broadcasts. The George W. Bush Administration, however, took a different approach to strategic communications. Its key concept was to "discipline the message." White House officials did not generally encourage subcabinet officials to do speeches, interviews, or op-eds in support of our Iraq policy or our war on terrorism strategy. They chose to rely almost entirely on the President, Vice President, Powell, Rumsfeld, and Rice. That made it easier to keep official pronouncements "on message," but it also meant writing off important audiences—including journalists, academics, and intellectuals— that could not be satisfied with generalizations delivered at a distance.[20]

Note that the worthy goal of "message discipline" undercut an even more fundamental premise of effective communication—adapt your message to different audiences. Message adapters or translators use the language of a particular audience and address their unique concerns. With as many audiences as the president of the United States must serve, it is physically impossible for a handful of people to carry out the translations. President Reagan used many translators; President Bush used few. Moreover, such a limited group has limited expertise to build a case in the language of the various audiences. That's a lesson all leaders can glean from Feith's candid assessment.

That leaves a lingering question: Isn't *agenda translation* fundamentally at odds with *message discipline*? In a word, no. They can actually coexist and enrich one another. The signature message forms the core; the translations for the various audiences branch off the hub. They reflect a deeper explanation of the fundamental agenda shared with every audience. They are NOT contradictory messages but mutually reinforcing ones. In Figure 15.3, a key agenda item for those ascribing to lean principles is "map the value stream" (e.g., chart all the specific steps involved in bringing a good or service to a customer).[21] That core principle can be translated into a variety of forms for different audiences without destroying the essence of the message. Corporate lawyers, for example, will identify very different value streams than their coworkers in the engineering department. Often the progress maker can start the translation process, but you need opinion leaders within a particular group to sustain and enhance

Figure 15.3   **Agenda Translations for Various Audiences**

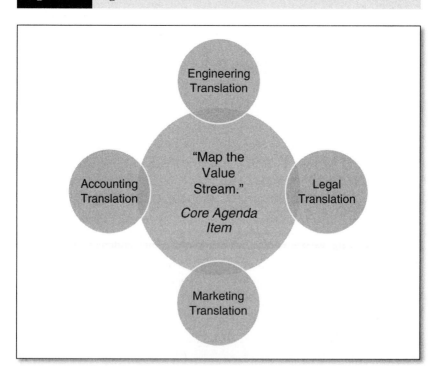

it. Lawyers know the hot buttons in the legal community better than others. Chief information officers know the concerns in the tech community better than others. And so on. These leaders may, in fact, be better positioned to act as translators and advocates than the CEO. What happens if some messages from different sources appear contradictory? Subsequent discussions can resolve the incongruency that clarifies and deepens the fundamental point.

Robustly Download Major Decisions

Often progress makers cannot keep everyone informed in real time about the decision-making process. For example, merger discussions or union negotiations are often conducted by a small group of people bound by confidentiality agreements. At some point, the group's decisions will need to be downloaded to others. In fact, the dynamics may resemble the challenge software engineers face when they create a terrific new application and want everyone to download the upgrade. The engineers eagerly endorse the upgrade because they have wrestled some pretty tough problems to the ground. Consumers, though, often respond with less enthusiasm because they have grown comfortable with the old, if flawed, platform. Learning something new—even if beneficial—exacts a cost they may be unwilling to pay.

Researchers discovered that leaders can *double* the likelihood of employee support if they download the decision by addressing seven key issues.[22] In fact, these issues provide a good foundation for communicating about *any* decision regardless of the level of employee involvement. Companies where these issues are routinely addressed tend to engender more support for the organizational direction and commitment to the organization. The elements highlighted in Table 15.2 provide a protocol for sharing a major decision with employees.

The protocol highlights the progress maker's thinking process and key facts that led to the decision. This promotes a deeper understanding of the progress maker's decision-making process (e.g., thinking routine) by transparently revealing the factors considered during the decision-making process, how evidence was weighed, and what proved to be the decisive factors. Do employees know what counts as evidence? Do they know what counts as a viable argument? If so, they will be able to properly evaluate evidence, participate in debates, and shape decisions.

The protocol also underscores the importance of striking the right balance between the organization's and employees' interests. Employees always listen to announcements with ears tuned to two channels: "WIFM" (What's in It For

Me?) and "WIFO" (What's in It For the Organization?). Leaders often make the mistake of broadcasting only on the WIFO channel. The temptations to do so often increase when there is news negatively affecting employees. Yet by avoiding the WIFM channel, leaders undermine their credibility and employees seek out other sources of information. Robust communicators acknowledge both the upside and downside of the decision for employees. If not, they know the result is likely to be unfounded fears and rumors.

Table 15.2	Robust Communication Protocol

- What is the decision?
- How was the decision made?
- Why was the decision made?
- What were the rejected alternatives to the announced decision?
- How does the decision fit into the mission or vision?
- How does the decision affect the organization (WIFO)?
- How does the decision affect employees (WIFM)?

Identify, Listen to, and Use Opinion Leaders

Every organization has informal opinion leaders who shape others' responses for good or ill. When compared to others, supportive opinion leaders tend be better informed, are more connected, enjoy higher status, and are more likely to mull over innovative ideas.[23] People with formal authority may or may not be opinion leaders. For example, military forces in Iraq quickly learned that government officials often held little sway over the local population; instead, local religious leaders shaped opinion.[24] Even in the blogosphere, where many celebrate egalitarianism, influence is unequally distributed. There are upwards of 133 million blogs available on the Internet with an estimated 175,000 new ones created each day, but only a handful receive regular traffic.[25] These bloggers are known as the e-influentials because they exert so much sway over opinion, even beyond the blogosphere. For example, news networks routinely consult the Drudge Report or Perez Hilton for story ideas.[26]

Progress makers identify the relevant opinion leaders whether they are in the mosque, blogosphere, or on the factory floor. Why? Because opinion leaders shape how other people interpret messages, evaluate information, and respond to events. While messages may flow directly to listeners through e-mails, presentations, or TV advertisements, the interpretations of those messages take a more circuitous route through the filter of opinion leaders. For example, consider what happened during the 2008 U.S. Republican primary election campaign that kicked off in Iowa. Mitt Romney spent six times as much on TV ads as Mike Huckabee. Yet he lost the primary. The reason: Opinion leaders within the caucus and neighborhood discussions held far more sway.[27] These opinion leaders, like those in organizations, disseminated additional related information, offered their views, and helped others make sense of official announcements. In short, opinion leaders often determine if an initiative glides into the fast track or drifts to a sidetrack.

Progress makers also listen to opinion leaders because they often identify issues that can be tweaked to make initiatives more palatable to others. Opinion leaders may identify ways to effectively promote the initiative as well. They can be a communicator's best friend or worst enemy. For example, in one large paper manufacturer, we discovered that opinion leaders often emerged from those in the maintenance crew. Why? They were the only ones who routinely moved from paper machine to paper machine. As they trekked from one job to the next, they disseminated information and opinions that often varied from the formal plant leadership and even their own union officials. Few initiatives could take hold without harnessing or at least blunting the undesignated leader's influence. When plant officials began to consult with these informal leaders, they met with more success.

As leaders craft their communication strategies, they would be well served by starting their discussions with the potential views of key opinion leaders. The opinion leader's lens should help shape messages, talking points, channel selection, roll-out schedule, and even the initiative itself. It's not a sign of weakness to ask, "How would Joe or Jane react?" Rather, it's a signal that leaders approach communication with a receiver-centric and strategy-based mind-set.

Harvest Concerns and Convert Them Into Action Items

This practice springs from a belief that if leaders fail to identify concerns, others will. And they may convert them into resistance or even subtle forms of sabotage. All too often, leaders are tempted to energetically offer their counterarguments when someone articulates a concern. That's a useful skill employed at precisely the wrong time. During the harvest, a vigorous debate often discourages further revelations, particularly from those who lack power or debating skill. In due course, the counterarguments can be voiced. Harvesting concerns requires the receptive mind of an inquirer, not the argumentative tongue of the debater.

The Associate Vice President for Institutional Effectiveness at Texas State University, Dr. Cathy Fleuriet, skillfully employs this practice. When formulating or launching a new initiative, she asks each staff member to "identify one potential concern or roadblock we will encounter when implementing the proposal."[28] Note several features of her request. First, she rightly assumes that there will be objections or concerns. She is not acting like a cheerleader but squarely faces the reality. Second, she insists that every staff member independently generate the objection. This provides a wonderful hedge against *groupthink* or the tendency to be overly supportive of the leader and not raise objections.[29] Third, she initially focuses on the identification of potential concerns *before* discussing the merits or possible retorts to the concerns. That's the way a progress maker harvests concerns.

The next step? Convert concerns into action items. The process may take any number of different forms. In some cases, objections prove so compelling it stops the initiative dead. Better to know sooner rather than later that the initiative faces insurmountable hurdles. More often, though, the discussion revolves around tweaking the initiative or crafting responses to concerns.

In some cases, the concerns take the form of discussion-terminating retorts or "remarks that stop further thought, discussion, and action" about the initiative.[30] When some senior-level managers at a *Fortune* 100 company were confronted with something new, they would often quip, "Here we go again." At other firms, employees use the phrase "program of the month" to describe any new initiative. In both cases, the discussion-terminating retort signaled to others it was time to disengage and wait it out because "this too shall pass." Progress makers spot discussion-terminating retorts and respond to the underlying sentiment in order to encourage deeper engagement in the initiative.

Encourage Upward Communication

Winston Churchill verbalized an ageless truism: "The temptations to tell a Chief in a great position the things he most likes to hear is one of the commonest explanations of mistaken policy. Thus the outlook of the leader on whose decision fateful events depend is usually far more sanguine than the brutal facts admit."[31] Professor of Leadership at the University of Kent Dennis Tourish put it this way: "Critical upward communication improves decision making in organizations. Without it, senior management teams become out of touch with the mood of their people, and underestimate or miss emerging problems in their marketplace."[32] Progress makers heed the statesman's and professor's implicit advice. They take active steps to circumvent the inevitable information distortions and reduce the number of missed opportunities. Fostering upward communication (e.g., up the chain of command) provides the remedy.

Effective leaders foster this special type of communication by building personal relationships with people at all levels of their organizations. The business press often gets enamored with meetings between various titans of industry. They often fail to take note of the day-to-day energy the titans devote to building and maintaining relations on the shop floor. Jack Welch, for instance, would always make a point to visit regularly with union workers and other employees on the ground floor of the business.[33] In the military, those in leadership positions are expected to learn "everything from the mundane to the profound" about their troops. "Nothing about them [is] too small to be overlooked and filed away for future reference."[34] Such practices, whether by the CEO of a *Fortune* 100 company or military squad leader, lubricate the upward communication lines.

Establishing and maintaining the communication lines shifts employees' cost/benefit ratio in the right direction. After all, it's easier to share a concern with someone you know rather than with a stranger—particularly one with lots of power. But it is not enough. As Churchill noted, power and status differentials have a way of destroying candor. So progress makers take the idea further by actively encouraging discussion about concerns. They even praise people for bringing issues to their attention that do not surface in other forums. These practices were not in place at Enron, and the company's failure was as predictable and it was preventable.[35]

Check the Effectiveness of Communication

The progress maker's commitment to a feedback-driven system translates into a desire to actively assess the effectiveness of communications. They seek to understand employees' reactions to their communications. They want to know at Internet speed about potential misrepresentations, misunderstandings, distortions, and rumors. They seek out information about what was discussed at the *real* meeting after the *official* meeting; after all, the real meeting is where opinions are shared, shaped, and finalized around the water cooler. Yet progress makers do not desire to pry and spy; rather, they seek to detect and correct communication errors.

How do they do it? One approach involves a Pulse Survey that is routinely (monthly or quarterly) administered to a rotating sample of employees. The short survey includes 10 to 12 numerically rated closed questions as well as one or two open questions. The Pulse survey often acts as an early warning device, uncovering employee issues that would not surface through other, more conventional communication tools.[36] Several years ago, The Boldt Company Pulse revealed that employees were concerned with the vacation policy. The issue emerged over the course of several months in comments to the open questions. Although the company had an open-door communication policy as well as a yearly climate survey, the issue never surfaced in those forums. The Pulse legitimized the issue and put it on the executives' radar screen. The company took steps to align the vacation policy with competitors, preemptively responding to the issue before it had a more severe impact on employee morale.

Other approaches include conducting focus groups, administering questionnaires after major presentations, and monitoring issues on company blogs. Each method (including the Pulse) has strengths and weaknesses. Focus groups, for example, provide rich data but can be overly influenced by a single individual. Consequently, wise leaders use a variety of methods and integrate the data from several sources before drawing conclusions.

CONCLUDING THOUGHTS

Progress makers define communication success as employee understanding and acceptance rather than disseminating a script. They perceive communication as a dialogue with negotiated meanings rather than a conveyer belt of transmitted symbols. They realize they have the power to initiate and encode messages, but employees have the power to decode and translate those messages in the context of discussions with their peers and opinion leaders. They recognize that effective communication is often the exception more than the rule and thus operate with guarded optimism when planning and announcing decisions. Progress makers may well be enthusiastic, but they don't overreach. They realize that the learning experienced by the decision makers can never be completely duplicated for employees. Yet they believe that cultivating understanding of the decision process—with all its tough calls, blemishes, uncertainties, and implications for the organization and employees—engenders the most important feature of sustained success: trust.

NOTES

1. Parts of this chapter are based on discussions with Professor M. Lee Williams of Texas State University as well as the following article: P. G. Clampitt and M. L. Williams, "Decision Downloading." *MIT Sloan Management Review* 48, no. 2 (2007): 77–82. Others parts were adapted from P. Clampitt, *Communicating for Managerial Effectiveness.* 4th ed. Thousand Oaks, CA: Sage, 2010.

2. The stereotype that women "gab" more than men does not hold up to scientific scrutiny. See M. Mehl, S. Vazire, N. Ramfrez-Esparza, R. Slatcher, and J. Pennebaker, "Are Women Really More Talkative Than Men?" *Science,* July 6, 2007.

3. "How Does IT Funding Affect Alignment?" *CIO Insight,* November 14, 2003, 26.

4. P. G. Clampitt and M. L. Williams, "How Employees and Organizations Manage Uncertainty: Norms, Implications and Future Research." Paper competitively selected and presented at the International Communication Association Convention, May 2003, San Diego.

5. See Chapter 11 of Clampitt, *Communicating for Managerial Effectiveness.*

6. Ibid., 260.

7. G. Orwell, *Animal Farm.* New York: The New American Library, 1946, 67.

8. H. F. Judson, *The Search for Solutions.* New York: Holt, Rinehart, and Winston, 1980, 100.

9. Clampitt, *Communicating for Managerial Effectiveness.*

10. K.M. Sutcliffe and K. Weber, "The High Cost of Accurate Knowledge." *Harvard Business Review* 81, no. 5 (2003): 74–82, p. 78.

11. P. Salem, *The Complexity of Human Communication.* Cresskill, NJ: Hampton, 2009.

12. Clampitt, *Communicating for Managerial Effectiveness,* 265.

13. P. Nutt, "Surprising but True: Half the Decisions in Organizations Fail." *Academy of Management Executive* 13, no. 4 (1999): 75–90, p. 75.

14. W. S. Churchill, *Speeches That Changed the World.* Edited by S. Montefiore. London: Quercus, 2006, 91–95, p. 93.

15. G. Fairhurst and R. Sarr, *The Art of Framing: Managing the Language of Leadership.* San Francisco: Jossey-Bass, 1996.

16. R. Tedlow, *Andy Grove.* New York: Portfolio, 2006.

17. B. Lane, *Jacked Up.* New York: McGraw-Hill, 2008, 99.

18. K. Keizer, S. Lindenberg, and L. Steg, "The Spreading of Disorder." *Science* 322 (2008): 1681–85, p. 1685.

19. For a more extensive discussion of this issue, see Chapter 5 of Clampitt, *Communicating for Managerial Effectiveness.*

20. D. J. Feith, *War and Decision: Inside the Pentagon at the Dawn of the War on Terrorism.* New York: Harper, 2008, 320.

21. J. Womack and D. Jones, *Lean Thinking.* New York: Simon & Schuster, 1996.

22. Clampitt and Williams, "Decision Downloading."

23. E. Rogers, *Diffusion of Innovation.* 5th ed. New York: Free Press, 2003.

24. M. Gordon and B. Trainor, *Cobra II: The Inside Story of the Invasion and Occupation of Iraq.* New York: Pantheon, 2006.

25. "State of the Blogosphere/2008." *Technorati,* August 2008. http://technorati .com/blogging/state-of-the-blogosphere/ (accessed June 7, 2009). See also S. Rosenberg, *Say Everything: How Blogging Began, What It's Becoming, and Why It Matters.* Crown: New York, 2009.

26. E. Keller and J. Berry, *The Influentials: One American in Ten Tells the Other Nine How to Vote, Where to Eat, and What to Buy.* New York: Free Press, 2003.

27. M. Mellman and M. Bloomfield, "Loose Lips Win Elections." *New York Times,* January 6, 2008. www.nytimes.com/2008/01/06/opinion/06mellman.html (accessed May 21, 2009).

28. Cathy Fleuriet, personal interview, May 21, 2009.

29. I. Janis, *Groupthink.* Boston: Houghton Mifflin Company, 1983.

30. Clampitt, *Communicating for Managerial Effectiveness,* 272.

31. W. S. Churchill, *The World Crisis 1916–1918* (abridged). London: Macmillan, 1941, 653.

32. D. Tourish, "Critical Upward Communication: Ten Commandments for Improving Strategy and Decision Making." *Long Range Planning* 38 (2005): 485–503, p. 485.

33. Lane, *Jacked Up.*

34. D. Cambell, *Joker One: A Marine Platoon's Story of Courage, Leadership, and Brotherhood.* New York: Random House, 2009. Location 73 on Kindle.

35. R. Lacayo and A. Ripley, "Persons of the Year." *Time,* December 30, 2002, 30–33; M. Miceli, J. P. Near, and T. Dworkin, *Whistle-blowing in Organizations.* New York: Routledge, 2008.

36. P. G. Clampitt, L. R. Berk, and T. Cashman, "Checking the Organizational Pulse." White paper, May 2006. Available at www.imetacomm.com.

⚝ 16 ⚝

CONCLUSION

———•◦•———

Three words leaders have trouble dealing with: "I don't know."
I think good leadership will often start with questions whose
answer is: "I don't know but we're going to find out."

—Warren Bennis

Many leaders derive immense satisfaction from the positions or titles they have attained. But progress makers take more delight in moving their organizations forward into the unknown future, where they don't know all the answers. Their fulfillment emerges from refining an established platform or establishing a new one. As they mature, the process of refining and exploring itself becomes even more intrinsically rewarding. Why? Because progress makers realize that all platforms—no matter how successful—are but temporary resting points on a quest to make the world a better place. They move beyond a desire to lead. They want to accomplish something significant, worthwhile, and meaningful to others. They strive to make a difference for the greater good.

In this book, we have introduced you to many leaders we consider progress makers. Some presided over *Fortune* 100 companies, others small businesses. Some were scientists and entrepreneurs while others were military officers and politicians. They came from all walks of life and from every country in the world. We have not tried to capture their essence with a string of superlatives—although they often apply. Nor have we tried to de-mystify their sway over others—although that is clearly evident. Rather, we focused on what they do and how they do it.

Progress making often involves tough choices. Former Xerox CEO Anne Mulcahy, for instance, had to lay off a significant number of employees in order to restore the company to profitability. She recounted one of her toughest decisions: "There were a lot of tough decisions. One of the most memorable was shutting down our consumer business. It's a business that I ran, I helped author. A business that could have had promise over time, but there wasn't time. Great people, a lot of promise."[1] Yet the difficulty of the decision did not deter her from the larger aim of saving the company. Sometimes progress makers must eliminate a platform (e.g., the consumer business) in order to move their organizations forward. And she succeeded in bringing the company back from the brink. In fact, her progress-making skills and leadership style have earned her numerous accolades, including the designation of "2008 Chief Executive of the Year."[2]

Progress making is about refining platforms and advancing from one platform to another. It is about providing enough stability to both *exploit* the current platform and *explore* new ones. Without that kind of dynamic stability, we cannot produce sustainability. And that's where some people in leadership positions, such as Ken Lay of Enron and Bernie Madoff of Madoff Investment Securities, fail the progress maker test. They not only made countless unethical choices but also failed to craft the kind of dynamic stability needed for sustainability.[3] In the end, they failed to accomplish something significant, worthwhile, and meaningful for others. They failed the most important test of leadership, which is "measured by the degree of production of intended effects."[4] Simply put, their ethical lapses eventually undermined their ability to make progress.

Collectively, the seven strategies reviewed in the book provide a guide for progress makers. Any single strategy will not suffice. John Mackey, the CEO of Whole Foods Market, was once asked about his philosophy for filling leadership positions. He responded,

> My philosophy . . . has definitely evolved over the years. I understand people a lot better today than I did 30 years ago. Back then, I was more impressed with people who were very articulate . . . I got snowed by a few of those people over the years. I still think communication is important, but I don't think there's a correlation between being a great communicator and other virtues that make a great leader.[5]

He underscores the dangers of focusing on a single leadership strategy.[6] We believe all seven progress maker strategies are equally important, and they synergistically strengthen one another. For example, how can leaders develop a focused and flexible organization without a world-class communication system? After all, leaders will need to quickly and effectively communicate about the ever-shifting focal points for their organizations' energies.

Table 16.1 summarizes all the strategies and related tactics we have discussed. These are not sacrosanct—particularly the tactics. Just like any other platform, they should be further refined and explored.[7] The strategies do, however, provide a starting point for a discussion about one of the most

Table 16.1   Summary of Progress-Making Strategies and Tactics

Strategy	*Tactics*
Envision the future with calculated boldness	Improve, develop, or acquire the necessary tools to monitor organizational health and direction Ponder and debate the gateway questions before proceeding Identify system-level roadblocks to progress Calculate the cost of failing to address critical issues Use the power of self-fulfilling expectations Learn to tolerate setbacks and recover
Cultivate a focused flexibility mind-set	Build frequent iterative loops Search for optimal environments Improve peripheral vision Manage the amount of stress placed on employees Declare war on the terrible triad (excessive planning, overconfidence, and cognitive bias) Legitimize strategic forgetfulness Designate "project pruners" and elevate their status
Enlarge the circle of engagement	Assemble a diverse but collaborative team Communicate in a collaborative manner Seek and discover the unifying point of commitment Moderate the influence of status and roles Sense and seize moments of acceleration Add talent to the team in a thoughtful sequence Routinely take stock and evaluate progress

(Continued)

Table 16.1	Summary of Progress-Making Strategies and Tactics (Continued)

Strategy	Tactics
Foster the growth of investment-worthy employees	Craft a talent investment approach
	Diversify your talent investments
	Make routine talent investments
	Regularly measure, analyze, and discuss the performance of your talent investments
	Routinely rebalance the talent portfolio
	Cut your losses
Seek, nurture, and evaluate actionable ideas	Build "discovery time" into the schedule, surroundings, and job duties
	Cultivate employee imagination
	Pay attention to "lead users"
	Use the right skills at the right time
	Articulate criteria used to evaluate ideas at different phases in the process
	Evaluate ideas by examining attributes rather than relying on initial impressions
Select, detect, and correct the proper errors	Conceptualize the errors you wish to monitor
	Systematically document and analyze errors to discern underlying patterns
	Evaluate, recalibrate, and adjust radar detectors
	Adjust error detection and correction responsibilities of stakeholders
	Champion productive—as opposed to defensive—learning
Practice receiver-centric, strategy-based, feedback-driven communication	Select a rich and meaningful signature message
	Use multiple, credible channels for important messages
	Translate your agenda for different audiences
	Robustly download major decisions
	Identify, listen to, and use opinion leaders
	Harvest concerns and convert them into action items
	Encourage upward communication
	Check the effectiveness of communication

important issues facing organizations today: How do we create sustainable progress? Putting that issue front and center shifts the spotlight away from power, titles, and egos and into the service of something greater. If you can do that, then you have moved "beyond the desire to lead" to something more consequential, significant, and enduring: You've taken the first steps toward becoming a progress maker.

NOTES

1. A. Mulcahy, "The Grill." *Computer World,* September 1, 2008, 22–24, p. 24.

2. "2009 Chief Executive of the Year." *CEO Magazine,* September/October 2009, 68–70.

3. J. Bandler and N. Varchaver, "How Bernie Did It." *Fortune,* May 11, 2009, 51–71.

4. J. Burns, *Leadership.* New York: Harper & Row, 1978, 22.

5. J. Mackey, "Ask John Mackey." *Inc.,* July/August, 2009, 112. See also D. Sacks, "The Miracle Worker." *Fast Company,* December 2009/January 2010, 83–87, 122–23.

6. Note that one of your authors devoted much of his career to the study of organizational communication.

7. In fact, this book actually represents a second platform for these ideas. The first was our book *Embracing Uncertainty: The Essence of Leadership,* published by M. E. Sharpe in 2001. We review much of the original research in that book.

APPENDIX A

Progress Makers Discussed or Profiled

———◆•◆•◆———

A. G. Lafley	Former CEO of Procter & Gamble
Albert Einstein	Theoretical Physicist
An Wang	Former CEO of Wang Computers
Andrea Jung	Chairman and CEO of Avon
Andy Grove	Former CEO of Intel
Anne Mulcahy	Chairman and Former CEO of Xerox
Atul Gawande	Surgeon and MacArthur Fellow
C. S. Lewis	Author and Middle Ages Scholar
Cathy Fleuriet[a]	Associate Vice President for Institutional Effectiveness at Texas State University
Chris Fortune[a]	Owner and President of Saris Cycling Group
Curt Herztark	Inventor of the Curta Calculator
David Stern	NBA Commissioner
Doug Hall	Founder of Eureka! Ranch
Duncan Smith	U.S. Navy SEAL
Edward Deming	Founder of the Quality Movement
Ernest Shackleton	Polar Explorer

a. We interviewed these progress makers. Their comments and profiles are highlighted in various chapters.

Franklin Roosevelt	32nd President of the United States
Frederick Taylor	Founder of the "Scientific Management" School of Thought
Freya Stark	Author and Middle Eastern Explorer
George C. Marshall	Former Secretary of State
George Reed[a]	Professor of Leadership Studies
Georgia O'Keefe	Artist
Gordon Moore	Former CEO of Intel
H. R. McMaster[a]	Brigadier General, U.S. Army
J. F. Kennedy	35th President of the United States
Jack Welch	Former CEO of GE
Jeff Bezos	CEO of Amazon.com
Jimmy Wales	Founder of Wikipedia
John Mackey	CEO of Whole Foods Market
Jonas Salk	Developer of Polio Vaccine
Laura Hollingsworth[a]	President and Publisher of the *Des Moines Register,* West Group President of Gannett's U.S. Community Publishing Division
Leonard Bernstein	Composer and Former Conductor of the New York Philharmonic
Mary Kay Ash	Founder of Mary Kay
Mike Cowen[a]	Chairman of Sportable Scoreboards
Nancy Thompson[a]	Executive Recruiter
Oprah Winfrey	Media Mogul
Oscar Boldt[a]	Former CEO of The Boldt Company
Pat Summitt	University of Tennessee Women's Basketball Coach
Richard Feynman	Theoretical Physicist

a. We interviewed these progress makers. Their comments and profiles are highlighted in various chapters.

(Continued)

(Continued)

Ron Reed[a]	Former Chief Education Advisor for The Discovery Channel
Rosalind Franklin	DNA Scientist
Ruth Kirschstein	Former Director of the National Institutes of Health
Sir Winston Churchill	Former Prime Minister of Britain
Steve Jobs	CEO of Apple (*Fortune*'s CEO of the Decade)
Tom Boldt[a]	CEO of The Boldt Company
Vicki Wilson[a]	Owner of Door County Coffee & Tea
Walter Wriston	Former Chairman & CEO of Citibank

a. We interviewed these progress makers. Their comments and profiles are highlighted in various chapters.

NOTE: Links to more biographical information on these progress makers are available on the book Web site at www.imetacomm.com/pm.

APPENDIX B

UMM and the Origins of Focused Flexibility

M. Lee Williams

Texas State University

———•◆•———

ocused flexibility is a notion that took shape as a result of research I conducted with Phil Clampitt several years ago.[1] In this appendix, I outline
the history of the research project and some of our major findings.

HISTORY

The tussle between certainty and uncertainty has concerned many researchers.[2]
Some scholars argue that humans have a fundamental need for certainty, even
if it is based on mythology.[3] Yet, others have argued that humans have coun-
tervailing needs to escape the "iron grip of predictability and monotony."[4] On
a behavioral level, the literature suggests that there are fundamental differences between employees who embrace and suppress uncertainty.[5] Those with
less tolerance for uncertainty tend to avoid ambiguous stimuli, rely on author-
ities for their opinions, and act in a dogmatic manner.[6] An employee who
avoids uncertainty may be hesitant to express a dissenting opinion, looking to
the supervisor for specific direction. On the other hand, those who embrace
uncertainty tend be self-actualized and flexible, preferring objective information.[7]

An employee who embraces uncertainty, for instance, would be comfortable critiquing a supervisor's decision because he or she entertains a different view of the facts.

Just as individuals vary in the way they approach and deal with uncertainty, so do organizations. Some organizations manage uncertainty by embracing it. They openly discuss changes in their customer base and competitors, foster innovation, encourage meaningful dialogue, and de-emphasize rigid planning processes. Others, however, tend to avoid uncertainty by following inflexible control procedures or policies, ignoring changing circumstances, overly relying on success recipes, and artificially bolstering organizational successes by overlooking shortcomings.

The Uncertainty Management Matrix integrates these two forms of uncertainty (see Figure B1).[8] This framework juxtaposes the individual employee's approach to uncertainty and how he or she perceives the organization's approach to uncertainty. Those individuals who embrace uncertainty see it as challenging, invigorating, and useful. They do not try to artificially drive the ambiguities and contradictions out of the situation. Conversely, those individuals who avoid uncertainty view it as threatening and undesirable. They tend to shun complexities and novelty. In like manner, individuals can perceive their organization as embracing uncertainty (i.e., being open to change and innovation) or see their organization as avoiding uncertainty by denying the presence or need for change.

Different climates emerge depending on how the individual employee approaches uncertainty and the way he or she perceives how the organization embraces or avoids uncertainty. As suggested in Figure B1, there are four basic possibilities:

- **Placid Climate:** Employees and the organization both avoid uncertainty. Employees want few surprises and they rarely get them.
- **Unsettling Climate:** Employees desire certainty, but they perceive that the organization embraces uncertainty. As a result, employees become unsettled and perhaps overwhelmed by the chaotic work environment.
- **Stifling Climate:** Employees embrace uncertainty, but they perceive that the organization avoids it. The result is that employees feel stifled.
- **Dynamic Climate:** Both employees and the organization embrace uncertainty. Employees want change and progress, and the organization promotes it.

Figure B1   Uncertainty Management Matrix

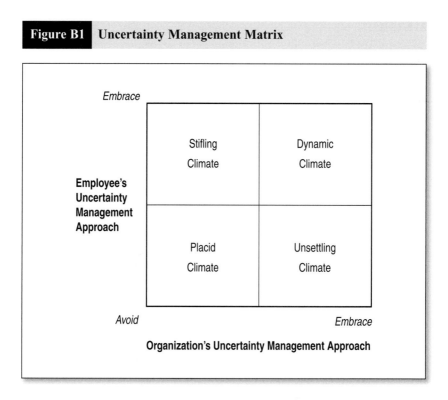

Each quadrant represents a different kind of organizational climate with varying beliefs, assumptions, and ways of communicating.

RESEARCH QUESTIONS

Since leadership and uncertainty management are important factors related to organizational outcomes, this research was guided by the following two research questions:

1. Do employees who perceive their organization as well led tend to operate in different uncertainty-embracing climates than those in not well-led organizations?

2. Do employees who perceive their organization as well led exhibit more favorable outcomes (e.g., satisfaction, commitment) than those in not well-led organizations?

METHOD

Employees were drawn from organizations, including financial institutions, medical facilities, retail organizations, manufacturing firms, government agencies, and educational institutions. A convenience sample of 249 participants completed and returned the questionnaire.

To answer the research questions, a survey composed of four parts was developed: (1) Uncertainty Climate questions, (2) Leadership Effectiveness questions, (3) Outcome questions, and (4) Demographic questions. A 7-point *strongly disagree* to *strongly agree* scale was used to measure all items except the demographic variables. (Contact either author for a copy of the questionnaire.)

Uncertainty Climate. Prior research has established reliable and valid techniques for ascertaining how employees perceive the uncertainty climate. Using the measurement scales developed by Clampitt and Williams, respondents completed a 24-item questionnaire.[9]

Leadership Effectiveness. One item on the questionnaire asked respondents to indicate on a 1 (*strongly disagree*) to 7 (*strongly agree*) scale if their organization was "well managed." Respondents who strongly agreed (7) that their organization was well managed were classified as working in a well-led organization ($n = 56$), and those indicating they strongly disagreed to slightly agreed (i.e., 1 to 5) were classified as working in a not well-led organization ($n = 98$). Those who responded "moderately agree" (i.e., 6) were not used in the study ($n = 95$). Therefore, this investigation is based on the 154 respondents who perceived their organization as well led or not well led.

Outcome and Demographic Variables. A variety of outcome variables were analyzed in this study. They included single-item measures of several types of satisfaction, communication satisfaction, commitment, productivity, organizational direction, and cynicism. Each was measured on a 1 (*strongly disagree*) to 7 (*strongly agree*) scale. The survey also contained a number of demographic variables, including gender, education level, and position in the organization.

RESULTS

Of the 154 employees investigated, 56 were in well-led organizations and 98 were in not well-led organizations. The chi-square test for independence revealed that the distribution of levels of education for well-led organizations was not significantly different from that of not well-led organizations ($\chi^2 = 7.30$, $df = 5$, $n = 148$, $p < .20$).

Seven percent were in top management, 22% in management, 56% in nonmanagement, and 15% other. Eighty-one percent were female and 19% male. For both job classification and gender, chi-square tests indicated no significant differences for the distribution in well-led organizations versus not well-led organizations ($\chi^2 = 2.99$, $df = 4$, $n = 149$, $p < .60$ and $\chi^2 = 3.53$, $df = 1$, $n = 153$, $p < .06$, respectively).

RESEARCH QUESTION 1

The answer to the first research question was clear. The data indicate that well-led organizations have very different uncertainty climates than their counterparts. In particular, well-led organizations promote either Dynamic or Unsettling climates. Note in Figure B2 that 78% of the well-led organizations were classified in those climates. Yet, only 29% of those organizations not deemed as well led were classified in the Dynamic or Unsettling climates.

By digging a little deeper into the data, we can glean further insights. The findings suggest that, in general, employees in well-led organizations *do not differ* significantly from their counterparts in other organizations regarding their *personal* comfort with uncertainty. On the other hand, employees in well-led organizations *do differ* significantly in their views of how their *organizations* manage uncertainty. In particular, well-led organizations *embrace* rather than *suppress* or *ignore* uncertainty. *In essence, employee personal comfort with uncertainty matters less than how they perceive the organization dealing with uncertainty.*

One caveat: While well-led organizations encourage a lot of discussion and debate upfront, the tolerance for ambiguity fades when it comes to outcomes and goals. Less well-led organizations tend to communicate muddled outcomes. For example, our data indicate that 50% of employees from well-led

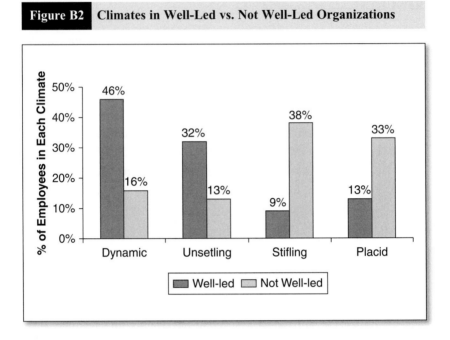

Figure B2 Climates in Well-Led vs. Not Well-Led Organizations

organizations agreed with the statement "My organization needs to know the specific outcome before starting a project." Only 26% of employees from the less well-led organizations agreed.

RESEARCH QUESTION 2

Overall, the answer to the second research question is that employees in well-led organizations express more favorable responses than those in not well-led organizations. They were more satisfied with their job, more satisfied with communication from their supervisor, more committed to the organization, and identified more with their organization's values. Furthermore, they felt their organization was headed in the right direction, said that it was a great place to work, and expressed less cynicism. They also perceived their coworkers as proud to work in the organization and that they were not overwhelmed by change. It would be an overgeneralization to say that leadership was solely responsible for all these positive outcomes; however, it is reasonable to assume that leaders in organizations perceived as well led contributed to and, to some degree, influenced these outcomes.

CONCLUSION

Uncertainty permeates organizational life. Leaders can choose to ignore it, suppress it, succumb to it, or embrace it and take action. That decision, to a large extent, will influence their organizations' level of effectiveness. Ignoring or suppressing it might provide temporary comfort. But employees instinctively know that uncertainty lurks just around the corner. Succumbing to or balking at uncertainty cultivates a sense of hopelessness and a perception of leadership weakness. Embracing uncertainty requires something special of leaders. It requires that they create appropriate policies, procedures, and cultural norms. It requires that they encourage employees to notice shifting trends and new ideas. And it requires that they encourage debate and dialogue. Yet, after the issues have been fully discussed, they tend to communicate specific outcomes. Such practices help instill the "focused flexibility" mind-set.

Effective leaders are not necessarily enamored with uncertainty but rather realize that uncertainty pervades all their information, knowledge, decisions, and actions. Rather than trying to rid their organizations of uncertainty, they seek to make it work for them. And they know their organizations can only transform uncertainty into action by properly communicating about it. Mastering this challenge shields them from ineffectuality, irrelevancy, and, ironically, instability.

NOTES

1. P. Clampitt and M. L. Williams, "Conceptualizing and Measuring How Employees and Organizations Manage Uncertainty." *Communication Research Reports* 22 (2005): 315–24.

2. K. E. Weick, *Sensemaking in Organizations.* Thousand Oaks, CA: Sage, 1995.

3. A. Fry, *Safe Space: How to Survive in a Threatening World.* London: J.M. Dent & Sons Ltd., 1987.

4. G. Gumpert and S. J. Drucker, "A Plea for Chaos: Controlled Unpredictability, Uncertainty and the Serendipitous Life in the Urban Community." *Qualitative Research Reports in Communication* 2 (2001): 25–32.

5. K. McPherson, "Opinion-Related Information Seeking: Personal and Situational Variables." *Personality and Social Psychology Bulletin* 9 (1983): 116–24.

6. A. Furnham, "Tolerance of Ambiguity: A Review of the Concept, Its Measurement and Applications." *Current Psychology* 14 (1995): 179–200.

7. P. Foxman, "Tolerance for Ambiguity and Self-Actualizing." *Journal of Personality Assessment* 40 (1976): 67–72.

8. P. Clampitt and M. L. Williams, "Communicating About Organizational Uncertainty." In *Key Issues in Organizational Communication,* edited by D. Tourish and O. Hargie. New York: Routledge, 2004, 37–59.

9. Clampitt and Williams, "Conceptualizing and Measuring How Employees and Organizations Manage Uncertainty."

INDEX

Supporting researchers for more than 40 years

Research methods have always been at the core of SAGE's publishing program. Founder Sara Miller McCune published SAGE's first methods book, *Public Policy Evaluation*, in 1970. Soon after, she launched the *Quantitative Applications in the Social Sciences* series—affectionately known as the "little green books."

Always at the forefront of developing and supporting new approaches in methods, SAGE published early groundbreaking texts and journals in the fields of qualitative methods and evaluation.

Today, more than 40 years and two million little green books later, SAGE continues to push the boundaries with a growing list of more than 1,200 research methods books, journals, and reference works across the social, behavioral, and health sciences. Its imprints—Pine Forge Press, home of innovative textbooks in sociology, and Corwin, publisher of PreK–12 resources for teachers and administrators—broaden SAGE's range of offerings in methods. SAGE further extended its impact in 2008 when it acquired CQ Press and its best-selling and highly respected political science research methods list.

From qualitative, quantitative, and mixed methods to evaluation, SAGE is the essential resource for academics and practitioners looking for the latest methods by leading scholars.

For more information, visit **www.sagepub.com**.